OTHER A TO Z GUIDES FROM
THE SCARECROW PRESS, INC.

The A to Z of the Welfare State

Bent Greve

The A to Z Guide Series, No. 54

The Scarecrow Press, Inc.
Lanham • Toronto • Plymouth, UK
2009

Published by Scarecrow Press, Inc.
A wholly owned subsidiary of
The Rowman & Littlefield Publishing Group, Inc.
4501 Forbes Boulevard, Suite 200, Lanham, Maryland 20706
http://www.scarecrowpress.com

Estover Road, Plymouth PL6 7PY, United Kingdom

British Library Cataloguing in Publication Information Available

Library of Congress Cataloging-in-Publication Data

The hardback version of this book was cataloged by the Library of Congress as
follows:

Greve, Bent.
  Historical dictionary of the welfare state / Bent Greve.— 2nd ed.
    p. cm. — (Historical dictionaries of religions, philosophies, and movements ;
  no. 63)
  Includes bibliographical references.
  1. Welfare state—Dictionaries. I. Title. II. Series.
  JC479.G74 2006
  330.12'6—dc22   2005020540

ISBN 978-0-8108-6837-3 (pbk. : alk. paper)
ISBN 978-0-8108-7003-1 (ebook)

∞™ The paper used in this publication meets the minimum requirements of
American National Standard for Information Sciences—Permanence of Paper
for Printed Library Materials, ANSI/NISO Z39.48-1992.

Printed in the United States of America

Contents

Editor's Foreword

Not so very long ago a book like this on the welfare state · uld mainly have praised such advantages as enhanced security, gre. · financial support, and a comfortable old age. The depiction would ha een generally positive. But the situation has changed, and although welfare state is still largely admired and widely aspired to, certa roblems have emerged, such as unwanted state interference, w dependency, a weakening of family and social ties, and especia. excessive fiscal burden. Thus, there is now a serious debate abou. what sort of a welfare state is best and how it should be managed in a more balanced manner. This debate pits those in favor of greater coverage and easier access against those insisting on more economic growth and freedom of the individual and, in so doing, adds the voices of the New Left and the New Right. This is actually healthy, and the result will probably be more rational and also more viable systems in the future.

However, for any debate to be constructive and productive, it certainly helps to know just what one is debating. That is the primary purpose of *The A to Z of the Welfare State*. It provides historical background through the chronology, introduction, and many entries, and brings the story up to date. It describes the often different systems existing in many of the advanced countries and some developing ones, with more examples than ever, especially for Eastern Europe. It includes information on early pioneers and present-day specialists, both those on the left and those on the right. Above all, it defines basic terms and elucidates crucial concepts, adding some of the most recent vocabulary. This is done primarily in the dictionary section. No less important, an expanded and updated bibliography—and a new section on Web sites—enables readers to find books, articles, and raw data on specific aspects and problems.

Bent Greve, the author of both the first and second editions of this volume, has continued a very active career as a specialist on the welfare state and its development, with some emphasis on Europe. Early on, this included working for the Danish Association of County Councils and then the Economic Board of the Danish Labor Movement. More recently, he has been serving as professor in Welfare State Analysis and head of the Department of Social Sciences at Roskilde University. Dr. Greve is the director of the Jean Monnet European Center of Excellence there and also a deputy member of the board of the European Institute of Social Security and vice-chair of the Danish Central Board of Taxation. This is a rather unique combination of activity in the public and private sectors, practical experience, and academic research, which allows him to take a well-rounded view of a subject that remains of great importance to everyone.

Jon Woronoff
Series Editor

Preface

This book tries to identify, describe, and define the core concepts that are fundamental to an analysis of the welfare state or welfare society. It focuses only on the definitions and concepts that are the most relevant, long lasting, and important, instead of presenting biographies of the many writers in these different fields. The presentation of biographies is limited to a very few and historically important thinkers. To those who thought that other figures should have been included, I apologize.

The central criterion for an entry has been the historical importance of a concept, not the individual researcher's contribution to the analysis of the welfare state and social policy. Furthermore, the dictionary describes how history has influenced the current development of theories and the analytical ways of dealing with the welfare state. It also describes the history, transition, and future of the welfare state.

I do not pretend to cover the whole field, but I have tried to present the information so that scholars interested in welfare states and welfare state analysis from different scientific viewpoints will find this dictionary of use. It attempts to provide insights from major areas in social science, including sociology, economics, political science, and social work. It tries to integrate the different disciplines and, by doing so, present a more complex and integrated view of the welfare state.

One goal is to describe and explain the items as clearly and precisely as possible. Some may find that the result is too simplistic, as many arguments for and against various standpoints and assumptions are left out in order to make a clear and hopefully crisp presentation.

I have tried to include the most important references to the welfare state literature. A core problem in doing this has been that a whole book could be filled simply with names and titles instead of information. The selection process is a result of my own research and using the databases at libraries about books and journals in the field. I know that this is sometimes not a full and sufficient way of selecting among the various authors. My argument for using this method is that I needed to narrow the field. Otherwise, the book would have consisted mainly of a bibliography, instead of what I hope to be valuable information and ideas, especially for the many students in the field who can use this dictionary as a first step in identifying areas of interest. Users can find important definitions, historical descriptions, and ways of interpreting welfare state development. This edition includes two new features, an appendix containing an overview of related Web sites and a bibliography of even more literature.

The book provides a few historical descriptions of the development of **social security** systems in selected countries. The countries chosen are core countries in different welfare state clusters, as well as those where important events for the development of the welfare state have taken place. Countries from different parts of the world have been included to broaden the picture and also to indicate the variety of approaches to welfare states and their development. This also implicitly answers the question of why mainly European countries are described. It would not have been possible to include all the countries in the world, and as the pattern of development often has been more or less the same among groups of countries, this seems to be a reasonable way of presenting historical trends in the development of the welfare state. My understanding of what constitutes a welfare state also influenced the choice of countries.

I have found it useful to cover the first year of legislation in many countries concerning central contingencies, such as pension, industrial injuries, unemployment benefits, sickness and maternity benefits, and family allowances.

Only a few illustrations are included. I had considered including a short, quantitative description of the development of the various welfare states—especially since World War II—but this would not have been precise and elaborate. It would be difficult to limit the illustrations while trying to cover the entire area of social security in the various countries and regions included in the book, and that description has therefore been left out. Readers interested in this topic should turn to statistics from the EU, IMF, and OECD. Many of the Web sites listed in the appendix provide collected data on welfare state issues from a comparative perspective.

List of Abbreviations and Acronyms

ALMP	active labor market policy
APW	average production worker
DRG	diagnosis related groups
ESF	European Social Fund
EU	European Union
GDP	Gross Domestic Product
HMO	health maintenance organization
ILO	International Labour Organization
ISSA	International Social Security Association
LIS	Luxembourg Income Study
MISSOC	Mutual Information System on Social Security
NAFTA	North Atlantic Free Trade Agreement
NAIRU	non-accelerating inflation rate of unemployment
NGO	non-governmental organization
NPM	new public management
OECD	Organization for Economic Co-operation and Development
OMC	open method of coordination
PAYG	pay-as-you-go
SAP	Social Action Program
SEA	Single European Act
UK	United Kingdom
UN	United Nations
USSR	Union of Soviet Socialist Republics

Chronology

The development of the welfare state has differed among countries th(
a heterogeneous path and strategy between different countries ha\
been and would have been expected to follow. This chronology presen
only the major core dates and events for the development of the welfa₁
state in general, including the first welfare legislation of the particul:
countries included in the dictionary.

sixth century BC   A narrow type of **social assistance** to soldiers wa
developed in Athens. This seems to have been the first legislative at
tempt to cope with a social problem.

1388   The first **Poor Law** was enacted in the **United Kingdom** to deal
with the labor shortage.

1601   The Elizabethan Poor Law was introduced in the United Kingdom to establish local areas' responsibility for the poor. This law was
the first to give specific groups with specified needs public support.

1698   The world's first life insurance company was started in the
United Kingdom.

1730   The Reformation began in many Northern European countries;
as a result of its changes, many poor were no longer supported by the
church; indirectly, this may have had an impact on the different types
of **welfare states** that emerged later.

1776   **Adam Smith**'s book *The Wealth of Nations* was published. This
book has since influenced many **liberals**' way of thinking about the
welfare state.

1791   In **France**, the constitution declared that citizens had a right to
social assistance. In the same year, a specific pension for seamen was
established in France as well.

1798 Poor relief laws were introduced in **Denmark**.

1834 The Poor Laws in the United Kingdom were changed to a more general law, with a more general level of support.

1838 Employers in **Germany** were made responsible for the railroad workforce.

1852 Mutual funds covering sickness and invalidity for specified groups were introduced in France.

1854 Compulsory insurance for mineworkers was introduced in Germany.

1883 **Sickness insurance** was introduced in Germany as the first in a series of new **Bismarckian** reforms establishing new principles for the welfare state structure and how to deliver and finance welfare state activities.

1884 The first law on **industrial injury** was passed in Germany.

1887 A law on industrial injury was passed in the **Czech Republic** and the dual monarchy of Austria-Hungary. This was the first area of **social security** to be covered in **Austria** and **Hungary**.

1888 The first social security law in Denmark, a law on child maintenance, was introduced.

1889 An injury insurance system was introduced in **Poland**. Also, the first law on **pension**s to be passed in any country was implemented in Germany.

1891 **Sweden** introduced the **sickness benefit** system.

1894 Mutual benefit societies were established in **Belgium** to cover sickness and **maternity benefits**.

1895 In **Finland** and **Norway**, the first laws on social security in the area of industrial injury were introduced.

1897 In the United Kingdom and in **Ireland**—even though the latter was not yet an independent country—a system covering industrial injury was introduced.

1898 The first **social insurance** system in France was introduced in the area of industrial injury. In **Italy**, a law on industrial injury was passed. **New Zealand** introduced a law on old age pensions.

1900 In **Spain**, a law on industrial injury was passed.

1901 **The Netherlands** introduced a law on industrial injury. The first study on **poverty** by **B. Seebohm Rowntree**, based on an analysis of poverty in York, England, in 1899, was published.

1902 Social security in relation to industrial injury was initiated in **Australia**. Total coverage was finally passed in 1946.

1905 For the first time in any country, an **unemployment** benefit system was introduced, in France.

1908 Social security coverage in **Canada** was introduced in the province of Quebec for industrial injury; other provinces soon followed.

1911 The first social security measures in **Japan** and **Switzerland**, for industrial injury, were introduced.

1913 **Portugal's** first social security law, covering industrial injury, was passed.

1914 In **Greece** and **South Africa**, laws on industrial injury were introduced.

1915 The first social security law in **Argentina**, on industrial injury, was passed. In the **United States**, the portion of the workforce covered by compensation reached approximately 30 percent.

1916 **Chile** introduced a law on industrial injury.

1919 **Brazil** passed its first law covering industrial injury. In the same year, the Weimar Republic in Germany was founded, securing certain rights for citizens.

1930 The first law concerning **family allowances** was passed in Belgium. This was the last social security area to be covered, and it was only gradually introduced in most other welfare states, often not until after World War II.

1931 **Mexico** introduced a law on industrial injury, the first area to be covered in that country. The Quadragesimo issued by Pope Pius XI included the now famous description of the concept "**subsidiarity**," which stated that what can be done at a lower level should not be taken over by a higher level.

1933   The New Deal under Franklin D. Roosevelt was initiated in the United States. These reforms sought to create jobs and introduced various social security laws.

1936   John Maynard Keynes published his now famous book, *The General Theory of Employment, Interest and Money*. It has had a profound impact on discussion and development of economic policy since World War II and also on the development of the welfare states.

1941   Archbishop Temple of the United Kingdom introduced the concept of the welfare state as an answer to the aggression and power of Germany.

1942   Lord William Beveridge published his report, *Social Insurance and Allied Services*, from which the **Beveridgian model**, characterized by universal provision of welfare, was developed.

1951   Arrow's impossibility theorem was published. **China** introduced laws on social security, including old age, **disability**, sickness, and maternity and industrial injury.

1952   ILO Convention No. 102 on **Social Security** was codified.

1957   The European Economic Community (now the **European Union**) was founded by Germany, France, Italy, and the Benelux countries. The treaty included labor mobility and social security for migrant workers.

1989   The Community Charter of Fundamental Social Rights was passed by the European Union.

1991   The Maastricht Treaty of the European Union included the Protocol on Economic and Social Integration and a **Social Dimension**. The United Kingdom did not adopt this protocol.

1997   The Amsterdam Treaty was concluded by the heads of state in the European Union. Social integration is part of the treaty and was endorsed by all members. The treaty also emphasizes to a greater degree than before that both labor market policy and social policy are areas of concern for the European Union as whole.

2000   The Lisbon Agreement, which calls for the use of the **open method of coordination (OMC)** in social policy, labor market policy, and pension policy in Europe, was adopted. This reflects the balance between the centralized and decentralized levels in the European Union.

2004 Ten former Eastern European countries joined the EU; nearly all European countries are now members of the European Union.

Introduction

The term *welfare state* is reasonably new, developed in 1930s and 1940s. Some see it as the opposite of the concept of w re of World War II. Opposite because warfare spends money on ry and war, welfare on social policy, health care, and so forth. Th ok goes farther back than the 1930s and 1940s, and aside from a eferences to ancient times and **poor laws**, the starting point for pr ng and discussing what we today would label welfare state ies is **Bismarck**'s reforms in **Germany** starting in 1883. Similar orms quickly followed in most European countries.

It is obvious that the concept has a relative meaning and will be interpreted differently over time and in different countries based on their economic, political, and cultural legacies and historical development. Definitions of the welfare state often focus on how and why a state intervenes in the economy and welfare of the individual citizen. A welfare state does not, however, have to mean state intervention; it may merely reflect the state's restrictions and the demands of the **labor market**, **families**, and the rest of **civil society**.

Some welfare states are fairly universal in their approach, whereas others have chosen a more selectivist approach. Many and very different types of the welfare state exist, as a result of the way different societies have chosen to develop their systems. Many welfare states came about in response to the Industrial Revolution, but others developed in response to changes in the **demographic** situation and structure, which gave rise to new demands for new protection. The initiatives were related to specific social areas, such as support for **pensions**, **education**, **housing**, and spouses. These developments were often in response to **market failure** and the market's inability to provide the necessary support for the individual's risk. This contrast between market and state has to a large extent also been part of the debate between, for example, the **New Right** and the **New Left**.

The systems in various countries are still quite different, and after the rapid expansion of the welfare state in the 1960s and 1970s, the **legitimacy** of the welfare state was increasingly questioned because of rising **unemployment**, increasing **dependency** on the state, ideological pressure for more individualism, state deficits, and state debt.

The economic consequences of the welfare state also came into question, including how the financing would influence individuals' behavior, as well as how different types of social security systems could have an impact on incentives to work and save. The state's role was and has been widely debated by, among others, the New Right and **public choice** theorists. The conflict between handling market failure and government intervention has yet to be solved. Given this criticism, it is difficult to foresee how the welfare state will develop. Basically, it can be argued that the welfare state will continue to exist, but the form, shape, and structure will also continue to vary among countries.

The interactions and borderlines among **state**, **market**, and **civil society** presumably will shift over time and the roles of various actors in the development can and will change over time and among countries.

HISTORICAL DEVELOPMENT

It is difficult to describe briefly the historical development of welfare states across countries, as the national strategies used when social policy and social security were initiated were highly nation specific. Nonetheless, it seems possible to identify some common features and also to see the development of welfare states in a framework in which certain periods have witnessed decisions that have had a stronger impact and influence on the developments of the welfare state than others. References are made here to certain key people in relation to the thinking about and development of welfare state activities, even though for many countries this means oversimplifying and neglecting national persons influence and national responses to change in economic and social conditions.

When looking at different countries and the complexity of their economic and social development, it is obvious why it is not easy to say exactly why and how different welfare states developed. National differences in economic, political, and cultural conditions have existed (and still do), and these differences have had an impact on the way the systems developed. This is why so many variations of the welfare state exist and why there are numerous interpretations of the why and how of welfare states.

The structure of the following discussion reflects the importance I have found in different historical periods of the development of the welfare state. The first period, briefly discussed, is ancient times and the development of the poor laws. Next comes the period of industrialization in the late eighteenth and early centuries (1870–1913), followed by the period between the two world wars and immediately after World War II. The golden age of the welfare state (1950–1973) is then described, followed by a discussion of the welfare state crisis, retrenchment, and new orientation since 1973. Central thinkers of the various periods are included, and the prevailing ideology of each period is also presented.

The first elements of the welfare state derived from many countries' support of specific groups that were seen as **deserving**. In ancient times, one particular deserving group was soldiers who had served their country. This implies that a core factor in public sector involvement has been opinions about who deserves support and who does not. This also indirectly acknowledges that, in order to involve some people in higher risk activities, some type of coverage is needed; for example, accident insurance for invalidity caused by work accidents. In ancient times, it was mainly men going to war who were covered, because the risk of not being able to support themselves after a war was high, and their war injuries were not their own fault.

Later on, more general approaches emerged, although they were weakly applied. The **Poor Law** Act of 1601 in the **United Kingdom** seems to have been the first law implementing support for specific groups in society aside from soldiers. There had been some earlier laws—such as the Poor Law Act of 1388—the main aim of which was to cope with possible labor shortage in the years after the Black Death. However, the 1601 act was the first under which a specified group, paupers who were old or sick, would receive support. On the other hand, others needing support would have to be employed in a house of correction. This law worked—on a decentralized basis—for more than 200 years, but communities were economically pressed by growing population and the beginning of industrialization, which began earlier in the United Kingdom than in many other countries. Due to growing pressure and changes in economic and philosophical thought, including **laissez-faire** attitudes and a belief in the need for incentives to the poor, a new poor law was implemented in 1834. Its main principle was less eligibility and inclusion of a strong test; it provided that most people should be discouraged from receiving poor relief. Here are the beginnings of the stigmatizing effects of **social policy**. The influence of **Adam Smith** and the free-market mechanism was clear in this period. In other countries, other poor laws with the same ideological emphasis as those in the United Kingdom were gradually introduced.

The **church** also played a central role in coping with the legal and administrative problems of society in many countries. However, this impact was quite different from country to country—mainly because of variations in religion. The Catholic Church emphasized its responsibility and also (even if first written down in the *Quadragesimo Anno*, 1931) the principle of **subsidiarity**, which implied a higher responsibility for the individual and the **family**. This has been an important factor in the diversity of welfare states in Europe. The Protestant church, on the other hand, has been more inclined to argue for state intervention and a smaller role for the church in relation to welfare state development.

In most European countries, development of the **welfare state** in the 19th century was brought about by growing industrialization and changes in demographics and societal structure, including increasing pressure on the cities. The welfare-related developments included poor laws, the establishment of mutual societies, and growing voluntary action and private charities. The role of the public sector was still limited.

From 1820 onward, the world economy grew more dramatically than ever before, and a comparison of the GDP growth rates for 1500–1820 with those for 1820–1992 clearly shows the difference. From 1500 to 1820 the growth rate was 0.04 percent, whereas from 1820 to 1992 it was on average 1.21 percent. Economic development also seems to have had an impact on the possibility of development of public support. Periods of rapid welfare state development correlate with periods of rapid economic development.

The most rapid economic expansion occurred from 1950 to 1973, the second most rapid was the period 1870 to 1913, and the third was the period from 1973 onward. Excluding the period from 1973 onward, when the debate over retrenchment and crisis was prominent, the two remaining periods are central to understanding the growth of the welfare states.

Between 1870 and 1913, many new types of legislation were passed addressing different and especially new social risks. Accident insurance, sickness, old age pension, and invalidity were among the areas covered. **Bismarck's** reforms in **Germany** in the 1880s emphasized **social insurance.** The first reform was a law concerning **sickness** in 1883, which was followed by **industrial injury** in 1884 and **invalidity** in 1889. These types of legislation were passed in many other Western European countries in the period until 1913.

Bismarck's social insurance reform was a response to the industrialization of Germany and fear of uprisings by the working class unless it were covered against new forms of risk. These new risks were caused not only by the new industries but also by population movements, which indicated that the **family's** responsibility was weakened. Without public sector intervention, many families would have been left without support in cases of industrial injury, sickness, and old age.

Reforms in Germany were based on mutual aid and combined the use of state intervention with employer responsibility. In this way, reform continued along the path already traced when employers' liability, personal savings, and private insurance were how individuals were covered before the reforms. Furthermore, this system used the capitalist production systems and combined it with state intervention. The tendency toward a more mixed economy was apparent.

In other European countries, in addition to personal savings and private insurance, mutual aid societies were of central importance. When these types of remedies seemed to lose strength and social problems increased, social security reforms evolved, and the state became more involved. It can thus be said that changes in demographics and economic conditions (industrialization and growing class conflicts) were the catalysts for the rising tide of welfare state reforms.

From a more ideological point of view, the **liberal** mode of thinking influenced the development of reforms in many ways. Collectivist approaches and thinking, especially Marxism, had an impact on various systems in the sense that the development of better living and working conditions was part of the class conflict in many countries. This conflict involved more than struggles between the traditional classes, that is, the workers and the capitalists. Especially in Scandinavian countries, coalitions were formed between workers and farmers with the aim of promoting decisions favoring both groups. Gradually, as compromises between different groups in society were reached that were not formed on the traditional lines between those owning the means of production and those without, it became apparent in many political democracies that these "coalitions" were driving forces toward a welfare state. The ideology behind the welfare state is thus not one-sided but has many different faces and often a mix of attitudes. Even though the term *welfare pluralism* first emerged late in the development of the welfare state, traces of it can be found early on in many countries.

Furthermore, the period until World War I was influenced by—and ran parallel with a gradual reduction of—voluntary work as part of social policy. Later on increased state intervention appeared in many welfare states.

When World War I started, reforms naturally came to a halt in many countries. Economic and political resources had to be used to cope with the war. After the war, the possibilities of and need for reforms gradually surfaced again. The process of, and wish for, changes and reforms of social security and increasing coverage of different needs, combined with state intervention in the economies, still existed, even though it had been difficult to implement new initiatives during World War I.

Expenditure for social protection and other welfare state activities continued to grow after World War I, although the classical way of thinking about public finance was a hindrance to any active stimulus to the economies. **John Maynard Keynes**'s work first made clear that the public sector economy could be used as an instrument for creating jobs and stimulating the economy. The economic **rationality** for growing pressure on the systems existed, partly due to the fact that ever more people were living in the cities in poverty and destitution without proper support.

Reforms were halted by the growing tensions in Europe and the outbreak of World War II in 1939. World War II and the preparations for what was going to happen after the war were important in the development of the welfare state after the war. The war seemed to inspire a more collectivist way of thinking, encompassing many who needed help through no fault of their own. Furthermore, there was a belief that the best way to reduce the possibility of another war would be to reduce tensions among countries, to create jobs, and to guarantee decent living standards. **Sir William Beveridge**, especially in his 1942 report, laid the foundation for many welfare state systems after the World War II. He proposed to reduce unemployment, provide a comprehensive **health care** system, and guarantee a minimum income. This more universal type of welfare system, which in **T. H. Marshall**'s understanding was implicitly built on citizens' rights, laid the foundation for the systemic development of the welfare state in many countries.

In the United Kingdom, Beveridge's ideas was combined with a more Keynesian economic approach to foster a slow but steady expansion of the public sector after the war.

The period from around 1950 to 1973 can be labeled the golden age of welfare state development. It combined high economic growth with a very rapid expansion of the public sector.

Welfare states around the world—with exceptions and differences pace—expanded very rapidly. All-encompassing systems and a great reliance on public sector provision than on the market and **civil soci** were the cornerstones of development. These systems included cov age of broader groups in society; better and a higher level of benefits; and new types of services for children, the elderly, and other vulnerable groups in society. Finally, health care systems were expanded in response to a growing need for treatment and new methods for taking care of different types of **need**.

Besides the possibility of expanding the public sector economically, a changed division of responsibility between family and society gradually took hold in many countries. This can be seen in the increasing number of women entering the labor market in many countries as well as the new types of care for which the public sector became responsible. The function of the family as a core unit for providing welfare diminished in many countries, although it still had an important role and in some welfare state types a very profound role, for example, in the **Southern European welfare state**.

The golden age of expansion thus experienced a high level of state involvement and a reduction in the role of the market and civil society—including voluntary organizations. The other side of the coin of this rapid expansion was growing taxation. The higher level of taxes and duties, combined with the economic recession in most of the world after the first and second oil crises in the 1970s, which quadrupled oil prices, brought into question the survival of the welfare state. In combination with the increase in oil prices, unemployment rates grew, **inequality** continued to exist, and public sector deficits started to rise in many countries. These factors led to a growing disbelief in the Keynesian fine-tuning of the economy and doubts about the welfare state's ability to guarantee decent living standards with so much public sector debt. Furthermore, the legitimacy of the welfare state was questioned by both the **New Right** and the Left.

The Left criticized the welfare state for not having honored its primary commitment to full employment and for not having brought about an equitable society. The state's role had become too weak compared to the markets, and a reformulation of the state's role in societal development was needed. The unfulfilled expectations increased the Left's criticism of the welfare state.

The New Right criticized the welfare state from the other side. The economic burden on society of a growing public sector crowded out private investment, and generous unemployment benefits reduced the incentive to work, especially at low-income jobs, creating problems in the labor market. Finally, the New Right questioned the role of the **bureaucracy** and **pressure groups**, especially within the framework of **public choice**. The argument was that the bureaucracy and pressure groups were mainly considering their own interests instead of society's and thus reduced society's overall welfare.

The growing legitimacy crisis and, some argued, financial crisis led to a new orientation of the welfare state in many countries, and the growth of the public sector came to a halt in many places, the exception being latecomers. Perhaps surprisingly, only a few real cutbacks in benefits or services in the various welfare states were implemented. A continuously high state level of involvement in welfare prevailed, and **convergence** seemed to be on its way. Thus the states' involvement in and financing of many activities can still be seen, although the focus seems to have shifted slightly toward health care and trying even more than in the golden age of the welfare state to target support to the vulnerable groups. Long-term consideration of **demographic** changes and the impact of **globalization** on the welfare state has opened new avenues for debate and discussion about the welfare state's future development.

The historical distinction between the **deserving** and undeserving was resurrected as a central element in the way the welfare states provide benefits to their citizens.

A more profound method of mixing **state**, **market**, and **civil society** has at the same time occurred in many countries. Voluntary groups and organizations also seem to have gained importance. The division of welfare into **public**, **occupational**, and **fiscal welfare** has also changed, with many welfare states relying increasingly on occupational welfare, sometimes supported by fiscal welfare; in this way a different role for the state has emerged.

Marketization and **privatization** were buzzwords for many conservative governments in the 1980s and 1990s and were combined with a more liberal approach to economic policy and greater reliance on the individual's commitment to society. Market elements were incorporated in public sector provisions, and the boundaries among state, market, and civil society underwent changes.

Retrenchment of the welfare state could be seen in several countries, although the real cutbacks were few and mainly hit the unemployed and those living on **social assistance**.

The welfare state still seems to be a cornerstone in many societies, and even more countries are trying to develop societies in such a way that access to care and social benefits will be possible, to ensure a decent living standard also for those outside the labor market. It can therefore be argued that there is no real welfare state crisis, just an adjustment of present ideologies and a less collectivist attitude. This is evident from the changes in many countries around the world.

A single definition of the welfare state still does not exist. Many different types of and suggestions for what a welfare state should be exist side by side. To some extent this has to do with the differences among the nation states' economic, cultural, and political developments. The interaction and mutual interdependence also create pressure for convergence among the various countries' systems, while trying to maintain respect for national traditions and differences in institutional structures. The welfare state emerged in response to new needs—and it continues to evolve as new needs arise and some of the old ones subside. The insecurity related to globalization and increased free movement of workers and capital also indicates a continued need for a welfare state.

Developments in many countries seems to underline that the citizens want welfare services—and they want more of them when they become richer. At the same time, the distinction between public and private delivery is less important as long as the quality is good and access is not dependent on income.

The Dictionary

– A –

ABSOLUTE POVERTY. This term refers to a certain "basket of goods" multiplied by the prices of those goods. The basket of goods consists of what is essential for survival or a certain minimum standard of living. The level calculated in this way could, depending on the wealth of the nation involved, be supplemented by a percentage to cover items not included in the basket (e.g., nonfood items). The calculation results in a line that the individual should be above to not be living in **poverty**.

The absolute poverty line has the advantage of making it possible to compare poverty in different countries in a certain year, at least if purchasing power is taken into consideration. One major disadvantage of using this measure is that it is difficult to use over time as prices change due to **inflation** and production methods change. Furthermore, it ignores the problems of being a poor family; that is, it may be difficult to buy goods cheaply by using the different bargains in the market when buying many of an item, and it overlooks nonmonetary considerations, such as personal security. Finally, it is difficult to decide which items should be included in the basket of goods before calculating the poverty line. Different goods, it is argued, should (or should not) be included, and they may vary among countries.

An absolute poverty line does not provide any information about the type of **welfare state**, nor does it give any indication of policies employed to reduce poverty. Different welfare states, depending on the relative wealth of the countries, will presumably also have different viewpoints about what goods are necessary for survival, not only in a nutritional sense, but also in the sense of being socially included in society, for example, to be able to participate in cultural and social life. In this way absolute poverty is a **normative** concept.

ACCIDENT INSURANCE. Accident insurance is taken out to protect against certain well-defined accidents, for example, a workplace injury. In most welfare states, this was the first contingency, besides support to the poor, to be covered by state support. This was achieved by making it an obligatory insurance, a state-supported insurance system or a state system in which those who were injured could be paid for a shorter or longer period. A dependent **family** may also be supported by accident insurance.

The reason this area was the first to be covered seems to be that it was a new risk, which emerged as a consequence of industrialization. Many families moved to the city, where relatives no longer supported them when injuries occurred. It was therefore impossible to maintain a decent standard of living. The injury was seen as being no fault of the individual, who therefore deserved support. It can be argued that, if no such support existed, it would have been difficult to attract more labor to the cities, where it was needed in the new factories.

Germany was the first country to introduce accident insurance, between 1881 and 1884, followed by **Austria** in 1887 and **France** in 1898. In Scandinavia, accident insurance was introduced around 1900, and in the **United States** and **Canada** in 1930. In many welfare states today different kinds of accident insurance still play an important role in covering families and individuals against specific kinds of risks. In addition, obligatory insurance against risk is a way of **financing** the welfare state that reduces the pressure on the more traditional means such as income taxes and duties.

ACTIVE LABOR MARKET POLICY (ALMP). This is an important element of many countries' welfare policies, as it can be a way of ensuring **social inclusion**; in addition, it is a way of helping the individual to be independent of aid from society. A reduction in people's dependence on society, for example, by reducing spending on **unemployment benefits** and **social assistance**, is an important element.

Active labor market policies can have many forms and variations; examples include on-the-job training, vocational training, and general **education**. Such policies can be in the public or the private sector and can include various forms of economic support from the we fare state to get people back to, or onto, the labor market. In the Sc dinavian **welfare states**, active labor market policies have been c tral to ensuring full employment since the mid-1950s. In m countries' social security systems, activation has been one of the c ditions for receiving social help.

ADVERSE SELECTION. When an individual with a significant i is able to hide this from an insurance company, the problem of verse selection arises. When analyzing the various ways of provid **social policy**, it is difficult to provide a market-based solution in face of adverse selection, and in areas where this risk is high pul intervention is needed. Insurance companies find it difficult to s correct premium, one that corresponds, for example, to the indi ual's risk of falling ill. This could result in a lack of supply, as possibility of calculating income and expenditures correctly is d i-cult, implying a high risk of losses for insurance companies when providing this type of insurance. In those cases, either obligatory insurance for all citizens or universal state insurance is often seen as the solution.

AFFIRMATIVE ACTION. This American term describes a method for supporting disadvantaged groups. This can be through special treatment or other types of help. Another way of describing it is positive discrimination toward specific groups. Affirmative action has especially been used in relation to gender and ethnicity issues, but it also arises in treatment of the handicapped, for example, in access to public buildings. In many welfare states, affirmative action has resulted in improvement of various groups' positions, including their **integration** into society.

AGING OF SOCIETIES. In the years to come, most mature welfare states will witness a change in their demographic composition. An increase in the number of elderly people and a decrease in the number of young people are the consequences of a falling birth rate and longer life expectancy. This has implications for welfare states, as the elderly in many welfare states receive public pensions, use the **health care** system more than others, and need more personal social care. In addition, it has implications for the **labor market**, which may be shrinking, thus, it has been argued, making it more difficult to increase wealth. The implications of the impact of aging vary depending on the change in birth rate and the level migration. An aging population may result in a variety of consequences, depending on factors such as changes in birth rates or changes in the levels of inward and outward **migration**. There is frequent discussion about how welfare states can cope with these changes. Views on the matter are very diverse, ranging from those who believe that radical changes need to be made to those who believe there is no need for change. In particular, it seems that there will be changes in the labor market emphasizing the need for an **active labor market policy**.

ALLOWANCE. This is a fund given to the individual by the state, the market, or **civil society**. The allowance can be based either on contributions or civil rights. Different types of allowance exist under different systems, including, for example, housing or child allowances. These allowances also have a different value in different countries, that is, some welfare states are more generous in certain areas than others.

ANCIENT TYPES OF WELFARE RIGHTS. In ancient times, there was no well-developed form of intervention and support for the needy. Still, in some sense the right and duty to share food with those, mainly elderly and children, who were unable to hunt or gather for themselves was a form of **social assistance**. In relation to benefits and services, taking care of those in **need** was based in the **family**.

In classical Athens (sixth century BC), a specific type of social assistance for soldiers was developed for those who had been wounded in war and were no longer able to take care of themselves. Support was later extended to citizens who had been determined eligible by a vote of the common assembly. In Rome, the state provided people in need with some grain, but it was not a well-developed system.

In many European countries, the **church** and monasteries later provided places where needy people could get some help, mainly **benefits in-kind**. With the onset of the Reformation in Northern Europe around 1730, the church began losing its property and therefore its ability to provide support for the poor. As a consequence, the state gradually took over this responsibility.

Insurance-based systems have existed in many countries for a long time. In Rome, for example, funeral insurance supported those expenses. However, only in 1698 was the world's first life insurance company started. In some countries "friendly societies" were created with the purpose of supporting each other in cases of severe need. This was mainly done among trade unions and other groups with specific needs. The **Poor Law** of 1601 in the **United Kingdom** (UK) was the start of a more institutionalized state system.

In most countries, the real development of social systems was a response to the Industrial Revolution and the breakdown of traditional bonds between families, as well as inflows into the cities, which were combined with new risks. Even today, systems like those developed in ancient times are in place in several welfare states, and the implicit distinction between deserving and undeserving plays a role in many countries' social policies.

APPEAL SYSTEMS. These are the systems in most welfare states through which citizens can complain about misconduct or ill or improper treatment by **street-level bureaucrats**. The appeal systems can have various forms and structures, but the main idea is that it will help to ensure all citizens the same treatment within the legal framework of a given society.

ARGENTINA. The first area of risk to be covered in Argentina, as in many other countries, was industrial injury, for which a law was passed in 1915. In the 1920s and 1930s, Argentina was one of the richest countries in the world and one should therefore have expected a more rapid development of **social security** laws than actually was the case. A law providing **maternity benefits** in 1934 followed the law on **industrial injury**, and the first **pension** system was created in 1944. The pension system originally targeted only a small group. In the late 1960s, it became a more general system. After World War II, Juan Peron governed until 1955, and from then on, a long period of economic and political problems followed, including dictatorships.

Unemployment benefits for construction workers were introduced in 1967; in 1991, they were provided more generally. **Family allowances** were introduced in 1957.

The Argentine system relies mainly on covering employed persons and therefore is not universal. It can be seen as a **conservative** system, in which only very limited public intervention and support are involved. It is also comparable to **Southern European welfare state models** in that it relies more on the **family** than the state.

ARROW'S IMPOSSIBILITY THEOREM. This is the most famous theorem in **welfare economics**, named after Kenneth Arrow's famous contribution in 1951. It states that, given certain conditions (described below), it is not possible to choose a **social welfare function** that will optimize society's welfare and that is unambiguous. The criteria are the following:

1. The **Pareto** criteria should be fulfilled.
2. There should be no dictatorship.
3. There should be independence of irrelevant alternatives.
4. There should be an unrestricted domain.

The first criterion is the traditional one in economics that changes should be made as long as one person's position can be improved without anybody else being worse off. It could also be more simply stated that the society should produce and distribute along the production function for the society.

The second criterion implies that the solution should not just be determined by one person, but should have broad support, and that the welfare function should represent all members of society.

The third criterion—independence of irrelevant alternatives—implies that an alternative should be a possible alternative, not, for example, something outside the production frontier.

The fourth criterion, unrestricted domain, implies that a ranking of different possible solutions should be possible. This means that all different combinations of goods and services in a society can be ranked and measured against each other.

The main problem with the measurement of welfare is the need to make **interpersonal comparisons**. One person's use of a good may give that person a specific **utility** that is different from another person's utility of the same good. Therefore, it will be difficult to find a solution.

Many have tried to solve the problem by relaxing one or more of the restrictions, but it still seems that it is not possible to objectively determine a society's welfare function and to make recommendations about the welfare policy in that country. At the same time, using elements from the criteria may help in prioritizing possible solutions.

ASYMMETRICAL INFORMATION. This refers to a situation in which the amount of information is not the same for all involved in a decision. This can be in an agreement or in administrative processes. This may be the case where an insurance company does not know whether an individual is a good or bad risk. Asymmetrical information is related to **moral hazard**. It also relates to the discussion about how to manage and steer different parts of the **welfare state**, such as the health care sector, where the professionals such as doctors have information that the principal agents do not. Asymmetrical information can also exist when individuals applying for a disability pension do not precisely inform about their abilities to take up a job.

ATTITUDE GROUPS. These are to a considerable extent the same as **pressure groups**. The main difference is that in an attitude group the individuals participating share the same beliefs, for example, a religion or ideology.

ATYPICAL EMPLOYMENT. Increasingly, many workers do not have regular jobs with a permanent contract but may work from a distance as tele-workers. Atypical employment can also refer to work that is short term and based on a specific contract or shifting between being employed and being self-employed. With new forms of work, new problems arise for social security systems, for example, how to provide unemployment insurance for those not working in the typical way with a fixed number of work-hours.

AUSTRALIA. Australia introduced **social security** later than did many Western European countries. Industrial injury was the first area covered, but it was not implemented throughout Australia at the same time—it took from 1902 to 1946. **Old age** and **disability** pensions were introduced in 1908, and widows' pensions in 1942. Then came **family allowances** in 1941; **sickness, maternity**, and **unemployment benefits** followed in 1944. Australia, as a member of the British Commonwealth, has been inspired by the **United Kingdom**, and its more universal approach is in line with **Sir William Beveridge**'s suggestions. Furthermore, the labor movement in Australia was strong and held office as a minority government in 1904 and 1908. By 1914, it had gained a majority. The strong impact of the trade unions seems to be one of the reasons for a more egalitarian approach in Australia than in many other welfare states.

Old age, disability, and unemployment benefits, as well as family allowances are, as a rule, paid by the government, and thus, in combination with the general criterion that it is covering residents in many areas. This system in these specific areas resembles the **Scandinavian welfare state** universal model. Some would describe Australia as a fourth world of welfare capitalism because of its combination of the means-tested and residual welfare state types on the one hand and the more universal types of benefits on the other.

AUSTRIA. After 1867, the former Austrian empire became the dual monarchy of Austria-Hungary. The first Austrian republic was established in 1918. The first **social security** law in Austria, the industrial injury law, was passed in 1887. It was followed by sickness and maternity coverage in 1888, then by **pensions** for salaried employees in 1906 and for wage earners in 1935. **Unemployment benefits** were first introduced in 1920, and **family allowances** began in 1948.

Austria was inspired by **Germany** and the **Bismarckian system**, which is also reflected in the Austrian system's strong reliance on participation in the labor market and contributions from the labor market. The system is thus mainly insurance based, although the family allowance system is universal. In certain areas, such as dental and medicine, user charges are applied. Austria can mainly be described as a Bismarckian welfare state due to the strong emphasis on and use of insurance funds in the system.

AVERAGE PRODUCTION WORKER (APW). This term is especially used by the Organization for Economic Co-operation and Development (OECD) when comparing the level of benefits in different countries. This is done by referring to the level of benefits acquired by a person who has the same income as an average production worker. It is thus a standardized way of measuring the level of benefits.

– B –

BASIC INCOME. Basic income is the level of economic resources that a welfare state will guarantee an individual person. It is most commonly understood as the minimum income that all citizens are guaranteed by the state. The level of social assistance can often be an indicator of the level of basic income, but only an indicator, because, for example, student benefits will be at a lower level, as they are expected to earn income later in life. Furthermore, the self-employed may for short periods of time have lower income levels due to variations in their ability to generate profits. Basic income can vary in amount depending on the type of benefits, for example, a basic pension.

BASIC NEEDS. These are the goods an individual and/or **family** needs in order to survive and have a decent standard of living. The International Labour Organization (ILO) has defined it as including two specific areas: (1) adequate food and clothing and some household goods; and (2) access to essential services such as water, transport, health care, education, and culture. It is stressed that basic needs should be understood within a country's historical and cultural tradition. This makes it difficult to measure and be precise about the concept, but it stresses that not only a minimum requirement, a certain basket of goods, should be reached.

The concept of basic needs has been used in the debates on **poverty**, and especially absolute poverty, but also on living standards more generally, for example, in Erik Allard's discussion of having, loving, and being. It is argued that basic needs should be fulfilled before an individual is able to move on to fulfill other needs. At the same time, there is no unanimous agreement on what the basic needs are in more concrete terms, and therefore it has been difficult to use in relation to policy recommendations for the development of the welfare state.

BELGIUM. The first welfare areas to be covered in Belgium were sickness and **maternity**; these benefits were provided through a mutual benefit society. In 1903, coverage against industrial injury was introduced. This was followed by **unemployment benefits** in 1920, and in 1924 a law covering the pension system was passed. Finally, in 1930 **family allowances** were introduced.

The Belgian system is mainly a continental **conservative** type with a high reliance on the labor market and only to a limited degree relying on the state as the main provider. Belgium's historically close connections with **Germany** seem to explain the development of its system. A major problem in Belgium has been its division into two separatist areas divided mainly by language, which has influenced the system and will probably continue to do so.

BENEFIT PRINCIPLE. This principle states that those who enjoy public service benefits should pay the taxes to finance them according to the degree of **utility** from the services received. It is mainly used when delivering public services, where it is possible to make a connection between users and the supply. Common examples are roads, bridges, public transport, water, and electricity. In some countries, the principle is partly used in relation to the payment for specific care facilities for children and the elderly. In recent years, there been an increase in welfare states attempting to combine **financing**, especially in **health care**, with increased user charges, although they do not always adhere to the general benefit principle.

BENEFITS IN CASH. This is money given to individuals who qualify for an income transfer when a specific risk occurs. It can be in the form of **unemployment benefits**, **maternity benefits**, **social assistance**, and so forth.

In different welfare states, various criteria govern receiving these benefits. The main ones are eligibility, a **means test**, and whether one is covered as a citizen or as a member of an insurance fund.

In most welfare states, the criteria must be analyzed in the historical, cultural, and national context in which they have developed. It seems that there is a tendency for countries to learn from each other, resulting in a tendency toward convergence; that is, the systems resemble each other, although not necessarily the whole structure and level of benefits.

Finally, the level of the benefits depends on the economic conditions in the country and the willingness of those not eligible for benefits to contribute if they are paid out of general taxation.

BENEFITS IN-KIND. These benefits are provided in the form of goods, such as bread and **housing**. In many welfare states, this was one of the first ways of delivering benefits, the argument being that those in **need** should have bread and someplace to live and not have a chance to spend the money on something else. It is also argued that by giving benefits in-kind instead of in cash the voters' or citizens' willingness to pay for these forms of welfare will be greater than otherwise.

Today, these benefits are still used in some countries, primarily in two specific areas. The first is (1) among certain groups that are not able to take care of themselves and (2) as assistance for those with very particular handicaps or sicknesses. The first group includes, for example, alcoholics and drug addicts. The fear is that if the benefits are not in-kind, the money support would be used to buy alcohol or narcotics.

The second area in which benefits in-kind are used is where the state can buy products (e.g., wheelchairs and help remedies for different **disabled** groups) at less cost than an individual could. This can also apply to certain types of goods, for example, medicine for those with lifelong diseases, where instead of doing an income transfer, medicine may be given directly.

It could be argued that, for example, homes for the elderly and **child care** are benefits in-kind, but these lie outside the definition given here, as they are mainly seen as social services. The criteria for receiving these benefits are outside the scope of benefits given directly, relating to certain characteristics of the groups receiving the benefit. Some countries use benefits in-kind to provide places where the poor can get a meal. In some countries benefits in-kind are issued as **vouchers** that entitle the individual to certain goods or services. The food stamp program in the United States is an example of this type of benefit in-kind.

BEVERIDGIAN MODEL. The Beveridgian model is named after Lord William Beveridge and his now-famous report, *Social Insurance and Allied Services*, issued in 1942. This report gave the name to a welfare state model that is characterized by universal provision of welfare and the intention of providing full employment. The basic idea was to provide comprehensive **health** services and specific **allowances** to children. Good housing conditions were also part of what was considered necessary to ensure a good and decent living standard.

The report argued (in paragraph 302) that a **social security** system should be built on three bases: (1) **social insurance** for basic needs, (2) national **assistance** for special cases, and (3) **voluntary insurance** for economic support on top of the basic level.

The report assumed that the social insurance for **basic needs** would be "as comprehensive as possible," and in that respect, it did not resemble the way we now think about insurance systems. It was not only those employed who were expected to pay into the insurance; the state should also contribute. This implied that some persons should be obliged to pay more through the tax system, even when the direct contribution was assumed to be a flat rate.

The report focused on want, disease, ignorance, squalor, and idleness. In this sense, it also reflected the ongoing debate about only giving support to those most in need, not to people who are just idle or want to live off the benefits of the welfare state. The distinction between **deserving** and undeserving recipients of welfare benefits has frequently been an element running through welfare state's principles for many years.

The Beveridge report, and its implementation in the **United Kingdom** after World War II, has to be understood in the light of the historical circumstances. There was a need after the war for security and stability. This illustrates that the model of welfare will not be the same over time but will change in the light of economic and political circumstances.

The main characteristics of the Beveridgian model can be described as an attempt to guarantee full employment, that is, a right to work; and a policy priority to provide jobs, a minimum level of subsistence, and a guaranteed standard of living. It proposes a **universal**

welfare state, implying that people will mainly be covered as citizens, and the transfer will consist of very low-level **flat-rate benefits,** financed through general **taxation.** This model has been implemented primarily in the northern parts of Europe, and it must be stressed that no country can be expected to follow the Beveridgian lines completely, making it more a typology than a concrete description of countries' systems. Still, the concepts behind it have had a profound impact on social policy and welfare state thinking in many countries.

BISMARCKIAN MODEL. Named after German Chancellor Otto von Bismarck (1815–1898), who established a compulsory insurance scheme in the 1880s, this system covered sickness, industrial accidents, and old age. The models were introduced to reduce political pressure from the growing working classes in cities and because of the fear of social uprisings. It was a new, but soon a well-developed, structure that emerged. It offered high coverage of the new risks stemming from the Industrial Revolution, such as **industrial injuries.** Furthermore, it helped to reduce social unrest and build a system in which mainly those in the labor market were covered.

Even today, the Bismarckian model can be characterized as relying on the labor market as the core provider of welfare and basing the right to transfers and their size on being in the labor market and having paid contributions. In this system, the degree of redistribution is small—going primarily from those not experiencing a social event to those needing help after being in the labor market. It builds on contributions from employers and employees, and the state's involvement is rather arbitrary. Today there is also some support for those outside the labor market.

The model was used primarily in continental Europe, with **Germany** as the prime example. Today it still prevails in Central Europe. It must naturally be borne in mind that the Bisckmarkian model is described here as a prototype. National variations stemming from various historical, cultural, and economic conditions in the different countries involved will thus exist. The Bismarckian model has also been labeled the **continental** model, referring to the countries from which it originated.

BRAZIL. Brazil was under Portuguese rule until 1899, when a republic was created. This may explain the late development of the **social security** system. In addition, for many years Brazil has been ruled by dictatorships. There was social unrest in the 1920s that created pressure for social development. Industrial injury was covered in 1919. This was followed in 1923 by pension and sickness schemes for railroad workers. In 1934, persons working in commerce were also covered, and in 1936, this coverage was widened to include those working in industry. **Family allowances** followed in 1941, and finally **unemployment** was covered in 1965.

The system is mainly based on being an employed person, but it also requires some public sector finance to support the different funds should there be a deficit in funding **pensions**, sickness, and maternity, and the main part of the unemployment system. Supplementary private pension systems also exist, and civil servants are covered under their own system.

The main criterion for eligibility is being part of the labor market, and in this sense, this is a traditional **Bismarckian** system. Today, there is still a very high degree of **inequality** and many poor people in the country.

BREADWINNER. This is the person who earns the money to support the other members of the household. In many countries and social systems, this has traditionally been the man, which has given rise to the "male-breadwinner model" in **gender** analysis of the **welfare state**.

BRIGGS, ASA (1921–). Briggs is a British sociologist and historian, primarily known for his writings about the welfare state from the historical perspective. His definition of the **welfare state**, found in that entry, is often used as a starting point for further discussion of what a welfare state is or will be. "The Welfare State in a Historical Perspective," in Schottland, C. (ed.): *The Welfare State*, New York: Harper and Row, 1969, is a useful starting point for discussion on this topic.

BUREAUCRACY. Although they date back a long time, bureaucracies originally were not well developed; their main purpose was to support the ruling king or emperor. In social science, the debate about bureaucracy is often related to **Max Weber** and the discussion about how to effectively organize production (including administration in both the public and private sector) and using people's different skills most efficiently. Bureaucracy in its original form should be capable of "attaining the highest degree of efficiency and is in this sense formally the most rational known means of carrying out imperative control over human beings. It is superior to any other form in precision, in stability, in the stringency of its discipline, and in its reliability" (Weber, 1947). Another way of stating this is that the "For bureaucratic administration is, other things being equal , always, from a formal, technical point of view, the most rational type. . . . The choice is only that between bureaucracy and dilettantism in the field of administration" (Weber, 1947).

The argument for the superiority of bureaucracy has been that those employed in the bureaucracy would know the precise rules for working and making decisions. This would reduce the time spent on finding solutions and therefore the time used on the production line.

Historically, bureaucracy was a response to the growing complexity of organizations and the need for delegation and control. The expectation was that it would make production more rational and produce fewer failures. The techniques it used were fewer personal relationships, rules for behavior, and a hierarchical decision-making process. It was expected that a very detailed description of how to behave would make all functions more efficient.

But this is only one of many different views of bureaucracy. Another is that bureaucracy is inefficient and a waste of resources and that its operations have been conducted more in the self-interest of the producers than to give the consumers better possibilities.

As the welfare state has grown, bureaucracy has had to administer, steer, and plan the benefits and services provided by the welfare state as well. This has led to a debate about whether bureaucrats overburden the welfare state and how the bureaucracy could have a negative impact on society's functioning. According to William Niskanen, bureaucrats act primarily in their own interest. This action of the bureaucrats it is argued has had a strong impact on the growth of the public sector.

Some theorists, mainly adherents of the **public choice** tradition, have argued that the main reason for the growth of the welfare state is that bureaucracy wishes to fulfill its own aims and not the clients' interests. The argument is that the status, power, and income of a bureaucrat depends on the size of the bureaucracy, and therefore only an increase in the bureaucracy will improve an individual bureaucrat's position.

Several arguments can be raised against this claim. First of all, the bureaucracy does not act alone. Many countries have elections, and there is usually a ministry of finance, which wants to reduce spending. Furthermore, from a historical point of view, given the development of the welfare state, it is not reasonable to assume that bureaucracies should have started to push for growth around and after World War II, and to a greater extent in the 1960s and 1970s. It is also not reasonable to assume, therefore, that they—at least alone—should be able to get the public sector to grow. However, this is not to say that it cannot be argued that in some areas and some cases bureaucracies have had an impact on the growth of the welfare state.

In addition, it should be noted that bureaucracies are a combination of the administrative bureaucracy, professional bureaucracy, and **street-level bureaucrats**. The administrative bureaucracy in the welfare state organizes and plans welfare state activities. The professional bureaucracy mainly focuses and concentrates on professional jobs, for example, doctors, nurses, etc. Professionals may have a special interest in and reason for wanting growth in their own specific area.

The street-level bureaucrat is the one whom the individual client meets and who is empowered to make decisions—including discretionary decisions. This means that the individual may be dependent on the person he or she talks to. This often happens with **social assistance** and other social benefits and services that are not bound by previous contributions or rely on discretionary decisions. This may pose problems for policy makers and clients, as it can result in different treatment of equal cases. On the other hand, street-level bureaucrats take the individual case into consideration and can be more helpful.

Ongoing methods of measuring the efficiency of the welfare state's activities also need bureaucrats to do the measuring. The evaluation of efficiency may thus in itself increase the need for more bureaucrats. In this way, welfare states are often confronted with a need to balance the need to know what is going on against the cost of administration. Moreover, administration is more expensive when the systems need to be very targeted and very just. Achieving a balance between justice and administrative costs is thus another challenge for most welfare states.

– C –

CANADA. Despite its historical connections with Europe, Canada developed its **social security** system at a relatively late stage. This may be explained in part by the autonomy of the provinces and the British North American Act of 1867, which united Canada as one country.

Industrial injury coverage was first introduced in Quebec and Newfoundland in 1908, then gradually in the other provinces over the next 10 years. A **pension** for the old was established in 1927, and **disability** coverage was added in 1954. In 1940, an **unemployment benefit** program was introduced. In the 1980s and early 1990s, systems relating to sickness, maternity, and **family allowances**, covering the whole of Canada, were introduced. Until then, there had been only a patchwork of systems in the various provinces and territories.

The Canadian system is a mixture of a universally based system for residents (pension, sickness, maternity, **family allowances**) and systems depending mainly on labor market contributions and finance. It is therefore somewhere between the more **conservative** type of welfare state and the **Beveridgian** type of welfare state.

CAPABILITIES. These are an individual's basic possibilities and his or her capacity to do something. The contemporary theoretical focus is on how individuals or groups can achieve or do certain things.

Amartya Sen has defined this theoretical approach as: "The approach concentrates on our capability to achieve valuable functioning's that make up our lives, and more generally, our freedom to promote objectives we have reasons to value" and furthermore it "represents the various combinations of functioning's (being and doings) that the person can achieve" (1992).

This way of looking at the concept reflects individual choices about different approaches to deciding on a specific living standard (given the limits) by choosing between different elements in life. It also posits that capabilities are within a given set of possibilities and the structure of society. The concept can be used to stress that individuals lack things. If individuals want to use or have a specific type of good, then the problem of not having access to it is a restriction and lack of capability. The concept can also be used to analyze **marginalization**, **social exclusion**, and **equality**.

CARDINAL UTILITY. This is the ability to compare the **utility** derived from consumption both between and among individuals. It means that we can state how much more utility, for example, a person gets from an extra unit of a product, and that we can compare the utility person A and person B have derived from a certain good. In practice, the concept is very difficult to apply, but in theory it is a useful assumption, as it enables comparing different levels of welfare in or between societies and discussing different solutions to specific problems.

CASH BENEFITS. *See* BENEFITS IN CASH.

CHILD BENEFIT. **Social security** systems include specific child benefits, and the criterion for receiving such benefits is that there is a child in the **family**. A benefit can be **means-tested** but does not have to be. It can also be of a different size depending on the age of the children. Most countries providing child benefits offer them as universal systems to support families with children, which frequently have a lower average income than other groups in society.

CHILD CARE. These are arrangements for taking care of the children when the parents are working. Child care can either be publicly or privately supplied. Furthermore, it can either be free of charge or paid for by user charges or a combination of payment from the users and public payment. In some countries, employers also offer child care as a way to attract labor.

The development of child care in some countries has been seen as a way of making it possible to expand the labor force by giving mothers the option of both having a job and taking care of a child. Reconciling work and **family** can be achieved by, among other things, a well-functioning child-care system, as it enables both parents at the same time to be in the labor market and participating in the family's daily life. The way a child-care system is organized largely follows the patterns of the various **welfare state** models. A well-developed day-care system is also expected to help ensure a more gender equal development of societies. Finally, day-care systems are seen in Europe as part of the strategy of increasing the labor force.

CHILE. Chile became an independent state, liberated from Spain, in 1818. But it was also one of the latecomers to develop **social security** and **welfare state** arrangements. Industrial injury was the first welfare-related law to be implemented, in 1916. Laws covering old age and **disability**, sickness, and maternity were passed in 1924. It was not until 1937 that laws concerning **unemployment** and **family allowance** were introduced. In the area of pensions, a mandatory private and social insurance system was introduced in 1981, but it was still mainly based on and paid by the employer and insured persons, although with some state guarantee for minimum pensions.

The system's main criterion for social security coverage is to be in the labor market. It is therefore a highly **conservative** model in which the coverage is only for the few, leaving all those not able to join the labor market dependent on private charity and **family** help.

Chile is a country with a relatively low income level, which may explain why the system is not more universal and also the relatively low level of benefits. Privatization and more market and less state involvement has been part of recent developments in Chile, which also helps explain the more rudimentary development of social security systems compared to other countries.

CHINA. The People's Republic of China belongs to the communist type of welfare state, in which the state bears the overall responsibility for all citizens, including guaranteeing jobs, which then gives rise to coverage under certain conditions. However, China has been introducing more market elements into society's development in recent years.

The first laws covering old age, **disability**, sickness, maternity, and industrial injury were introduced in 1951. The late development of a welfare system must be viewed in relation to the long period before and after World War II of civil war and war with Japan, which occupied parts of China for long periods. In 1986, a law on **unemployment benefits** was introduced, which covered all workers in state enterprises. This must be seen in the light of the possibility of company bankruptcy from this period on which implied that workers could become unemployed.

The system is in a sense universal, offering everyone access to health care, etc., but it also implies the duty to take up a job, which thereafter generates one's **social security** rights. The present system, which has more market elements, and the new risks this implies, seems to be moving toward a more residual welfare system in which the government provides a safety net when other means have been exhausted, in order to ensure some minimum standard of living. Increasingly China is using the safety-net approach to supplement the insurance systems developed in several areas. This can be seen as a response to changes in the economy but also to the restructuring of society, with more people living in big cities.

CHURCH. The church is a religious organization that in many countries has played a pivotal role in the development of welfare state systems. In some countries, the church has been the first to help the poor and needy, but it has also emphasized the distinction between the **deserving** and undeserving. It still has an influence on the thinking of different parties and people and thereby indirectly on the welfare state system. For example, the emphasis in some countries on the family can be attributed to the role of the church. In some countries, the church also plays a role in formulating social policies and can be seen as a **pressure group**, especially for the most vulnerable.

CITIZENSHIP. This is an individual's legal connection with a country. Most people are citizens of the country in which they were born. Others may change their citizenship due to either voluntary **migration** or involuntary migration (refugees). Citizenship is often connected to civil, political, and social rights (*see* MARSHALL, T. H.).

The possibility of individuals being granted different citizenship depends on the law in the target country. Most countries have rules about how to be naturalized. These rules often involve the person's connection to the country and the number of years that individual has stayed in the country. In some countries, double citizenship is allowed. The concept of citizenship is important in the social policy debate because part of the distinction between different social policy systems depends on whether or not an individual has citizenship. Rights to **social security** may depend on citizenship, although in parts of the world regional and local agreements provide that rights can be transferred to other persons without them becoming citizens. This is the case in the **European Union** (EU) and among the Nordic countries. A citizen who has been working in another country collects rights to, for example, a pension. International agreements of this kind make the concept of citizenship more blurred, and in the EU, for example, the idea of having European citizenship as well as national citizenship has been discussed.

CIVIL SOCIETY. This is the area and functions of private individuals or families or organizations that are not subject to state intervention or regulation. It is a way of describing institutions and organizing activities that are not inherently built into the more formalized structures of society. The concept has been defined as a "set of social practices outside the state and outside the relations and forces of production" (Urry, 1981). The civil society is thus not a single entity but a broad variety of individuals and groups who, for different reasons ranging from altruism to **family** bonds, in various ways often help each other and thereby form part of the **solidarity** of society. It is presumed, although not always certain, that family members help each other.

Historically, civil society has been seen as a way of living in a civilized political community and was therefore more of a term for civilized society. Around 1750, the perspective on civil society changed, and observers started to look upon civil society as being the dichotomy of the state. Gradually the distinctions among state, market, and civil society emerged.

In the past 20 to 25 years, civil society has been brought back into the analysis of the welfare state. Highlighting the problems and reasons why something happens outside the state and the market has made this possible. Furthermore, it is obvious that part of social problems tends to be solved and clarified outside these two areas and without any need for public intervention or market-based solutions. The debate about civil society also covers the question of whether individual or collective solutions with a higher emphasis on civil society will involve less need for collective solutions and more individualistic solutions. It can be said that civil society is a sphere in which self-interest and egoistic, rational behavior will and can occur.

The relations among **state**, **market**, and **civil society** can also be labeled the welfare triangle, the welfare mix, or the mixed economy. Within civil society, **voluntary** organizations and self-help groups have been developing, which may result in different and therefore unequal treatment of groups in **need**. In this case, a higher reliance on civil society may impose greater **inequality** and injustice. Finally, institutions in civil society are not necessarily open to information from and control by independent authorities.

CLAIM. A claim is a demand to receive certain benefits or services from the system, which can be, for example, the state, a fund, or an insurance company. A claimant is therefore a person claiming certain rights in the **social security** system.

CLASS. Class is the division of the population into different groups in society. The main criterion to distinguish among classes is their position in the economic hierarchy.

One such division is the **Marxist** distinction between those who own the means of production and those who are employed by the owners of these means. In this view, it is to be expected that the inherent conflict between the two classes will end in conflict and give rise to revolution.

Others argue for a broader concept of class, which could include the working class, the middle class, and the upper class. Contemporary analysis tends to avoid using such a simple description because production methods have changed so much that one cannot just set off workers as a specific group. There are many different types of work, and there are many different ways to acquire income and wealth. Furthermore, the distinctions between the different classes may have vanished in some countries. This is not the same as arguing that no differences exist or that the stratification of societies and analyzing different classes' position in society is of no use in social science analysis. This type of research emphasizes the relative position of the individual in society and tries to analyze how different policies have an impact on various groups. The strata may be defined by looking at **employment**, single households versus families, ethnic minorities, migrant workers, or different income groups and the distribution of persons/families among them.

Class analyses have often been used to describe the historical development of the various welfare states by examining the way in which the working class and the middle class may have had an interest in that development. An example of a service those classes might have an interest in is providing (or guaranteeing) and delivering certain basic **needs** to the citizens.

Recently, the term *class* has also been used indirectly, by using the word underclass as a concept for those at the bottom of the social ladder and also those who are receiving **social security benefits** from society. If the concept emphasizes specific groups as being members of the underclass (single parents, the elderly, the unemployed, the disabled, the chronically ill, etc.), the term describes certain special vulnerable groups, without indicating that they will be there permanently. Gender analysis often has a dimension that replaces the original class-based analysis, as women in many welfare states have been an underprivileged group.

The use of the word *underclass* has been criticized as representing a concept that gives the political decision makers a moral right to reduce that underclass's benefits and make demands on the way its members contribute to society's development.

The concept of class has therefore not vanished from the analysis of the welfare state. It seems instead to have changed its focus to specific vulnerable groups and their position in society.

CLASSICAL ECONOMICS. This is a specific school of economic thought in which the individual's self-interest is seen to be the main driving force, which should create growth and prosperity. Classical economists argue for little public intervention, although some would be necessary in order to have stability and reduce conflicts between different people's interests. Classical economists believe in the market as the main regulator of the economy and that growth would be ensured through a combination of accumulation of capital and division of labor. Furthermore, classical economists maintain that the various markets would clear in the long run. For example, the balance of payments would be in equilibrium due to changes in the gold balance. If there was a deficit, gold would flow out and export prices would rise, while import prices would fall. This would then restore the balance of payments. Monetary policy and control are therefore essential for the classical economics model.

The main theorists in this tradition were **Adam Smith**, David Hume, John Stuart Mill, and David Ricardo.

COLLECTIVE BARGAINING. This is the process of negotiating working conditions (including wages) between the employer and employees' organizations collectively. In many welfare states, collective bargaining includes elements of social policy and what has been labeled **occupational welfare**. In many countries, for example, **pensions** are partly organized and financed in the labor market.

COLLECTIVISM. This is a specific way of thinking about societal development. In collectivist thinking, **equality** and equal treatment have a very high priority. Examples of collectivist thought can be found in **Marxism**. In relation to the **welfare state**, the collectivist approach would prefer state intervention to ensure that all citizens have a decent standard of living. For example, in the collectivist view, insurance-based health care would be unacceptable, as two persons with the same needs would be treated differently. Collectivists would also try to redistribute society's profits to promote greater **equality**.

COMMUNITARIANISM. This is an American-inspired viewpoint that criticizes the modern welfare societies for not being able to fulfill the requirements of both freedom and equality. Communitarians argue for more **solidarity,** including the use of local institutions such as the **family,** or local communities, which can ensure liberty. They therefore also argue in favor of the development of **civil society**.

COMMUNITY. Sociologically, this is a group of persons who are linked together by some common characteristics, such as culture or religion. Living in a certain geographical area can also link people by creating some specific social relationships or a common interest. A community can also be understood to have the same feelings or thoughts. Therefore, a community can be members of a nation, immigrants, religious groups, or just people having the same interest. The historical archetype of a community is the **family**.

In welfare state analysis, the idea of community is more often used as a way of interpreting a specific distinctive geographical area in which social services can be delivered.

COMMUNITY CARE. Local or decentralized units in the welfare state supply community care. In sociology, the term *community care* may be interpreted broadly as the care provided by a group of people in a local area. When looked at in this way, community care can be difficult to measure and analyze. In most welfare state analyses, community care is interpreted as the local provision of a part of the welfare state's delivery of goods and services. The care delivered is mostly for the elderly and children, but care for the vulnerable and disabled can also be part of community care. To what degree the care is delivered by the community or by civil society or the market depends largely on the specific type of **welfare state**.

COMMUNITY WORK. This term describes how a collective (the **community**) solves the problems of the specific community. It can include work within the **family** as well as neighborhood work and other local initiatives that try to solve local problems.

COMPARATIVE ANALYSIS. This type of analysis refers to the comparison of countries, **welfare state** types, or systems. The use of comparative analysis has grown within the last 20 to 30 years to get a better grasp of both individual countries' welfare state development and comparisons between and across countries. In addition, it places welfare states in a broader context and clarifies similarities and differences between countries. These studies often compare the different types of welfare states (**Bismarckian, Beveridgian, Scandinavian,** etc.) in specific countries or among broader sets of countries.

These analyses are often quantitative; that is, they compare the amount of money spent on different areas in social policy or in total public sector expenditures. Comparing the level of benefits, economic living standards, the number of people living in poverty, etc., are common studies. Studies comparing the systems and different criteria for receiving benefits have also emerged within the last 10 to 15 years. The **European Union**, for example, now regularly publishes an overview called *Social Protection in the Member States of the Community* from the Mutual Information System on Social Security (MISSOC), which is a European information system on social protection in the member states. It includes comparative tables on organization, financing, health care, sickness, **benefits in cash, maternity**, invalidity, old age, survivors, industrial injuries and occupational diseases, family benefits, **unemployment**, and guaranteeing sufficient resources. Comparative analysis is often difficult, as the available data are often not comparable, and if they are comparable, only at an aggregate level, which makes detailed conclusions very difficult to reach.

In the last 15–20 years, comparative analyses have also been supplemented by qualitative analyses, which examine the administration of the systems and how the individual perceives and gets support from the public sector. These analyses take into account the administrative impact of the **bureaucracy** and the **street level-bureaucrat**.

Some of the analyses have pointed out that in fact there is no country that fits exactly into any one welfare state type. This is due to differences in national systems, which is why they are treated as prototypes in this dictionary. Prototypes make it possible to make at least some comparisons and draw some broad conclusions about different types of countries and their differences and similarities.

Individual countries often also use comparative analysis as a mirror for their own development, and it is also used by **pressure groups** as support for why a system should be improved.

CONFLICT THEORY. This theory points out that as resources become scarce there will be conflicts about how to distribute them among different groups in society. In conflict theory the outcome of the **welfare state** is a result of the conflict (or, more mildly, competition) between different groups or **classes** in society.

Karl Marx's analysis of the state was based on a conflict between labor and capital. Modern conflict theory distinguishes between systemic and social conflicts. The systemic conflicts are between institutions, whereas social conflicts are between persons and can be, for example, within **families** or at a working place. Among proponents of this theory, there is no agreement about whether conflict is positive or negative. It may be positive in resolving problems; it may be negative in that it creates opposite interests that can only be resolved by use of physical power.

CONFUCIAN MODEL. This is a welfare state model developed mainly in the Far East, in countries, such as Japan, Singapore, South Korea, Hong Kong, Thailand, and Malaysia. It is not a very specific model and includes several elements from different European types, but it maintains its own historical flavor and status. One of the primary distinctions between the European and Confucian models has been a historic tradition of relying much more on families in the Asian countries than in Europe, perhaps with the exception of some Southern European countries.

Countries in East Asia have combined conservative corporatism with **subsidiarity**. But the corporatist structure lacks the workers' involvement that is present in traditional European countries. The use of the subsidiarity principle lacks the strong role of the **church** as in Europe. The **family** and extended commitments of individuals toward certain groups are the main means of delivering social welfare. This also explains why the role of the state has been minimal in comparison to other welfare state types and why charity and voluntary action have been prominent.

Many of the countries that exemplify the Confucian model initially developed their welfare states in the late 1960s and 1970s in response to political and economic problems that arose in the aftermath of World War II. But economic growth has made it possible to develop new forms of social welfare, although at a much slower pace and lower level than in Europe.

Confucian systems are top-down, rather than bottom-up. This is in contrast to many European countries, where the struggle between the working class and capitalist ruling class was one reason for developing a welfare system. So, even if the Confucian model resembles some European types of welfare state systems, it has its own features and stands out as a model combining different European types with Confucian learning.

CONSERVATIVE MODEL. This model emphasizes the market as the institutional provider of social welfare. It stresses that the public sector should only intervene when all other possibilities have been exhausted. The conservative model further stresses that market is the main provider and financer of the welfare state. This implies a strong emphasis on the labor market, especially local labor markets, as they can develop systems and welfare for those who need it. Support for those covered by the systems is high, whereas those outside and supported by the public sector will receive rather less.

In some sense, the conservative model resembles the **Bismarckian** model, with its strong emphasis on the labor market and low support to those outside it. Countries characterized as conservative are, for example, **Germany** and the **United States**. There is no real commitment in the welfare systems to develop and maintain full employment.

Redistribution in countries following this model is minimal. Such a country is sometimes referred to as a "night-watchman" state, as it only intervenes to a very limited degree and leaves most activities outside its scope.

CONSTITUTIONAL LAW. This law is made up of the rules by which a given society will have to act. In some countries, constitutional law states the right to have a job but not necessarily how to achieve that goal.

CONTINENTAL MODEL. This refers to a welfare state model geographically placed in the center of the European continent. It resembles the **conservative model** and have many common elements with the **Bismarckian model**.

CONTINGENCY. This is a risk, often specified beforehand, that may occur. For example, a contingency can be **sickness**, **unemployment**, or invalidity.

CONTRIBUTORY BENEFIT. This benefit is only available to those who have contributed to financing it. In many countries, such things as **unemployment benefits**, **sickness benefits**, and pensions are contributory. The size of the contribution and how it is calculated can vary among various countries, different **welfare state** models, and type of system. A contributory system, especially when it relates to benefits related to the size of previous payment, as for example in the pension system, can be a disadvantage for persons working on temporary contracts and will often also be a disadvantage for women, since they may bear and raise children and thus spend less time in the labor market or accept part-time employment. In this sense, the contributory benefit is not gender neutral. Furthermore, persons with low income tend to get lower pensions than persons with higher income. In this sense, such a system also reproduces the inequalities in a society.

CONTROL GROUP. In research, a control group is a group of people who are not given the same treatment as those in another group. The control group offers the possibility of testing whether or not the outcome of the activity is due to the initiative taken or just a random outcome. A control group can help in measuring the effectiveness of an initiative. In social science, including welfare state analysis, control groups are seldom used because they are looked upon as being unethical.

CONVERGENCE. This concept relates to a debate about whether or not countries, at least in the same regional economic area, such as Europe or Southeast Asia, will move toward some common type of welfare model, or at least are moving in a direction where the differences between institutional structure and level of spending of the countries are decreasing.

Convergence can be considered from various angles. Harold Wilensky (1975) was the first to argue that convergence was part of natural, long-term economic development. The power resource school criticized this standpoint, arguing that politics matters. **Globalization** has been the basis for another argument that convergence would occur in welfare state policies, given that globalization would make it more difficult for individual countries, especially the smaller countries, to pursue independent policies.

Data from Europe seem to indicate that convergence may occur or already be occurring on the level of overall spending, but that, at the same time, it is possible at the national level to maintain a variety of institutional structures and approaches. Thus, this view maintains that convergence will occur but that it need not be through either a race to the bottom (i.e., the lowest level of spending and/or level of benefits) or by catching up to the highest level in a region. It may be, for example, the result of different historical patterns of welfare state development.

CORPORATISM. Corporatism involves the **integration** of labor market partners in the decision-making process. It is interpreted in different ways, ranging from full co-optation of the partners in the states' decision-making process to a more partial inclusion in the process. Corporatist states can grant a varying degree of autonomy to the partners involved in the process. The Italian period of corporatism, for example, resembled a dictatorship, where the partners were only formally included and had no autonomy.

In other countries, the corporatist strategy has been used to build a consensus about societal development, especially in labor market policy. In these countries, the partners have frequently been involved in the administration of labor market policy as well.

Corporate structures can be found in many welfare states, especially in relation to integrating labor market partners in decision making. This is also the case within the **European Union** (EU), where the partners play a pivotal role in formulating and discussing new initiative in these areas. In the EU, integration of the partners is seen as essential for the **open method of coordination** on Employment and Social Exclusion.

COST-BENEFIT ANALYSIS. This process considers both the costs and benefits of a specific project. A project can then only be recommended if the benefits exceed the costs. If more than one project is evaluated, the analysis will compare the surplus of the various projects and choose the one for which the general positive value is highest. This, of course, assumes that the projects are comparable.

Although it is reasonably simple to calculate the costs of a given project, it is very difficult to calculate the benefits of a given project. Naturally there are some problems related to cost calculations, including insecurity in the longer term for project costs, how the project will develop, and the cost involved in maintaining and running it. But the problem of benefits is even greater, because benefits in different projects include, for example, the well-being of individuals, or longer life, shortening of traffic time, etc. Included are all the benefits that involve the individual's **utility**, and **welfare economics** does not give us any specific and well-known way of aggregating them.

For both costs and benefits, there are further problems in deciding which discount factors to use. A high factor will reduce the value of future income at current prices, and a low factor will mean a relatively higher value for the future income compared to a situation with a high factor. As costs and benefits arise at different times—in big projects, often with expenditure first and income afterward—the size of the discount factor can be very important when calculating whether or not a project ends with a surplus or deficit at current prices.

The reason for using analysis like cost benefit is that it enables the decision-making process to take other than purely economic criteria into consideration. This means that broader social aspects can be considered when making decisions. However, this raises the problem of and need for making **interpersonal comparisons**, which is difficult because it is impossible to know all the affected individuals' personal preferences. For example, individuals' valuation of spare time will vary. The same is the case for a cleaner environment, etc. Therefore, a cost-effectiveness analysis is often carried out because it only compares costs of different projects and does not use information about benefits.

CZECH REPUBLIC. In the geographic area of the Czech Republic, many different types of **social security** programs were originally introduced, following the **German** example. The first elements were introduced when the Czech area was part of the dual monarchy of Austria-Hungary. In 1919, Czechoslovakia became an independent state. Coverage against industrial injury was established in 1887, against sickness and maternity in 1888, and for old age and **disability** in 1906.

Family allowances followed in 1945, and finally, **unemployment** benefits were introduced after the fall of the Berlin Wall in 1991. The Czech system is based partly on being in the labor market, partly on being a citizen. It therefore has a combination of universal rights with specific benefits relating to being in the labor market. The system has been changing since the breakup of Eastern Europe, and it seems to be moving toward a more **Scandinavian welfare state** approach, with general coverage in many areas, but at the same time, labor market participation seems central.

– D –

DAY CARE. *See* CHILD CARE.

DECENTRALIZATION. This refers to both the process of dividing and the actual division of competencies in different countries. In several welfare states, a decentralization of responsibilities to lower administrative levels has taken place.

DECOMMODIFICATION. This relates to the degree to which individuals or families can maintain a decent standard of living without being dependent on labor market participation. In recent times, this concept has been used especially by Gøsta Esping-Andersen (1990) in his attempt to classify welfare state types. Others have questioned the use of decommodification as a starting point for welfare state analysis, pointing out that history and culture play an important role. Furthermore, some systems provide a high degree of coverage by using the concept of **citizenship** as the main criterion when delivering welfare, thus avoiding the idea that the individual's protection is dependent on the ability to be in the labor market. In these systems, decommodification has been important in the development of the welfare state.

DEFAMILIZATION. This refers to how **welfare states** help women to be independent of the **family**, especially in terms of economic independence. This can be accomplished in various ways, such as day care for children and family allowances. In welfare state literature, the concept is often connected to the concept of **citizenship**.

DEFINED BENEFIT PLAN. This refers mainly to the level of **pension** in a pension system in which the pension is dependent on the number of years with paid contributions in the labor market, the size of the contributions, and often also the final year's salary or the average salary.

DEFINED CONTRIBUTION PLAN. This is a **pension** plan in which the benefit is dependent on the contributions and capital income earned on those contributions.

DEMOCRACY. The word *democracy* comes from the Greek "demo, which means the poorer people. When discussions about democra started in Greece, the poorer people were those without any influei on the decision-making process.

In this form of government, the majority of people in a society make decisions about their leaders and laws through either direct or indirect voting. It includes elections in which different groups or groupings can participate and nowadays also access to the media. An election with one candidate may therefore not be considered democratic, unless it is clear that no others want to be elected and have had a fair chance to participate in the election.

Some of the main questions in relation to democracy are which decisions should be made at which level, whom to elect as representatives of the different groups in society, and how the system should take care of or accept the political minority. Should democracy, for example, give a small majority the possibility of not respecting a minority's specific interests?

In many countries, democracy has historically been followed by a period of dictatorship and then, after a certain period, a return to democracy. Examples of such countries are **Germany, Italy, Japan,** and **Russia**.

One of the questions that arise when discussing democracy is how to elect representatives. Should all the small groups be represented in the parliament, with the risk that it may not be possible to form a majority coalition, thus making it impossible to steer the country effectively? The expression a "Polish parliament" originates from the situation in **Poland** in the 1920s when there were so many parties in parliament that it was not possible to form a coalition, and no decisions could be made.

On the other hand, some types of electoral system have been criticized for not being sufficiently democratic. For example, in the British system, one party can govern with only around 35 percent of the population supporting it. This is because of the first-past-the-post system (i.e., only one representative from each constituency). Furthermore, it is nearly impossible for new parties to emerge, which tends to result in a dual party system. The electoral college in the **United States**, through which a minority of the voters can elect a president, has also been criticized.

The relationship between the media and elected officials and candidates has come more into focus because of the media's increased influence in democratic elections.

In social policy, democracy has been tied particularly to how to integrate the more vulnerable in society, that is, to prevent them from social exclusion from decision making.

Finally, the question has been raised within social policy in the past 10 to 15 years of how to involve people in the decision-making process of the various institutions and at the local level in general. Democracy, therefore, is an issue not only on the macrolevel but also on the local level.

DEMOGRANT. This **social security** scheme is financed with public money and, when a specific social contingency occurs, there is a right to benefit. This implies that no means test is taken into consideration. The aim of the demogrant has been to supply a minimum, flat-rate level of benefit for groups that without doubt are **deserving**, therefore requiring no means test. Typical examples are **child benefits** and invalidity pensions.

DEMOGRAPHY. This is an analysis and description of a given population, describing the population in different age groups, the number of births, number of deaths, and **migration**. It provides information about the population at a specific time (stock) and the movement during, normally, one year (flow).

Demographic figures are calculated in various ways, because the number of deaths and births is not enough in itself to describe a population and its trends. The number of elderly, for example, affects the absolute numbers of deaths. The overall change in population is influenced by deaths, births, and migration. The absolute figures present only part of the picture; therefore, relative numbers are calculated including, for example, the number of children a generation of women is expected to give birth to. This makes it necessary to know the number of fertile women, that is, women between the ages of 15 and 49. This information can then form the basis for a calculation of expected trends in population in the years to come.

Demographic information about changes in different groups of the population is used in a number of disciplines and for various purposes. For example, it is used to forecast the consequences of the demand for **health care** and **day care** for children and schools. Furthermore, the **dependency ratio**, and changes in it, can be used to estimate either a need for retaining money for these purposes in the future or for finding ways to reduce dependency and related costs.

In relation to the private **pension** market, changes in demography, and especially life expectancy, have played a vital role in developing adequate solutions to the risk insurance companies incur when covering specific groups. How high should the group's premium be if an individual is entitled to receive a pension when retiring, and what is the risk of paying out life insurance if the individual dies before reaching the age of retirement? Knowledge about mortality and the causes of death has a high value for those offering this type of insurance.

Finally, knowledge about demographic changes may play an important role in how public sector expenditure will change and how private producers may also need to change their production. In most countries, a lot of demographic statistics are readily available. Certain demographic information is sometimes seen as an indicator of the level of welfare in a given society. This is the case, for example, with the average life expectancy and infant mortality. A long average life expectancy is seen as proof that, among other things, the welfare state is providing a good **health** system, good nutrition, etc.

In recent years, demographic analysis has been used especially to predict and analyze the consequences of the aging of societies, which will take place in most Western countries through the year 2050. There has been a growing concern about the impact on public sector spending and the ability to have a sustainable welfare state, and this have been raised in the discussions in many countries. Demographic information is thus also important in analyzing and making decisions about the long-term development of welfare states.

DENMARK. Denmark follows the **Scandinavian welfare state** type. The origin of the Danish welfare state goes back to the poor relief acts of 1798. However, in the first Danish constitution of 1848, poor people were deprived of their political rights when receiving poor relief.

In the period before the Industrial Revolution, some voluntary sickness insurance funds where established. But it was only in the late 1880s that new laws where introduced. In 1888, a law on child maintenance for children born outside wedlock was enacted. In 1891, a new poor relief law was enacted, in 1892 a sickness insurance reform was passed, and 1898 saw the introduction of **accident insurance** reform. **Unemployment** insurance reform followed in 1907. **Bismarck** inspired the changes, but from the beginning, the Danes tended to adopt a more universal approach. In 1933, a coalition between workers and farmers (which also had a majority in parliament) introduced a whole new set of laws, which were passed. These included the Public Assistance Act, the National Insurance Act, the Employment Exchange and Unemployment Insurance Act, and the Accident Insurance Act. These new laws can be seen as a first attempt to create a welfare state based on universal coverage and paid for by general taxation. These changes were combined with a wish to fine tune the economy through public intervention.

After World War II new areas were covered. The most important was the old age pension without a means test, introduced in 1956. Reforms were made in sickness insurance and public assistance. Unlike what had happened when the first constitution was adopted, there was no loss of civil rights as a consequence of receiving public assistance. As an example of the move toward a general welfare state, the government assumed marginal responsibility for unemployment funds in 1967. Furthermore, the state's overall spending in the field of social policy grew rapidly—from around 10 percent of GDP in the late 1940s to around 17 to 18 percent in the late 1960s.

The reforms continued, albeit more slowly, in the 1970s, and gradually stopped in the 1980s. Still, the Danish welfare state can be characterized as a model of the universal approach, also based on broad societal agreement among different groups and a **corporatist** way of dealing with many problems. This is especially so in relation to labor market policy. The trend in the 1980s included a more highly decentralized welfare state model.

It could be said that the Danish welfare state has matured and therefore is only making gradual changes in light of pressure for both reforms and cuts in expenditures. However, at the same time a system with relatively high public support continues to exist.

DEPENDENCY. This is the economic, physical, or psychological need of an individual person for the delivery of services in-kind or cash that the person relies on receiving. Dependency can be either material or nonmaterial, as the dependent person may, for example, have the necessary economic means but still feel lonely. Often dependencies focus on various kinds of support from the **welfare state**. *See also* DEPENDENCY RATIO.

DEPENDENCY RATIO. This ratio calculates the relationship between those who are dependent on welfare services and those who are not. It is a way of describing the burden of those who have to pay for those receiving benefits from the public sector. Those paying may naturally at other times in their life cycle be receiving benefits.

The dependency ratio is frequently defined as the ratio between those aged 15 to 65 and those younger and older. A dependency ratio of 1 indicates that there is a balance between the number of those able to participate in production and the number of those not able to. It is not possible to state just from the dependency ratio anything specific about the possibility of **financing** a welfare state, as this also depends on the total level of production and internal decisions about how to finance the welfare state. However, the dependency ratio may provide valuable information about the future consequences of changes in **demography**.

Dependency ratios may also be calculated to compare those having a job with the rest of the population and may use groups other than ages 15 to 65 when making comparisons. In recent years, dependency ratios have mainly been used to analyze how the change in the number of elderly may affect either total public sector expenditure or **pension** funds. Furthermore, the figures have been used to discuss possible future problems of the **social security** systems of an **aging** of society.

DEPRIVATION. When a person or group does not have the possibilities considered "normal" in a given society, that person or group is considered to be deprived. Such people or groups usually have a very low standard of living compared to the average for that society. Deprivation is closely related to the concepts of **inequality**, **poverty**, **social exclusion**, and **justice**. Deprivation can be in one specific area or occur in several areas. It can also be interpreted in both absolute and relative terms. *Absolute deprivation* refers to a situation in which the individual is denied certain rights, whereas *relative deprivation* mainly refers to a situation in which the individual does not have full or sufficient access to a set of specified goods and services.

DESERVING (AND UNDESERVING). The deserving are those who, through no fault of their own, are poor and have a right (deserve) to receive benefits from the public sector. Historically, the use of the concept of deserving and undeserving poor has had different connotations. The undeserving poor in some countries lost their right to vote when receiving **social assistance**. The level of benefits to the undeserving poor has always been lower than to the deserving poor. In some systems, only the deserving poor could receive benefits; the undeserving poor were left to beg on the streets and live off the charity of other people.

The notion of deserving versus undeserving can still be found in discussions about social policy. While the deserving poor (e.g., the elderly, disabled, chronically ill) receive benefits without any counterclaims being made from the public sector, the undeserving poor have to prove that they need assistance and should often be prepared to do something in order to receive a benefit. It is not always possible to differentiate the deserving from the usually undeserving; only in a few objective cases is it possible to distinguish clearly between the two.

The unemployed may be both deserving and undeserving. They are considered deserving in most countries if they have actively been searching for jobs or were laid off because the company closed down or reduced the number employed. If, on the other hand, they quit their jobs, only searched briefly for new jobs, and had not been willing to move for work, then they could be thought of as undeserving. In cent years in many Western countries, migrants from the third work have often been looked upon as undeserving, and issues of ethni and welfare state benefits have thus often arisen. Between the categories are many gradations, and it also seems that the distinci is closely bound to a moral standpoint, which may change over and within different cultures.

DIAGNOSIS RELATED GROUPS SYSTEMS (DRGS). Diagnos related groups are standardized sets of treatment for specific di In health care, a DRG fee will be paid to the provider for the vi delivered. **Health care** systems in different countries use different sets of DRGs. DRGs relate to differences in the costs of health and also to different priorities in the management of the health care system.

DISABILITY. A disability is the inability to do something that one could do before. Disabilities can be either physical or psychological, that is, that the disabled individual faces a certain disadvantage. This disadvantage can take the form of a direct physical handicap or be the inability to be part of a group or to interact with other people in a given society. *See also* DISABILITY BENEFIT.

DISABILITY BENEFIT. This benefit is provided by the welfare state to people with certain physical or psychological handicaps as determined by medical examination. The criteria for receiving a disability benefit can vary among countries, and the provision can be either public or insurance based. In most countries the criteria are primarily focused on physical handicaps as decided by medical examination of the individual, but psychological disabilities are covered, although to a lesser degree. *See also* DISABILITY.

DISCRETION. Discretion is the ability of those administering social systems to make an independent assessment of the needs of the applicant when making decisions. This issue is often debated in relation to **street-level bureaucrats**, as it is possible that the individual client's level of benefit will be dependent on which bureaucrat he or she has contact with.

DISINCENTIVE. A disincentive is a benefit in cash or kind (or a service) that reduces the individual's willingness to do something, primarily either save or work. The disincentive can be a high level of benefits, high taxes and duties, a low wage level, or a combination of factors.

A high combined marginal tax rate and reduction in **social security** benefits can result in a situation where an individual who becomes employed will have no increase in disposable income. This is described as a disincentive to take up a job, and it can also be labeled the poverty trap. Changing the level of benefit can reduce disincentives, as can changing the period during which an individual can receive the benefit or benefit by the marginal income tax. Finally, reducing disincentives can be done by training to improve the individual's position on the labor market or by a general **active labor market policy**.

DISTRIBUTION. Distribution refers to how income and wealth are divided among different groups in a society. Besides describing the division of money, it may also include a description of how other goods are distributed as well as the nature of access to different types of services (mainly public) in a society.

Distribution can be analyzed in two ways. **Functional distribution** shows how income has been divided among those production factors participating in the production process, whereas personal **income distribution** focuses on different people's shares of the total annual income in a given society. The personal income distribution can sometimes be considered for individuals, families, and various occupational groups. The emphasis is on people instead of factors of production.

The theory of how income is distributed in a society often takes as its starting point demand and supply, **human capital**, productivity of different persons, and production factors. However, it can also analyze the strengths of different groups involved in the production process and in society in general.

Distribution is often measured as deviations from a strictly equal division. This may have different starting points by emphasizing different perspectives in a distribution, for example, those who are farthest away from the average or median income in a society. The distribution can be measured by the **Gini coefficient**. Most analyses take as their starting point the statistics for income and wealth. However, they also acknowledge that this is not a very good and precise measure because some income is not declared and the hidden economy may produce different results.

Distribution and the description of distribution are also used to analyze the number of people living in **poverty** and how many are living below a certain poverty line.

Finally, distribution and information about it are used in comparing various countries and within individual countries over time. These figures supplement the information given by the per capita production presented in national statistics, that is, the gross national product per inhabitant.

DOMICILIARY CARE. In social services, this is the care delivered in people's own homes.

DUAL LABOR MARKET. This is a specific way of describing the labor market that emphasizes that there is a core and a periphery. In the core, the stable and well-paid jobs are available to the core labor force, which often, but not always, are those with the highest level of education or long-term employment for the same employer. On the periphery, only low, insecure jobs are available. Those jobs often require a lower level of education or no education at all, and working conditions are rather poor. The periphery has generally been in sectors of a society's industrial production, but it has recently been moving in the industrialized world to the service sector, where many jobs offer little security and low pay.

The theory of the dual labor market has been used to explain why certain groups have a higher risk of living in poverty, why wages are stagnant, and why labor markets are not clearing to let the unemployed back in. The argument is that those at the core of the labor market—which is most of the labor force—are not willing to give up their demands for higher wages to allow those who are perhaps less able to gain a place in the labor market, which they will only have access to if minimum wage levels are lowered.

This concept should not be taken too literally but rather as a way of thinking about how the labor market functions, because most countries have many different **segments** in the labor market, and it would be difficult to describe each of these with any degree of precision and even more difficult to analyze the position of many different groups.

– E –

EARLY RETIREMENT. This occurs when someone leaves the labor market before reaching the normal pension age. In some countries, early retirement schemes have been developed. The intention of those schemes is to allow those who are not able to continue in the **labor market** for a very long period to leave it with specific **benefits**. These benefits have also been used as part of active **labor market policy** as a way of reducing the supply of labor and thereby reducing **unemployment**. Facing changes in **demography** and the need for more labor in the future, several countries have tightened the eligibility conditions for receiving early retirement benefits. Still, with countries becoming richer, more people tend to leave the labor market early in order to enjoy a "third age" with time to do other things, such as traveling, reading, and enjoying other cultural activities. This is an example of how a noneconomic **incentive** can have an impact on the individual's behavior. *See also* STATUTORY RETIREMENT AGE.

EARNINGS-RELATED BENEFITS. These benefits are dependent on one's previous income. In many cases the benefit is a percentage of the previous earned income that qualifies for that benefit. This percentage may be combined with an upper ceiling. In many countries, this has been the case for benefits in relation to **unemployment** and sickness and more often now in several countries in relation to **pensions**. This is because in some pension systems, the connection to earnings has been built on the contributions paid during the years in the labor market.

EASTERN EUROPEAN WELFARE STATE MODEL. This describes the state and social policy systems in Eastern European countries until they were broken up in the late 1980s. Before this happened, the systems mainly relied on state provision, delivery, and financing of social policy. Some of the countries in Eastern Europe have had a history of being involved in social policy in ways similar to other Central European countries and through **church** provision. Therefore, in addition to the state benefits, some have been provided by **families** or churches and have been based on the labor market with the system's commitment to full employment.

The systems that existed before the late 1980s could be characterized as having job security and universal free **health** care services. In addition, they subsidized food and **housing**, which greatly reduced insecurity. Also included were well-developed maternity systems. But due to job guarantees, there was no **unemployment benefit** system, no **social assistance**, and only a very rudimentary way of dealing with more specific problems in the fields of **social policy**. The individual had a right as a citizen to a job, and support was based on this, even if part of the employment was "hidden unemployment."

The main advantage of these systems was this set of guarantees. The main disadvantages were the lack of development of a real **social security** system and the lack of support for those who did not really fit into the labor market or who had other social needs. **Pensions** were often very low, and the state apparatus granted privileges to certain groups, making society unequal. **Inequality** was therefore not— as in the rest of Europe and the **United States**—related to being in the labor market or having capital income but more on whether or not one belonged to the "ruling class."

The changes of the late 1980s and 1990s have had far-reaching consequences for these countries' systems. At present, they are developing in a variety of directions. In reaction to the old state bureaucratic systems, many countries have relied more on market provision and therefore have moved toward a more **liberal** approach to welfare state development. Because some have historical ties with Central Europe, they have developed systems that resemble the **Bismarckian** one, which, however, due to financial pressure look more like a **Southern European model**, with high dependence on families as the main providers and only marginal intervention from the state. *See also* CZECH REPUBLIC; ESTONIA; HUNGARY; LATVIA; LITHUANIA; POLAND; SLOVAKIA; SLOVENIA.

EDUCATION. Historically education has not been thought of as an element of the welfare state's delivery, but at the same time it has always been considered a **merit good,** in the sense that individuals, if given the choice, may prefer less education than what from the society's point of view is the optimal level.

In modern welfare states, education has become more centralized as a mechanism for ensuring both that all citizens actively participate in society's **democratic** life and that the society has an educated workforce. A highly educated workforce is seen as an instrument for ensuring competitiveness against other countries but also as a way of reducing pressure on public spending, because in most **welfare states,** the degree of **unemployment** is related to the level of educational attainment. **Active labor market policies** in many countries therefore include education as one of their essential elements. Education has become increasingly important because resorting to the most traditional economic instruments has become more difficult in individual countries due to economic **globalization.**

ELASTICITY. This is the degree to which a change in one factor will have an impact on another factor. Elasticity of demand and supply refers to how the quantity of a good demanded and supplied will react to a change in the price of the specific good. Welfare state analysis examines labor market elasticity, which indicates how a change in wage level or taxation could have an impact on the labor force supply.

EMPLOYMENT. This is time spent by a worker in the production process. It is seen as the individual's participation in the labor market to produce goods and services and thereby provide a labor input (there is also input from land and capital) to production.

National employment statistics only include that which can be measured and registered. Therefore, time spent on production in households is not regarded as employment; the same is the case for voluntary work and work in the hidden economy.

Besides giving rise to income for a person or family in many societies, employment also brings social esteem and **integration** into societal life. Those without work are therefore, besides being without income, often also deprived of contact with many others and socially excluded.

Full employment is defined as all those willing to work and wanting a job being able to get one. In neoclassical economics, full employment is defined as being the point at which all those willing to work at the going wage-rate can get a job. In **Keynesian** economics, it reflects whether or not there is a full utilization of productive resources and **unemployment** is therefore minimal.

Unemployment will often exist, but the amount will vary over time. There may also be underemployment, which is the case when someone wanting work is not actively searching for it due to conditions in the labor market that make the chance of getting a job relatively low. Furthermore, people may work part-time but really want a full-time job. In developing countries, many will have to live off agricultural production, which frequently is done on plots of a very small size. They are employed, but if possible, they would want to have either more land to work on or to get a job in another sector.

ENTITLEMENTS. This concept describes what the individual in case a certain contingency occurs can be expected to receive. Entitlements can be based upon citizenship, contribution (voluntary or obligatory), and can then be either based upon rights or discretationary decisions by the administration.

EQUAL OPPORTUNITY. This is **equality** in the sense that equal groups should be treated equally. Equal opportunity can exist between different groups in societies (e.g., migrant and nonmigrant workers) or between different sexes. Equality of opportunity can also be related to the **educational** system. This means that a individual has the same chances. However, the result may still be **inequality** due to different **capabilities** or individual work, either because of difference in working hours or differences in wages in the different segments of the labor market. *See also* GENDER.

EQUALITY. Equality refers to the **distribution** of resources in different societies. It can be interpreted in different ways and is often interwoven with moral judgments. The definition of equality stated below has implications for the political decisions made in a given society. It can take different forms: **equal opportunity**, equal treatment, and equal outcome.

Equal opportunity refers society's efforts to ensure that all citizens have the same chances in life. This means that society should intervene when, for instance, monopolies threaten to reduce the individual's opportunities. It can also be used as an argument for state involvement in **education** to ensure that individuals from different social backgrounds have the same chances.

Equal treatment refers to equal cases being treated in the same way. This means that people experiencing the same situation should be treated in the same way as others. This does not necessarily imply an equal distribution of income and wealth but is more a guideline for how to behave in specific situations in society.

Equal outcome focuses on the evaluation of the situation by different persons in society where the outcome of different activities, for example, in the labor market, has an impact on the individual's situation. In cases where very different outcomes are measured, for example, in money terms, then this means that the public sector should intervene to try to make the situation equal for all persons.

None of these definitions of equality gives any indication of which type of intervention should be used in various situations. Nor do they give any **normative** indication of which type of equality will be preferable and which may be in a conflict with other societal goals or the time over which it should be measured. They merely point to how equality can be interpreted in different ways and how, in a given society, equality will depend on normative viewpoints. Finally, the concept of equality can be used as a framework for comparing different situations in or between countries.

The concept of equality can also be interpreted by comparing it with concepts such as **inequality**, **functional distribution**, **income distribution**, and so forth. *See also* GINI COEFFICIENT; LORENZ CURVE.

EQUILIBRIUM. In economic theory, equilibrium refers to a balance between supply and demand. In purely market-based countries, the expectation is that the market will lead society toward equilibrium, which includes full **employment**, no surplus of certain goods and services, and full utilization of production facilities.

In real life, equilibrium does not exist, or if it does, it is difficult to measure and normally society is on the way from one equilibrium to another. As a concept, is it useful as an analytical tool to describe how different types of interventions and disturbances may affect behavior and the market's functioning.

ESTONIA. This is a small Baltic country with around 1.5 million inhabitants, which became independent again in 1991 after having been part of the Union of Soviet Socialist Republics (USSR) since 1940. In 1922, Estonia was one of the first countries to introduce the family allowance. This was followed in 1924 by laws concerning **pensions**, **sickness** and **maternity benefits**, and **industrial injury**. The present day social security system resembles to a high degree a continental welfare model built on a social insurance system. Employers pay one-third of the costs for old age, disability, sickness, maternity, and industrial injury benefits. The state finances **family** allowances, unemployment benefits, and **health care**.

In 1994, Estonia became a member of the **European Union**. Estonia's economy has grown rapidly since it gained independence from the Union of Soviet Socialist Republics.

ETHNICITY. This refers to the shared ethnic background of a group. In **welfare state** analysis, it has been shown that in many countries there is discrimination based on ethnicity, such as higher **unemployment** rates and less access to public services. Ethnicity has assumed an increasing role in welfare state analysis because migrants, especially, are often not well integrated into societies and therefore often have worse living conditions than those coming from the society originally.

EUROPEAN SOCIAL MODEL. This model is conceived of in the **European Union** as one welfare state model that could be used to compare the **United States** and Europe. It is not yet exactly clear what type of welfare state model this should be. One reason for this may be that, in general, it is difficult to reach agreement within the European Union in areas concerning social and **labor market** policy. The fact remains that national differences exist, and various approaches to the welfare state exist.

However, some core elements exist, including the guarantee of a decent standard of living for all and an agreement that an inclusive society should be built. Moreover, access to the labor market is expected, and goals for the participation rate of men and women, young and elderly, have been set. Thus, in many ways, the European Social Model can be understood as a combination of various traditional welfare state models.

EUROPEAN UNION (EU). Formerly called the European Economic Community and the European Community, the EU now consists of 25 members (**Italy, France, the Netherlands, Belgium,** Luxembourg, **Germany,** the **United Kingdom, Ireland, Denmark, Spain, Portugal, Greece, Finland, Sweden, Austria, Estonia, Latvia, Lithuania, Poland, Hungary, Czech Republic, Slovakia, Slovenia,** Cyprus, and Malta). The first six countries in the list founded EU in 1957. In 1973, the next three countries joined; in 1980, Spain, Portugal, and Greece entered; and in 1994, it was the turn of the Finland, Sweden, and Austria. On May 1, 2004, the last ten countries entered, coming mainly from Eastern Europe. More countries from Eastern Europe are expected to join in the coming years.

The European Union originated from the idea of a customs union facilitating trade and using the various countries' comparative advantages when trading with each other. The EU was also seen by some as a way of reducing conflicts in Europe, especially the historical conflicts between France and Germany.

The development of EU social policy is a long and complex story. It started with the initial treaty in 1957, which increased labor mobility and **social security** for migrant workers. In 1971, a reform of the European Social Fund (ESF) included funding for vocational training, and the reform continued in 1974 with the Social Action Program (SAP), which among other things included promotion of employment and a social dialogue in Europe, including the first EU **poverty** program. This was followed by a long period without any new initiatives, which ended in 1987 with adoption of the Single European Act (SEA). The SEA introduced recommendations about **health** and safety of workers and stated the intention of economic and social cohesion. In 1989, a Community Charter of Fundamental Social Rights was adopted, including 47 initiatives, one of which was concerned with **employment** and remuneration.

In 1991, the Maastricht Agreement was concluded, which had a Protocol on Economic and Social Integration and a Social Dimension (which does not include the United Kingdom). This was followed by recommendations on convergence and guaranteed minimum income in 1992 (recommendations are not binding on the member states in contrast to directives).

Labor market policy was included in the Amsterdam Treaty in 1997, and the aim of the European Union was described not only as including traditional economic aspects but also to ensure a high level of employment. Based on the Amsterdam Treaty, in 1997, guidelines for National Action Plans for Employment were adopted in Luxembourg. These action plans, which later would be labeled the **open method of coordination (OMC)**, were an attempt to encourage a common understanding of the need for an **active labor market policy**. Later more areas of **social policy (pension, social exclusion)** became part of the OMC.

Still, the European Union does not have any real impact on welfare state policies in the individual member states, because social and labor market policy, including financing of the welfare state, is decided by the nation-states. Only in relation to the free movement of workers, health and safety at the workplace, and equal treatment of men and women does the EU have a direct impact on the nation-states' policies.

However, the increased awareness on the supranational level of social and welfare policy, as well as the more economic aspects that the EU addresses may influence the member states to pursue a more common policy, leading to at least some degree of **convergence**.

The EU's initiatives have already had a huge impact on the development of social policy regarding health and safety and equal treatment of men and women. The same is true for spending through the ESF and other regional and structural funds, where the economically weaker areas of the European Union especially are supported.

The EU's impact on the development of the welfare state cannot be overemphasized and should not be neglected. The ongoing enlargement of the European Union could indicate a trend toward more uniform welfare states in Europe, especially if it evolves into a more integrated economic and monetary union. Some have labeled this a **European Social Model**.

EVERYDAY LIFE. As a sociological term, this describes **family** life. It is a way of examining roles and relationships in day-to-day life. It is often used in sociological analysis to describe the home, neighborhood, and local community and the individual's lifestyles within them.

EXIT, VOICE, AND LOYALTY. This concept was developed by Albert Hirschman (1972) to describe the ways that individuals in society can respond to decisions and find solutions to different problems. They can exit (i.e., **migrate** or move to another area of the country). They can raise their voice, either in debate or by voting for a party at the next election who takes an opposing standpoint. Finally, they can be loyal and agree with the decisions made.

In the welfare state debate, this term has been used to argue in favor of a more decentralized way of organizing the welfare state. In a highly decentralized system, it may be possible to develop different combinations of services, transfers, and local **taxes** that the individual will have the opportunity to choose and combine as he or she prefers.

– F –

FABIANISM. This movement was formed by people in the **United Kingdom** who advocated a **collectivist** approach to **social policy** and argued that the capitalist system would inevitably crumble. They believed that a universal and collectively decided welfare state would be developed out of the old system. Fabians saw the **Beveridge** approach as confirming their ideas about and visions of society's development.

FAMILY. This is an institution within which many different activities take place. It normally refers to parents and their children. In a larger framework, the family can include all those who are relatives, mainly in a biological sense. The term nuclear family refers to families consisting of parents and immature children. This is seen as the narrowest way of defining a family.

The concept of the family is related to different **welfare states** and their way of functioning. In many welfare states, and especially those where the state only intervenes as the lender of last resort (i.e., **sub**sidiarity exists), the family plays an important role in the delivery of care and different types of income transfers. In these systems, the family structure will have a strong impact on whether or not a person is covered (or supported) in the event a specific contingency occurs.

The role of the family can be analyzed from various viewpoints, but the analytical unit generally tends to be the household instead of the family. The reasons for this are both practical and theoretical. The practical reason is that many statistics are based on the special the household. The theoretical reason is that a household is the the individual is living in, and although this may consist of relatives it may also consist of many other people, including friends, lovers and companions. *See also* DEFAMILIZATION; GENDER.

FAMILY ALLOWANCE. This is support to **families** with children. The way it is structured and the criteria for receiving it vary among different **welfare states**. It is also known as **child benefit**.

FAMILY REGIMES. This term describes how various societies place different emphases on the role of the family. These range from full **defamilization** to reliance on the family as the main provider, as in the **Southern European welfare state** type. Regimes often describe the difference between the male **breadwinner** and dual breadwinner types of household.

FEMINISM. This is both a theory and a movement based on the belief that women are treated in a systematically different way (and disadvantaged) compared to men in the welfare state. Feminist researchers have claimed that most research has not taken into consideration the specific sociological impact of differences in **gender** when analyzing the outcomes of the welfare state.

Feminist researchers adopt different dividing lines in their research compared to other types of welfare state research such as **liberal** and **Marxist**. In many countries the issue of gender has been used, among other things, in relation to the analysis of labor market development, as in most countries women earn less, do more part-time work, and are often in more insecure jobs, than men.

FINANCING. This is the means through which support is funded. There are many different ways to finance the welfare state. It is important to understand these different approaches and their relation to welfare state development and how the different ways of financing in different models can be interpreted.

In principle, it is not necessary to collect **taxes** and duties, but not doing so has economic consequences such as problems with the balance of payments, public sector debt, inflation, and bottlenecks in the labor market. All taxes and duties collected will have an impact on allocation, stabilization, and distribution in the economy. Furthermore, they will all cause some distortion, for example, the choice between work and leisure, saving and consumption, and the use of capital and labor in the production process. Taxes and duties may further change the consumption patterns of various goods and services. They could, for example, switch the consumer's spending from tobacco to milk by putting a high duty on tobacco and none on milk.

Taxes and duties can, in principle, be imposed in all parts of the economy. They can be levied on households, firms, markets for goods (consumer or capital), or factor markets. Furthermore, they can be placed on wealth, inheritances, and so forth.

User charges and obligatory insurance membership can also be thought of as a way of financing the welfare state. Social insurance contributions may also be another way of financing welfare programs rather than using income tax or duties.

The core elements of a good tax structure include that:

- It will provide adequate revenue.
- It will ensure an equitable distribution of the tax burden.
- It will minimize excess burden and can be achieved with low administrative cost.
- It can be used to achieve economic goals (stabilization, allocation).

Taxes and duties often take the form of

- Income taxes
- **Social security** contributions

- Value added taxes (VAT)
- Duties
- Others (e.g., property, bequest, wealth).

The most frequently used are income taxes, social security contributions, and value-added taxes. The combination of these varies to a very great extent between countries. One could argue that user payments and user charges are a way of financing part of public sector expenditures. Obligatory insurance, privately organized and delivered, could indirectly also be a way of financing the welfare state.

Welfare states that have a more universal approach often rely on income taxes and value-added taxes, whereas welfare states with a more selective approach tend to use social security contributions. Welfare states taking a minimalist approach rely mainly on private charity.

The manner of financing the welfare state also depends on the historical traditions and development of welfare states. The more mature welfare states seem to have a higher overall level of taxes and duties as a proportion of Gross Domestic Product (GDP) than do the newer welfare states. Many Western European welfare states spend from 45 to 50 percent of GDP on public sector expenditures. Not all of this is spent on social policy in its broad meaning, but it indicates the influence of the public sector on the economy and the need to finance it.

Different ways of financing public sector expenditures have different social policy implications with respect to who pays and who receives benefits from the public sector.

Using contributions—and not making them obligatory—implies that only those who contribute will be covered. The criterion for coverage will often be having a job in the labor market, but it could be something else, such as voluntary payment to life insurance. A consequence of relying on contributions is a tendency toward a more polarized society, dividing those inside and those outside the labor market. In the field of **health care**, the difference between those paying into a contributory system and those not paying—as in the U.S. system—results in an unequal treatment of individuals, and for some, no treatment at all.

Using income taxes and duties may indicate a more universal system in which the right to a benefit or service depends on being a citizen in the given country. In addition, taxes and duties may have the consequence of changing the **distribution** of resources as a result of their impact on individual choices. This can happen in two different ways. The first is between generations (intergenerational) and the second is within generations (intragenerational).

Intragenerational redistribution through the tax and duty system has the aim of ensuring that those with a high income pay more in taxes than those with a small income. This redistribution will be combined with public sector spending mainly devoted to those with a small income, resulting in redistribution from rich to poor. How effective this redistribution is depends not only on the level and composition of the tax and duty systems but also on how the public sector spends its money.

During their lifetimes, some people may be among both those paying for and those receiving benefits. This is intergenerational redistribution. Frequently this is mainly within areas such as care and benefits for children and the elderly. Those who are elderly and now perhaps receive a public pension or are in care have previously paid the taxes and duties. In this sense, one generation is paying for the next generation and expects that the coming generation will do the same.

Taxes and duties are therefore of great importance to the welfare state and how it fulfills its goal. Furthermore, taxes and duties will have an impact on the society's overall economic functioning and on redistribution between and within generations.

Countries cannot just impose whatever types of taxes and duties they would like if they are open market economies. **Globalization** has an impact on how an individual country can chose its tax packages. Taxes on companies, for example, will have an impact on the firm's location, and in order to attract foreign investments, countries are often willing to change to a lower level of these taxes compared to neighboring countries. Higher duties on goods that can easily be traded across borders are also more difficult to impose. Thus, although globalization has not created serious difficulties in financing the welfare state, it has imposed certain restrictions on choices about taxes and duties.

FINLAND. The welfare state in Finland started with a law on **industrial injury** in 1895. This was followed by an **unemployment** insurance law in 1917 (changed to unemployment assistance in 1960), a law on **pension** and **disability** in 1937, a law on **family allowances** in 1948, and a law on sickness and **maternity** in 1963. Finland has gradually developed its system and has been a latecomer in many areas compared to the other Nordic countries. This may be explained partly by its history. From 1809 to 1917, Finland was under Russian rule and thereafter a two-year civil war prevented a real development of social policy.

Finland was hard hit by the changes in Eastern Europe in the late 1980s, and therefore it tightened the welfare system during the 1990s, although without making very dramatic changes in its overall composition. Today, Finland's welfare state resembles in many respects the other **Scandinavian welfare state** types but with a much more direct influence from the **Bismarckian** type.

FISCAL POLICY. This is the government's intervention in the economy, either through taxes and duties or government expenditure. The intervention can have the purpose of expanding or contracting the economy.

Fiscal policy was seen by **John Maynard Keynes** as one way of managing the economy to achieve stable economic growth. The use of fiscal policy could help achieve a more balanced economy, including balance of payments equilibrium and low **unemployment** rates. This approach was mainly inspired by a belief in macroeconomic policy. Questions were raised later about how the microeconomic level was affected by changes in fiscal policy, that is, the impact on incentives and the willingness to work and save.

As economies have gradually become more open, it has become harder to use fiscal policy in individual countries, especially the expansive version of fiscal policy, without creating balance of payment problems. Still, fiscal policy does play a role in preventing huge swings in the economy, so fiscal policy on a smaller scale can be used. A country facing deterioration in the balance of payments or in the level of unemployment may use fiscal policy in a limited way to ensure better overall macroeconomic balance.

FISCAL FEDERALISM. This is the understanding of which level of government has the right to tax and levy duties. It is often supplemented by a discussion of at which level taxation or duties are best imposed: supranational, state, regional, or local.

FISCAL WELFARE. This is welfare distributed through the tax system. Fiscal welfare can, for example, be the support to homeowners through a right to deduct interest payments. Fiscal welfare can be an alternative way to achieve certain welfare goals as opposed to **public** or **occupational welfare.** *See also* SOCIAL DIVISION OF WELFARE; TAX EXPENDITURES; TITMUSS, RICHARD MORRIS.

FLAT-RATE BENEFITS. These are benefits paid at the same rate to all who are eligible. These types of benefits are not **earnings related.** Even flat-rate benefits may be means-tested based on income and wealth; that is, only those with an income or wealth below a certain level will receive the benefit. Flat-rate benefits were part of the **Beveridgian** description of a new social policy in the **United Kingdom** after World War II. The extent of these kinds of benefits varies among different types of welfare states.

FLAT-RATE PENSION. This is a **pension** that does not depend on contributions or previous earnings. It can therefore also be labeled a **universal** benefit. Its level may depend on the number of persons in the household, and it can also be **means-tested.**

FLEXICURITY. This term refers to a situation that combines a highly flexible **labor market,** as in the **post-Fordist** production system, with a high degree of social security, which is attained through welfare state benefits and by ensuring a decent standard of living.

FRANCE. The history of social policy and **social security** in France has had a long-lasting impact on social security development in many other European countries. This is true even though we usually compare the development of welfare states with the situation in the **United Kingdom** and **Germany.**

The French Revolution drastically changed the picture of charity and the role of the **church** in France. Furthermore, in the 1791 constitution, it was declared that citizens had a right to assistance. In 1791, a right to **pensions** for seamen suffering invalidity was also established. In 1852 and 1856, France developed systems that provided subsidies to certain mutual funds covering sickness and invalidity for certain groups.

Mutual assistance and insurance for a very few groups were developed in the beginning and the middle of the nineteenth century, but they did not provide sufficient support to those in need, and many groups were left out. Therefore, in 1898, a **social insurance** system to cover **industrial injury** was introduced. It was a special system for very few groups, but it was an all-encompassing system. These changes were followed in 1905 by an **unemployment** insurance law, then a law concerning old age and **disability** in 1910, and then sickness and maternity laws in 1928 and **family allowances** in 1932.

During World War II, there were plans in France—as in Britain—to develop a more comprehensive system, but it was never implemented in France the same way it was in Britain. There does not seem to be a very satisfactory explanation for this.

France has a mixed type of system in which some aspects—**family allowances**, for example—are of the universal type, and compared to other **European Union** countries they are generous. Other aspects build primarily on the social insurance system. The French system has been developed within France's structure of central administration and is therefore highly centralized compared to other European countries.

However, it is mainly a continental model, and most of the financing comes from payments from those in the labor market and those who are insured. The government is not directly involved in the payment of social security in France, leaving this to the above-mentioned partners. But this does not mean that the government is not actively involved in deciding the levels of benefits and the structure of the system.

In recent years debates have focused especially on the pension system and how to finance it given ongoing **demographic** changes. Lower pensions and more years in the labor market have been discussed as solutions.

FREE RIDE. This is when someone enjoys the benefits of a good or service or agreement but pays nothing for it. In welfare state analysis, the concept has been used as an argument for state provision in certain areas where it is not possible to ask for payment—urban street lighting is an example—and therefore it is not possible to exclude someone from enjoying the good. A free ride is especially possible in relation to **public goods**. The possibility that some are getting a free ride makes it difficult to know the exact preferences and demand for many public services.

FREEDOM. Freedom is the state being independent and free to make one's own decisions. In welfare state analysis, this concept has been used when analyzing **capabilities**, but the conflict between state and market and its impact on the individual's ability to make his or her own decisions has also played a central role. The debate between advocates of **public choice** and advocates of a more central role for the state plays a role in this conflict.

FRIENDLY SOCIETY. Friendly Societies were established in the nineteenth century in many countries to support and protect their members through mutual aid. They can be viewed as an early type of insurance-based solution.

FUNCTIONAL DISTRIBUTION. This is the distribution of income from production among the factors of production: land, labor, and capital. *See also* INCOME DISTRIBUTION.

FUNCTIONALISM. This theory describes the development and growth of the welfare state as a response to changing needs of either citizens or capital interests. In a historical context, this theory asserts that the development of the welfare state will mainly be explained by industrialization. Thus, capitalism needs to be revitalized and receive continued support from the state in order to develop and maintain high profit rates.

FUNDED SYSTEM. This is a specific way of **financing** and developing **pension** systems. Under this system, those who want to have a pension will have to pay a contribution. This can be either voluntary, part of a collective agreement made in the labor market, or compulsory by statutory law. In most countries, the system is based on voluntary or collective agreements. The voluntary systems will frequently be helped and given incentives to develop through state tax subsidies. Collective agreements can take many different forms: agreements in individual firms, collective agreements for a whole sector or industry, or nationwide agreements for specific groups of skilled or unskilled workers.

Funded systems are based on the idea that the individual receives a pension in accordance with what he or she has paid in. Funded systems may be built into a collective agreement covering certain risks, such as invalidity or life insurance. The individual will normally also receive a pension in accordance with what he or she has paid into the system.

Various arguments exist in favor of and against the different types of pension systems. One advantage of a funded system is that it is possible to increase capital stock and thereby presumably also the future level of output, because this capital stock can be invested in productive capacity. The system will normally not be seen as a tax by the individual and will therefore presumably cause fewer distortions between saving/consumption and work/leisure than taxes and duties are normally assumed to create. Finally, another advantage is that the government will know the future size of public sector expenditure in the area, and this will not fluctuate much as a result of the proportion of elderly in society.

The problem with the funded system is that it takes a very long time to implement. For example, decisions about improving the level of benefits may take 30 to 40 years to be fully implemented. The value of pensions can be easily reduced because higher taxes reduce the buying power of the pensioners. Another problem is that if savings are not used to increase production, there may be a balance of payments problem when the pensions have to be paid out. The pensions, as seen from the whole society's point of view, can only be spent if the production capacity is in accordance therewith.

Some would argue that a funded system has the built-in disadvantage that when a government has reduced pressure on expenditure for the elderly, then the government will be able to spend more in some other areas. If the saving is very high, it may depress the overall rate of return due to the very large amount of money used to buy stocks and bonds. Despite increasingly open capital markets, this seems to be a problem only for countries with a more restricted access to international capital markets.

Unless very strict restrictions are imposed on pension funds, there is a risk for the members of the funds if those administering them abuse them or do not invest the money in the best possible way. Members of well-run pension funds may then have higher pensions than those in poorly run ones. In the case of a company-based pension fund, where it is not possible to transfer pension rights when changing jobs, there may also be severe restriction on the way the labor market functions.

Finally, it has been argued that very big pension funds may apply political pressure—"pension fund socialism," as some has labeled it. It is that such large amounts of money collected together could have an impact on society, at least in terms of pressure on the decision-making process.

Ultimately, each country will develop its own combination of these systems. Most countries use a combination of the **pay-as-you-go system (PAYG)** and a funded system to pay for pensions.

– G –

GENDER. A person's sex may affect that person's position in society, and decisions can also be influenced by different perceptions of gender. A growing body of literature has tried to describe and explain how gender has had an impact on welfare states and their development. This type of research tries to explain many different developments in society. It emphasizes the positions of men and women more than **class** or differences in status and income.

In many states, the position of women is often seen as weak, although there has been a movement toward more gender-equal societies in several countries. In welfare state analysis, different concepts of a male-**breadwinner** (strong or weak) model of the welfare state have been introduced. *See also* FEMINISM.

GERMANY. The current German welfare system is still inspired by Otto Von Bismarck and the so-called **Bismarckian model**. Coverage for sickness was introduced in 1883, followed by support for **industrial injury** in 1884 and **invalidity** pensions in 1889. But even before the 1880s, certain groups had industrial injury and sickness insurance in parts of Germany. In 1838, for example, employers were made responsible for labor on railroads. In 1854, compulsory insurance for mineworkers was introduced, and in 1871, employer responsibility for workers in specific parts of the industrial sector was enacted. With the introduction of these laws in the united Germany in the 1880s, the state as an entity took over in areas of social policy that had previously been either ignored, only partly covered, or left to voluntary assistance. The reason for the successful development of the German system was that it was piecemeal and based on mutual aid, which for some already existed. Finally, it did not rely on state intervention alone; the system used a combination of state and private financing and organization.

The development of the welfare system was also a response to growing unrest among the working class in Germany, which arose due to the increasingly difficult and bad working and living conditions in the cities. So the case of Germany exemplifies one of the explanations of the emergence of the welfare state—fear of social upheaval. In addition, economic insecurity after industrialization was taken into account when developing systems by giving better coverage to those families that could no longer rely on other types of income or their own food production.

The structure of the Bismarckian system has, to a very large extent, stayed with the system since it was built, and therefore it still relies on labor market participation, combined with some state financing and intervention. With the founding of the Weimar Republic in 1919, citizens were partially recognized as having some rights, but still the main criterion was, and is, that the individual was in the labor market. It was only in 1927 that a law on unemployment was passed, and **family allowances** were first introduced in 1954.

These late developments can to a certain degree be explained by Germany's defeat in both world wars, which naturally hindered the rapid and continued development of the social system. Furthermore, the role of the **church**—although weaker than before—still existed, and **family** responsibility was—and still is—a factor, as evidenced by the fact that children can be forced to pay their parents.

The German welfare state model follows a more traditional **male-breadwinner** approach than many other Western European welfare states.

The system in Germany is still in most areas building on the Bismarckian reforms, using contributory financing from employers and employees, although nowadays with broader support especially for the very vulnerable groups. Social insurance systems still remain the most central, including a specific system of Plegeversichering for long-term care.

GINI COEFFICIENT. This measures the degree of **inequality** in a **distribution**, which can be income, wealth, or something else. It describes how far away or close a country is to a hypothetical situation of having an **income distribution** where each decile has an equal share (decile) of society's income. It can be illustrated on a diagram with the proportion of the population measured along the horizontal axis and the proportion of income along the vertical axis. If the line in the diagram is straight from the left bottom corner to the upper right corner, then the income distribution is equal, and it has a Gini coefficient equal to 0.

The Gini coefficient can vary between 0 and 1, and the closer it comes to 1 (which is a situation in which one person has the total income or wealth), the more unequal the situation is. Most Western countries experienced a gradual move toward a more equal distribution, measured in this manner, in the period after World War II. This stopped in the 1980s, when the degree of inequality remained almost the same, but some countries experienced a slight decline. Inequality variations are still measured by the Gini coefficient in various welfare states. The Gini coefficient is highest when measured before taxes and transfers in all welfare states. It is only one among various measurements of the degree of equality, although the most commonly used. *See also* LORENZ CURVE.

GLOBALIZATION. In economic terms, globalization refers to increased trade and travel, more open capital markets, capital's ability to move quickly from one point to another, and companies' willingness to relocate production to where labor is cheap. It has been argued that globalization will undermine the nation-states' ability to form and develop their own social policies. There is also concern that global **market failures**, global monopolies, and global economic problems will persist.

The argument for globalization having an impact on welfare state policies centers on the loss of autonomy of the individual nation state, as well as that global competition will weaken those forces in societies that have been the main advocates of welfare. It has been argued that competition, at a constantly lower level of social security by reducing contributions, will gradually undermine the welfare states.

The counterargument is that in a global world there is an even greater need for **social security** as insecurity increases in many areas. The demand for welfare state policies will grow and, at the same time, many countries have become richer as a result of increased global interaction, which has also increased the demand for welfare benefits.

Despite the fact that open market economies have been under pressure from other countries' production, this has not led to a decrease in spending on social welfare; furthermore, programs throughout the world have predominantly been increased, although some retrenchment can also be found. At the same time, globalization should also be expected to deliver different kinds of services and medicine at a cheaper price and thus reduce the economic pressure on the welfare states.

GOVERNMENT. This concept has no clear and unambiguous meaning. There are a variety of forms of government. In Western countries, it usually means that there is a body (the government) which, due to a constitution, has the right to make decisions about governing and should do so in agreement with an elected parliament. In some **democracies**—such as the **United States** and **France**—an elected president has a great deal of influence on the decisions and the appointment of the government.

"Government" may also be given a broader interpretation, encompassing those making legislation, those responsible for implementing the law, and the courts interpreting disputes concerning the laws. Used in this way, it describes a way of ruling a country where power is divided between different organs with different powers in the system.

The focus of welfare state theory has shifted from concentrating on the functions and institutionalized structure of the government to analyzing the built-in consequences of governance on societal development and micro- and macro-decisions. Such analysis examines the impact of the **bureaucracy** and **pressure groups** on the growth of public sector expenditures. Attempts are made to analyze how the system itself contributes to growth in the public sector.

GOVERNMENT FAILURE. This is the opposite of **market failure** and refers to a situation in which **government** intervention in societies and expansion of the public sector becomes larger than is optimal. It is public choice theorists who especially argue the possibility of government failure. They refer to the Leviathan monster of the Bible, implying that the public sector may be crowding out the private sector.

Other arguments for government failure revolve around the impact of **pressure groups** and the **bureaucracy**. It is not possible to measure the possible size of government failure, but it is obvious that as long as market failure exists so may government failure.

GREECE. Greece was a relative latecomer in developing **social security** systems and a broad, all-encompassing welfare state. In the sixth century BC, there was some support for soldiers who had been disabled in battle, and in the fifth century BC it became possible for some persons to receive a specific benefit if an assembly decided that they were eligible for it. This was an early variation of the **means-tested benefit**, and a stigma was attached to receiving it.

With the decline of the old Athenian state system, these benefits apparently vanished. Not until 1914 was a law on industrial injury presented, followed by a law on sickness and maternity in 1922, old age and **disability** in 1934, **unemployment** assistance in 1945, and **family allowances** in 1958.

In recent times, during the period from 1967 to 1974 under a military junta, no real development of social policy occurred. Then in the late 1980s and early 1990s Greece experienced a rapid development of the welfare system in an attempt to match the developments of the rest of the **European Union** (EU). Part of this was financed by regional support from the EU.

Despite its historically close links to **Germany**, Greece belongs more to the **Southern European welfare state model**. Greece spends less on social security than do other EU countries, and it thus also has more rudimentary coverage than other EU-welfare states.

GROWTH OF THE PUBLIC SECTOR, THEORIES. There can be, and are, several explanations for the growth of the public sector—and in most countries the **welfare state**. They range from socioeconomic, ideological, and political institutional perspectives to consumer, financial, and producer perspectives. They include demand and supply arguments for development of public sector expenditures. The need to correct **market failure** can be given as a reason for increasing public sector spending. In the years to come, changes in **demography** may require an increase in spending for health care and pensions.

A useful typology could take its starting point in four dimension with an impact on the growth of the public sector, all dealing with direct or indirect impact. These four dimensions are voters, exogene factors, costs, change at decisive a level. In the following, this typology is shown, and examples of what have the impact is given:

Voters	a) Directly	Ex: Demography
	b) Indirectly	Ex: Voting
Exogene	a) Directly	Ex: Business cycle
	b) Indirectly	Ex: Displacement
Cost	a) Directly	Ex: Baumol's disease
	b) Indirectly	Ex: Fiscal illusions
Decisive level	a) Directly	Ex: Change in ideology
	b) Indirectly	Ex: Bureaucracy and pressure groups.

In various countries and welfare state types, there will be different reasons behind the growth of expenditures. It seems, however, that a mixture of reasons is needed to explain the development of the public sector.

A specific reason for the growth of many more mature welfare states has been the change in the division of labor between **family** and society. Taking care of children and the elderly moved away from the family sphere as women gradually entered the labor market. In this respect, the growth of public sector expenditure can be seen as a response to a change in demand for public sector services and transfers.

It is not possible to provide a single explanation and comparative analysis of the growth of the public sector because frequent changes in the definition of what the public sector is in different countries has resulted in a lack of comparable data. Furthermore, **tax expenditures** are not included in all countries' statistics, and this creates major problems for comparisons between countries.

– H –

HANDICAP. *See* DISABILITY; DISABILITY BENEFIT.

HEALTH. Health and health care are central areas in the **welfare state** that in most countries are paid and delivered on a universal basis. In some countries, health care is financed by different kinds of insurance schemes, often in a combination with user charges. The level of user charges varies between countries, but generally user charges tend to have a negative impact on the distribution.

Health is of central importance for most people, and therefore public support for state intervention tends to be high in many welfare states. The problems within health care involve many ethical questions and also questions with regard to **justice** and **equality**. They raise issues of how to set priorities among persons with different types of illness and also stress the need for measures to prevent people from becoming sick.

In the twentieth and twenty-first centuries health has, in general, been improving, as evidenced by the increase in the average life expectancy. This is a result of both curing sicknesses and reducing infant mortality.

Health care ranges from the direct delivery by general practitioners to specialized treatment at highly specialized hospitals. There are therefore many different types of treatment involved and many different types of persons with different educational backgrounds. This also makes the area of health care a difficult and complicated field to analyze.

Voters' support of spending on health care is often very high, lending support to the **Rawls**ian argument that nobody knows whether or not they will one day be on the other side of the veil and will need treatment. *See also* HEALTH CARE and HEALTH ECONOMICS.

HEALTH CARE and HEALTH ECONOMICS. These are broad topics of importance in **welfare states** regarding their delivery of services to individual citizens. Health care refers to the individual's health independent of who is delivering the services. Health economics is a special discipline within economics that attempts to explain and analyze the development of health care expenditure, the individual's choice among different solutions, and the consequences of different combinations of public, private, and insurance-based solutions with regard to the problems of health care.

Most welfare states offer free access to hospitals, but in some, a private provision also exists. The individual will often have to pay (partly or fully) for medicine and visits to the general practitioner. Some areas are provided for by both the public and the private sectors, and the distinctions are not always clear.

Health care often has the greatest public support when measuring support for specific aspects of the welfare state in different societies, presumably because many people expect to use the system. It is organized quite differently in different countries, and the mix of public and private is very diverse. At the same time, the demand for health care seems unlimited.

Analyzing the area involves ethical, economic, **justice**, and philosophical questions. For example, given scarce resources, who should be treated first, should we treat all diseases, and, if so, which should be treated by the public and which should be treated by the private sector? Will the public sector, for example, supply abortions, and pay for change and manipulation of genes? Should new technologies always be used, and how can one make sure that the costs are covered efficiently? Furthermore, how long should treatment continue for a person with no chance of a continuation of life? Is it acceptable to experiment with human beings to improve life chances for other persons by testing different methods and different medicines?

As societies in more and more countries are graying, the economic pressure in the health care area has become more evident and has led to a need for greater prioritization of the resources available.

Comparative analyses of health care activities are often used to try to make the health care system as efficient as possible. This includes not only the administration and planning of the system but also how users react to different ways of organizing and financing the system.

HEALTH INSURANCE. This is a mechanism for individuals to cover risks of illness and injury if they are not covered by state welfare. The individual, by paying a premium, is covered for the cost of treatment. If the insurer knows about them, "bad lives" will have to pay a higher premium than "good lives." In this way, the use of an insurance system may create **inequality**. Naturally by pooling the risk, which can be done by collective insurances or by the state, this inequality will not arise as the individual is then covered not depending on his/hers own health and risk.

HEALTH MAINTENANCE ORGANIZATION (HMO). This is a system of controlling healthcare costs found primarily in the **United States**. The HMO, through its member providers, provides medical services to member patients, who pay a fee. HMOs assume different forms, and the services provided vary. A critical element is that it is difficult to estimate how to balance the fee and the use of the system, combined with the fact that some are not covered at all.

HEGEMONY. In this system of government, the ruling class in a society dominates specific norms and values. Hegemony can be maintained either by political or ideological means. State hegemony means that the state's economic and military power and ideology are maintained over a period of time.

HIDDEN ECONOMY. This refers to unrecorded economic activity; for example, when people evade paying taxes or avoid deductions in their **social security** benefits by not reporting their income.

There is no clear indication that the hidden economy should be larger in **welfare states** with a high overall tax burden, although economists sometimes claim this is so. The **incentive** not to record economic activity, it is argued, is higher when taxes are high. Others argue that the combination of the risk of being caught and the fines attached have an impact on the size of the hidden economy. Yet others emphasize that societal norm and values and whether it is in general considered acceptable to cheat the rest of society is more important in relation to the size. The distinction between the hidden and official economies is not always clear-cut. Helping friends and relatives, for example, can be considered tax evasion if it takes the form of an exchange of work. The hidden economy is often referred to as the "black economy."

HOMELESSNESS. This is the condition of people who have no living accommodations or have only unsatisfactory and temporary accommodations. Homelessness is becoming an increasingly prevalent urban problem in many welfare states, with many people living on the streets and thereby often also **marginalized**.

HORIZONTAL EQUITY. This is a distribution in which equals a treated equally. In policy making this means that persons in the san situation should be treated in the same way, or the outcome of the di tribution will not be equal. Horizontal and **vertical** are both concepts used in describing equity. *See also* GINI COEFFICIENT.

HOUSING. This term refers to provision of living accommodations. Housing and housing policy are a special area of the welfare state with the purpose of either delivering or supporting accommodations for people. The policy can be aimed at reducing the cost of living by different means. This can be through direct economic support to those who are building accommodations or through **housing benefits**. It can also be done indirectly through **tax expenditure** by allowing the deduction of interest payments on mortgages. In addition, it can include the use of physical planning to make areas available to build affordable new houses. Housing policy can also include the right of the public sector to rent out certain living quarters to, for example, single mothers and homeless people, at reduced or nominal rates. *See also* HOMELESSNESS.

HOUSING BENEFIT. This is support provided to families to pay all or part of the cost of their living accommodations. In most countries, this is **means-tested** (based on income and the cost of the accommodation) and directed toward low-income earners. The ability in many countries to deduct interest payments on a house can be looked upon as an indirect housing benefit. This, however, is not means-tested. *See also* HOUSING.

HUMAN CAPITAL. Human capital refers to the individual's personal **capabilities**, that is, skills, talent, and knowledge. These abilities can be acquired in different ways, such as through **education**, training, or on-the-job experience, but for some, they are also something the individual is "born" with.

Human capital will often be reflected in individual income, but some of it may not be transferred from one job to another. This is usually the case for the more specific forms of human capital. Furthermore, human capital cannot be transferred directly from one person to another, although of course persons using their human capital when teaching others may be able to transfer their skills.

The theory of human capital, often connected with the works of Gary Becker, implies that an individual can invest in him/herself by education and that this type of investment will yield a return through higher income on the labor market.

Requests for support of different types of education, for example, as part of **labor market policy**, implicitly use arguments from human capital theory, assuming that people obtaining more or better education will have a higher chance of getting a job and then be better able to take care of themselves. Human capital is different from **social capital** especially because of its clear focus on the individual's personal competencies.

HUNGARY. Hungary's **social security** system followed two different paths and was markedly different before and after World War II. Hungary's history has undoubtedly had an impact on the development of these systems. From 1867 to 1918, it was part of the Austro-Hungarian double monarchy. From 1919 to 1949, it was a kingdom, and then until 1989, it was an Eastern European communist country.

Until World War II, Hungary was strongly influenced by the **Bismarckian** system, and as a result, its early social welfare measures were based on **social insurance**. This was the case for sickness and maternity in 1891 and industrial injury in 1907. Old age and invalidity support was also originally built on the basis of social insurance, but from 1957 onward **unemployment benefits** were the assistance system in these areas. Family allowances were introduced in 1938 as a universal system and remain a universal system today.

After World War II, the social security system was based on the right to have a job and thereby social rights in the communist system, which was closely connected with having a job. Pension rights were connected to having been on the labor market for a long period. The system today to a large extent is based on payments from the insured and the employers. The state only takes responsibility for family allowances and to guarantee against deficits in the insurance system.

Since the collapse of communism, Hungary has returned to the traditional **conservative welfare state model** corresponding to a Bismarckian system, with a high reliance on the social insurance system and the necessity for the individual to gain social rights by being in the labor market.

– I –

INCENTIVE. This is an encouragement for a person to perform a certain action. Analysis of incentives in the welfare state has concentrated on two areas: incentives to save and incentives to work.

Incentives to save can take the form of tax relief or lower taxation of interest income. This has especially been used to get people to save for their own retirement. It has also been argued that saving for periods of **unemployment** is important.

The debate about work has focused on **unemployment benefits**. Some see a low unemployment benefit as a better incentive to take up a job when offered one than a high level of unemployment benefit would be. There is, however, no clear and firm evidence that this is the case.

Incentives can also exist in relation to movement from one geographical area to another, for example, to pursue **education**. Incentives are mainly economic motivations but can include nonmonetary attractions such as good working and living conditions.

INCOME DISTRIBUTION. This describes the way money income is distributed in a society. There are two forms of money distribution, functional and personal.

Functional distribution is how gross factor income is distributed among the different factors involved in production: wages (labor), profit (capital), and land. Personal distribution is how income is distributed among different persons in society. It is often measured using the **Gini coefficient**, which describes how big a share different deciles (a tenth of the population) receive and how far this distribution is from a hypothetical distribution in which each decile has exactly a tenth of the personal income in a given year. Another way of measuring personal distribution is by comparing the income of the 20 percent of the general population with the highest income with the 20 percent with the lowest income. Other methods emphasizing different aspects of distribution are also used.

Many different problems are encountered in the measurement of income distribution in different countries—especially when discussing how the impact of this measurement on the degree of **inequality** can be interpreted. Some problems relate to that not all can be measured, that is, the statistical background for the data. The data will usually not include gifts and bequests. Furthermore, the **hidden economy** will not be included. Because such factors vary among different groups in a society, their impact on the distribution is obvious. If the income distribution is calculated by comparing income after tax deductions, then a further problem arises due to the differences between groups in the types of, and ability to obtain, tax deductions.

For comparisons between countries—and in some cases also within countries—differences in purchasing power parities also must be taken into consideration.

Moreover, income has an impact on consumption. This is also the case for transfers and services from the public sector, which influence the individual household's ability to buy various goods and services and thus its relative position in the income distribution.

Besides measurement problems, difficulties in analysis arise as a result of behavior differences among families. In some families, the savings may be high and thereby give rise to interest income, whereas others might spend the money during the year and not have any interest income. Differences in consumption may therefore not be a consequence of the income stemming from the labor market but rather a result of different consumption patterns.

Individuals may also be at different stages of their life cycles. Income statistics typically include all persons in society: those who are undergoing education, have just started in the labor market, those who have been in the market for a long time, and pensioners. Changing income during these periods may give rise to a misleading interpretation of the impact of the differences in the income distribution if these are not considered.

Finally, differences in **family** size may have an impact on consumption per person, depending on how many have to live on a specific income. Traditional statistics do not—and it would be difficult for them to—include differences among individual needs and how this may affect their economic position in society. For example, an individual who has a large income but needs to spend a very high proportion on medicine or **health care** due to permanent **disability** may not have the same consumption possibilities as a healthy person with the same income.

When looking at income distributions over time and making comparisons between countries, these aspects must be included in the analysis to obtain a coherent answer to questions about the degree of **inequality** in and description of income distribution in those countries.

Besides comparing income distribution, one can also compare the distribution of wealth, and increasingly, degree of access to the democratic decision-making process as indicators of the degree of equality in different countries. *See also* HORIZONTAL EQUITY; VERTICAL EQUITY.

INCOME MAINTENANCE PROGRAM. This type of program is designed to alleviate poverty by providing **cash benefits, social security**, social services, and/or **benefits in-kind**, such as food stamps and school lunches. These programs attempt to repair the damage caused by market forces.

INDEXATION. This is the way in which the level of benefits changes. In some systems, indexation is linked to prices, in others to wages.

INDIVIDUALISM. This is the opposite of **collectivism** and is based on the individual's choice and connection to the state and society. Individualism has been a major element in the development of various

liberal versions of the welfare state. *See also* METHODOLOGICAL INDIVIDUALISM.

INDUSTRIAL ACHIEVEMENT MODEL. This model in many ways resembles the **Bismarckian** notion of the **welfare state**. It relies on the individual's participation in the labor market, to which rights are connected. Payments into the system may be compulsory, but they may also be voluntary or part of collective agreements. Systems may and will often be insurance based. Benefits are related to income and previous contributions. In this type of model, social welfare institutions are only partly developed, and those outside the labor market are only covered to a small degree.

INDUSTRIAL INJURY. This is an injury that occurs at the workplace. Industrial injury was the first injury to be covered in most countries, because it was a requirement of industrialization and many families were not covered against this type of risk when moving into the cities and taking up jobs at the new workplaces.

INEQUALITY. This concept concerns the way that resources are distributed in a society. Analysis of inequality should, in principle, include all resources available in a given society, but it often focuses on the economic distribution of resources in a society. There are various types of inequality: inequality in opportunity, inequality in economic income or wealth, unequal treatment, etc.

Inequality is often measured by calculating the differences in income or wealth among various groups and persons in a given society. Different measurements of inequality exist. The indicator most often used is the **Gini coefficient**. Some of the other indexes used are the Herfingdahl, Atkinson's index, Theil's entropy, and Dalton.

Although adequate statistical information—even with its shortcomings—is available about differences in income and wealth, it is much more difficult to obtain information about other types of inequality. Studies will sometimes describe differences in access to **education**, the labor market, etc. These will often be based on case studies and therefore cannot be repeated as often as indicators of inequality based on income and wealth, for which statistics are available each year. *See also* EQUALITY; HORIZONTAL EQUITY; VERTICAL EQUITY.

INFLATION. This is the increase in prices from one period to another, for example, if a basket of goods costs 100 units in the first period and 105 units in the next, the inflation rate is 5 percent. In many social security systems, a correction for inflation is built in so that people receiving benefits will have the same buying power from one period to another. During periods of rapid inflation, systems that are not index-linked will experience fast deterioration for those living on benefits, who could eventually end up living in **poverty**.

INSERTION. This is the French term for **integration,** mainly relating to the labor market. Insertion policies are those that can reintegrate **marginalized** or socially excluded groups. Having better social contacts can do this, but it is often achieved through programs that get people back into the labor market. *See also* FRANCE.

INSTITUTIONAL MODEL. This model originated from the Beveridgian way of thinking about welfare states. In this model, a more universal approach is developed, and the individual's living standard is seen as part of society's responsibility. **Citizenship** is recognized as criteria when receiving benefits, and a decent standard of living is part of the goal. Furthermore, the model is mainly financed through general taxation, and the right to benefits is therefore not only for those participating in the labor market. Redistribution is in general high in this type of model. It also has many characteristics in common with the **Scandinavian welfare state model.**

INSTITUTIONS. Institutions are places, organizations, and entities, such as hospitals, day care institutions, prisons, **families,** and **churches** and also concepts, relationships, and practices, such as the law, the state, the family, and religion. Therefore the understanding in the social sciences of what institutions are is not unambiguous. Capitalism, practices, rules, **norms,** and markets can all be seen as specific types of institutions.

Following are some of the many definitions used in the social sciences and the main area they are related to:

• Institutions are a set of rules, compliance procedures, and moral and ethical behavioral norms designed to constrain the behavior of individuals in the interest of maximizing the wealth or **utility** of principals (historical institutionalism).

• An institution is a social arrangement regulating the relationships of individuals and collective groups to each other. This includes laws, customs, traditions and "administrative guidance's," while excluding biological fundamentals from sex to epidemiology (institutional theory).

• An institution is collective action, control, liberation, and expansion of individual action (institutional economics).

These definitions all have in common a description of how institutions can be seen as a set of organized structures, which can have different goals and institutional structures. They stress further that institutions are not only formal organizations but can also be structures of a whole or part of society.

INTEGRATION. *Integration* comes from the Latin; "integer" means whole or complete and in welfare state analysis this refers to how individual's or groups can be part of society's development. Integration can be done at both the micro- and macro-levels.

On the macro-level, it can involve the joining of different countries or groups in a society by making them have the same possibilities. It has mainly been used as a way to create common markets in which the free trade of goods and services can take place. It can also involve a higher and more common way of solving different problems within an area, for example, in the **European Union** or through the North American Free Trade Agreement (NAFTA).

On the micro-level, integration involves the individual's ability to be a part of the way society functions. An individual without a job may not be integrated. But lack of integration may also exist in relation to social contacts, culture, policy, and other areas. This type of integration is labeled social integration.

It is difficult to define and measure whether or not integration has taken place. Analysis can therefore focus on whether or not an individual is socially excluded (*see* **social exclusion**) instead of trying to measure the degree of integration. Furthermore, it can focus on either social or system integration, and also on how to move the society or individuals in such a way that they will be bound together (integrated) better than before.

In welfare state analysis, integration has often focused on how different groups, such as women, migrants, and young people, are positioned in society. In recent years, greater emphasis has been placed on integration in the labor market due to the higher impact on people's welfare of being in the labor market in relation to both income and social contacts. Furthermore, with the **migration** of refugees and illegal immigrants from outside the **European Union** and the **United States** into these areas, new elements of integration have been raised. Integrating those coming from another cultural background has proven difficult in several welfare states, but it appears to be necessary to cope with the change in **demography** and to reduce the conflicts and tensions in various societies between those who are integrated and those who are socially excluded. *See also* GENDER; INSERTION; MARGINALIZATION.

INTEREST GROUPS. These are groups of persons who wish to promote or argue for a certain decision who join together to apply pressure on decision makers. They are manifold and exist in many countries. In welfare state analysis, interest groups have been seen as part of the explanation for expansion of the public sector, which has responded to various interest groups' desire for influence in specific areas.

It is very difficult to know how big the interest groups' impact really is, as they form a part of the societal decision-making process, and different groups have different interests. Some apply pressure for increases in specific areas, while others may argue for a lowering of taxes and duties. An asymmetrical decision-making process has been used as an argument to suggest that interest groups have an impact on the growth of public spending in relation to welfare areas, because those gaining a positive value from expansion in a specific area are few, whereas those paying for it are many.

Undoubtedly interest and **pressure groups** have had an impact, but it is not possible to make a quantitative assessment of that impact.

INTERNATIONAL LABOUR ORGANIZATION (ILO). The ILO was established in 1919 as part of the Versailles treaty to be an international organization with the purpose of working for social justice, which it was believed could help in ensuring peace. It is a tripartite body in which employers and employees as groups each have 25 percent of the votes, and the governments have 50 percent. Since 1946, the ILO has been part of the **United Nations (UN).**

Among the important functions of the ILO is issuance of conventions, which are used as guidelines for structuring and organizing social and labor market policy in many countries. An important example is Convention No. 138 on the working environment. Conventions have also been issued on social security and discrimination. Countries that have ratified the conventions are bound to follow them.

INTERPERSONAL COMPARISONS. These are comparisons of different **utility** levels among many individuals, which raise the question of whether it is possible to find a **societal welfare function** on the basis of which normative advice can be found to make the best choice among possible options.

As individuals, we are able to reflect on and know the utility we receive from a specific good or bundle of goods. It will be much more difficult to know on an aggregate level—that is, for all individuals—what utility each individual derives from different goods. One person's pleasure in a good bottle of French wine cannot be compared with another person's dislike of French wine because of, for example, political reasons or taste.

To compare utilities, one can compare levels of utility and changes therein. When comparing levels, the present situation for different persons will be compared. When comparing change, what will happen to different persons when moving from one set of solutions to another is examined.

Ordinalist comparisons only compare the different levels of utility, whereas a cardinal approach compares both levels and changes therein.

The problems involved in comparing utility may be fewer when referring to more traditional goods, for example, the basket of goods necessary to survive. But it is difficult—or perhaps impossible—to compare people's tastes or pleasure in many cultural events. Some like to watch football, whereas others hate it. It is impossible to find an overall societal welfare function because individuals' preferences will have a great impact and are difficult to combine. For example, when comparing apples and pears, some would call both fruit, but that is not enough if one wants to find an overall societal welfare function.

INVALIDITY. This refers to a person's inability to take care of himself or herself. In most **welfare states**, it is possible to receive an invalidity (disability) **pension.** The size of the pension may depend on the degree of invalidity and the ability to work in the labor market.

IRELAND. Ireland has been highly influenced by Catholicism, but its historical links with the **United Kingdom** have also had an impact on the development of the welfare system. In 1921, Ireland received the status of a dominion within the British Commonwealth, and in 1922, it declared itself an independent state but remained within the Commonwealth. In 1949, it became a fully independent state outside the Commonwealth.

In Ireland, welfare systems, such as those covering industrial injury in 1897, old age in 1908, and **disability** in 1911, were established early. Sickness and **maternity benefit** systems and **unemployment benefits** were also introduced in 1911. **Family allowances** came along in 1944. To a large extent, the system is based on the criterion that the individual must be in the labor market, but at the same time, there is state involvement and coverage of vulnerable groups.

The Catholic influence in Ireland has not only brought a rudimentary development of the welfare state, as in other Catholic countries; it has also been a factor arguing for the social responsibility of the state. The Irish system has state involvement, a high degree of responsibility within the **family,** and many voluntary organizations involved in supplying social help for the various groups in need.

The system is a mixture of the **Beveridgian** model and the **Southern European welfare state model.** Financing is mainly a combination of state financing and contributions from employers, employees, and the self-employed. Ireland experienced very rapid growth in its economy during the 1990s, which has continued in the first years of the twenty-first century. This has reduced unemployment but has also increased inequality. Within the **European Union**, Ireland spends the least proportionately on social security.

ITALY. Italy followed many other Catholic countries in its development, but its social policy was also influenced by its close connection to **Germany** and its fascist government. At the same time, Italy has had a strong working class and for a long time also one of the strongest communist parties in Western Europe. These factors, in combination with the influence of the Catholic **Church**, have profoundly affected the development of the Italian welfare system.

Italy became a unified kingdom in 1860. It participated on the losing side in both world wars. The fascist period from 1922 to 1943 was doubtless a reason for the presence of **corporatist** elements in the system. Political instability in Italy can be seen as an explanation of the limited and sporadic development of social policy in the postwar period.

Laws on industrial injury were introduced in 1898, followed by maternity in 1912, and **unemployment benefits** and old age pensions in 1919. Legislation on **family allowances** was enacted in 1937 and on **sickness benefits** in 1943. The Italian system is built mainly on participation in the labor market, but at the same time it has universal components such as **health care** and family allowances. Still, in all areas, the main financial principle is contributions from either the inhabitants or employer or employee.

Different parts of Italy employ different welfare models. The northern part of Italy has been increasingly developing toward a more continental **conservative** welfare state model, whereas the southern part of Italy still has many features and structures that resemble the **Southern European welfare model** of very limited state intervention. Care for those in real need is first and foremost the responsibility of the **family**; the state only rarely steps in to help the individual.

Italy has undergone rapid economic development in the past 20 to 25 years. During this period, the welfare system has been expanding, and it is therefore in a period of transition. However, its main characteristics, despite the increasing level of coverage and universal health care system, can still be described as a **Southern European welfare state type.** Reforms in recent years point even more in that direction, although contribution and participating in the labor market, as in the more continental model, seem to be more important for the individual's coverage.

– J –

JAPAN. Historically, Japan was isolated for long periods until 1867 and has been involved in several wars since, which means that it h? been difficult to develop a welfare system. On the other hand, t growth in the economy since the beginning of the 1950s has m? Japan a very rich country.

Japan belongs to what has been labeled the **Confucian** welf? state type. Its welfare state has been developed quite recently. Ind? trial injury was the first **social security** system to be introduced, 1911. It was followed by **sickness** and **maternity** in 1922, **old a** and **disability** in 1941, **unemployment benefits** in 1947, and m? recently **child allowances**, in 1971.

In Japan's constitution of 1947, it is stated that the individual h a right to a decent minimum standard of life and access to health ca? Japanese social policy is based on a highly centralized model, wi part of it managed by the employers in the labor market. The **fam lies** also play a very important role in the Japanese system in taki? care of those not able to help themselves. This is partly the reas?n why it was so late before **pensions**, for example, were introduced. It was also only in 1973 that the Japanese government declared J?pan to be a welfare state.

With families, companies, and societies structured hierarchically, the system relies on a very top-down approach to social policy. The Japanese work ethic and strong commitment by companies to life-time employment have also reduced the need for a public welfare state system. If, as recent developments indicate may happen, more people are left without lifetime employment and families assume less responsibility, new needs will arise.

A large part of the system is market based, and it is therefore difficult to say that the system resembles anything seen in other parts of the world. Rather, it is a specific kind of Southeast Asian model with a strong emphasis on family values but also reliant on the market in a more **liberal** sense.

JUSTICE. This is one of the core concepts of many social science disciplines. It is also often used in political debates to argue for a specific solution, which will be more "just" than other solutions. The problem is that it is difficult to define what justice is—and it is even more difficult to measure it. The term will therefore often be used interchangeably with **equality** and the negation thereof, **inequality**.

Two major types of justice are distributive justice (how to distribute goods and services among citizens) and commutative justice (referring to the treatment of individuals who do not follow certain rules). Welfare state analysis focuses especially on distributive justice. This concept can be found in the old Athenian society and Aristotle.

Distributive justice can also be defined as absolute or relative. Absolute distributive justice means that everyone gets the same goods given the same situation. Relative distributive justice refers to different criteria for deciding how to distribute goods in a society, such as:

1. To each according to what he or she deserves
2. To each according to what he or she has done
3. To each according to what he or she needs
4. To each according to his or her abilities
5. To each according to his or her position in society.

It is clear that these criteria will give rise to quite different recommendations for the distribution of goods in a society—and even if a society agrees on one of the criteria, it may still be difficult to interpret and decide what, for example, the individual deserves.

Nevertheless, the concept of justice is often used in many fields of social science. For example, the argument for progressive taxation rests on it, that is, those who are most able to pay should pay higher taxes than those without the same ability.

Another way to achieve distributive of justice is to make a distribution according to:

1. property rights,
2. whether one is **deserving** or **undeserving**, or
3. **needs**.

It is obvious that a distribution according to property rights could be very unequal, because it will have its conservative roots in the historical distribution of goods in a society. The other two principles would also be very difficult to apply, as it is quite difficult to decide what the individual deserves and what needs the individual has. Moreover, it could be argued that not all needs should be satisfied. An individual who has a need to fly to the moon, for example, cannot expect the rest of society to pay for this. Using property rights as the starting point in relation to justice could also be said to rely on a libertarian notion in which the individual's freedom is the central element in a just society.

John Rawls, in his famous book *A Theory of Justice*, suggests that the concept of justice should be viewed in terms of some basic principles and before the individual knows his or her position, that is, behind the veil of ignorance. His argument is that if the individual does not know his or her future place in society, then he or she will be more prepared to take into consideration the position of weaker persons.

Rawls applies two basic principles in his analysis:

First Principle: Each person is to have an equal right to the most extensive total system of equal basic liberties compatible with a similar system of liberty for all.

Second Principle: Social and economic inequalities are to be arranged so that they both: a) to the greatest benefit of the least advantaged, consistent with the just savings principle, and b) attached to offices and positions open to all under conditions of fair equality of opportunity. (1972, 302)

These principles include both equality and liberty but also that certain minimum conditions should be taken into consideration when distributing resources in society.

More libertarian theorists argue that justice is the outcome of the way market forces work. Furthermore, they hold that difference in economic or other conditions due to the market's behavior is not a reason for intervention. A more **Marxist** approach would be to argue not only for just possibilities but also to distribute to each according to need. The concept of justice is also used when trying to create a **social welfare** function in which equal distribution is one goal—or at least maximizing **utility** in society.

Obviously, no simple and one-dimensional definition of justice exists. Therefore it is not possible to apply the principle as more than a concept in arguments for or against different types of state intervention and the development of the **welfare state**.

– K –

KEYNES, JOHN MAYNARD (1883–1946). Keynes was born and lived in the **United Kingdom** and was educated at Cambridge. He first became widely known with the publication of *The Economic Consequences of the Peace* in 1919. During the 1920s and 1930s he dealt primarily with monetary policy and how to use it so that full employment would also be possible. His thoughts on this were published in *Treatise on Money,* published in 1930.

From then on he worked on his major contribution to economics: *The General Theory of Employment, Interest and Money* (1936). This book has become one of the most influential of the twentieth century and has had a profound effect on the role of the welfare state, by stressing the possibility of a macroeconomic approach and the use of **fiscal policy** as a way to counterbalance the cyclical movement in economies with the use of public investment. However, Keynes did not dismiss the use of monetary policy. Furthermore, he questioned the functioning of the **labor market**, money, and the way investment decisions were made.

Keynes's theoretical work opened up new ways of thinking, which had an impact on economic and social policy after World War II. In 1940 Keynes published *How to Pay for the War*, suggesting new methods as opposed to just using the classic economic approach.

– L –

LABOR FORCE. This is defined as those employed and unemployed in the labor market. Often it is described as those in the labor market between the ages of 15 and 69, but in principle, it should include all who want to and actively are searching for work. The reason for the age range is mainly that (in most Western countries at least) most people under 15 are still living at home and undergoing education, and most of those over 69 are retired. However, changes in time spent in the educational system and early retirement policies in many countries make the validity of this age range debatable.

Changes in the labor force have an impact on the number employed and unemployed. Growth of the labor force means that even if there has been an increase in the number of jobs, the number of unemployed has also increased. *See also* LABOR MARKET POLICY.

LABOR MARKET POLICY. This policy involves measures designed to improve the functioning of the labor market in the welfare state and to reduce **unemployment**. Labor market policy can be either passive or active.

Passive labor market policy has two different aspects—compensation and matching. Compensation takes the form of **unemployment benefits**, **early retirement** benefits, and early social pensions. The amount and duration of unemployment benefits have been widely discussed in relation to the impact on people's willingness to take a job. They have also been discussed as a core issue in securing and avoiding large-scale **inequality** and with regard to **stigmatizing** effects from being unemployed. Passive labor market policy has as its overall aim compensation for any damage the individual incurs by being unemployed.

Active labor market policy will ideally ensure that the labor force has the necessary qualifications to fulfill the requirements of the employers when demand is shifting from area to another. The necessary qualifications will exist if productivity is equal to the wages paid. Active labor market policy will thus only increase employment in the long run if there is a market for the goods produced and a marginal profit from increasing the number of people employed.

Active labor market policy can influence both demand and supply in the labor market. Influencing the supply of labor can be achieved through various leave schemes; vocational training and mobility grants can also do this. Demand can be influenced by qualification programs in companies, on-the-job training, subsidized employment, quotas, and finance policy. Matching labor market policy involves employment services, which have the purpose of trying to make demand and supply in the labor market meet.

The effects of different types of active labor market policy depend on the economic environment in general, the possible deadweight losses of a new activity, and the long-run **demographic** situation in the labor market. It is in general assumed that active labor market policies will have a positive effect if they raise the **human capital** and the economic environment is positive for changes in the level of

unemployment, including changes in the international economic conditions.

Finally, in relation to the welfare state an active labor market policy may reduce **marginalization** and also the **dual labor market**. Labor market policies also often have a regional dimension to ensure the balanced development of a society.

The use of active and passive labor market policies varies widely among welfare states. They are most developed in the **Scandinavian welfare state model**. *See also* KEYNES, JOHN MAYNARD; LABOR FORCE.

LAISSEZ-FAIRE. This is a policy of nonintervention by the state. It is therefore often a **conservative** policy in which the existing **inequalities** in a society will prevail. Moreover, the consequences of market forces on, for example, **unemployment** and **inflation**, will not be counterbalanced by public intervention.

LATIN RIM. *See* SOUTHERN EUROPEAN WELFARE STATE MODEL.

LATVIA. This small Baltic country first gained its independence from the the Union of Soviet Socialist Republics (USSR) in 1991, and in May 2004, it became a member of the **European Union**. Changes in the economy and the movement toward a market-based economy have resulted in unemployment and poverty for many Latvians.

The first laws concerning social security were passed in the 1920s, but all the legislation was rewritten after independence, and laws on **family allowances** and **unemployment benefits** only came into effect in 1991. The system is built mainly on social insurance, with the exception of health care and family allowances, which are paid by the state. It is thus mainly a **conservative model** but with some elements drawn from the **Scandinavian model**.

LEAVE SCHEMES. Leave schemes are intended to give people **incentives** to temporarily exit from the labor market. They exist in various countries, with different benefits and criteria attached to them. The schemes can be designed to give incentives to undertake **education** or training. The idea is that the individual with a state grant can leave the labor market for a given period, living off the leave scheme benefit, and ultimately increase **human capital**. There are also parental leave schemes whereby individuals can take care of childreɪ or other relatives needing assistance.

Finally, leave schemes also exist where the main purpose is a saʲ batical leave, that is, an individual can leave the labor market foɪ previously agreed period, without specifying the cause. Faced wⅰ expected shortages in the **labor force** due to **demographic** changⅽ leave schemes have been reduced in many countries over the last fⅽ years.

LEGITIMACY. This means having broad societal support. Quesⁱ often arise about whether decisions and developments in the welⁱ state do have broad societal support, that is, whether somethinɡ done in the right way and whether those making the decisions haⅰ the right to do so. The problem with this concept—as others—is th it involves **normative** value judgments about whether decisions haⅴ popular support.

In welfare state analysis, the concept has been used to discuˢ whether the state has sufficient support for the continuation of the welfare state project or if support has decreased over time, opening the question of its continuation.

The crisis of legitimacy, due to an inability to fulfill the expectations of the welfare state, has been widely debated. It has been put forward as an explanation of the emergence of the **New Right** and the fact that it has been possible in some countries to make major cutbacks in welfare state benefits. The expectations of the welfare state were, among other things, which unemployment would be permanently low and that growth in the economies could improve living standards for most people and at the same time reduce **inequality**. Given the high level of unemployment in many countries from the mid-1970s onward and the increase in unstable economies, confidence in the welfare state has been diminished.

On the other hand, the expenditures on social policy in most countries have either continued to rise or been stabilized at a high level. Seen in this light, there may have been a legitimacy crisis, but it must be over or at least be of reduced importance compared to what it was before. Support for the various welfare states' activities varies. The highest support in most countries is for **health care** and **pensions**; there is less support for social assistance.

LIBERAL. This is a believer in **liberalism**, a particular approach to societal development. Liberals were originally in opposition to the conservatives, but today the difference is less clear-cut. Liberals argue for slow but gradual change, believing that the individual is the best person to know his or her own interests. Given such an **individualistic** approach, there is less scope for state intervention. Still, liberals accept intervention to promote stable economic development and guarantee internal and external security.

LIBERAL MODEL. This model places a large degree of emphasis on the market as the main provider of welfare and is therefore based on **means-tested benefits**, for which the level of compensation is low. It is based on limited state intervention, for those "really" in need. The public sector is mainly responsible for financing in these limited areas, and often also, at least to a certain extent, for health care.

This model puts freedom and individual property rights high on the agenda and before intervention. It is not committed to intervention to create full employment, relying on the market to accomplish this task. It has its historical roots in the Protestant work ethic and therefore as a rule finds that the individual should be able to take care of himself or herself. Countries in the liberal model group therefore often also spend less public money on welfare than do other countries, and a higher degree of social insurance can be found there. The **United States** and **United Kingdom** are such countries.

LIBERALISM. This political ideology that argues that people can and should be free to act in their self-interests, and only in a few and very well-defined cases should state intervention take place. It favors **democratic** rule but with a view that the state should not be expanded too much.

French philosopher Jean Jacques Rousseau, the Scottish economist **Adam Smith**, and the English philosopher John Stuart Mill inspired liberalism.

In relation to **social policy**, liberals argue that too much welfare provision could reduce people's **incentives** to become employed and thus create distortions in the labor market. Intervention to create jobs is seen as a hindrance to long-term stable development, and the market should have a chance to clear by making changes in real wage levels instead of intervention, which may build on more rigid structures and less flexibility in the labor market. Social welfare should be minimal, and the public supply of welfare should be limited as much as possible. On the other hand, liberals acknowledge that those in need should be helped, but they make a distinction between the **deserving** and the **undeserving** poor. *See also* NEW RIGHT.

LIFE CYCLE. This is the individual's changing position over his or her lifetime, starting with being dependent on others and often ending with being so again. In between, the individual will usually be able to take care of himself or herself. In certain cultures and societies, different phases of life are endowed with certain duties and tasks and, for example, in certain cultures, the elderly are seen as being wise.

In relation to social policy, this life cycle gives rises to different problems. The first is whether everyone should be supported if they have been able to save money to use when they become pensioners. Furthermore, it opens up the question of who the poor are. Is an elderly person who has had the ability to save for retirement poor if he or she has not done so? Should those, such as young people, who only for a short period of their lives are unable to finance their livelihood, be considered poor and needing support?

The second problem that part of the welfare state consists of agreements between generations; for example, it is possible to receive services and benefits during different periods of the life cycle that are paid for by another generation, but it is then expected that the new generation will pay for the next. As long as these intergenerational agreements hold, they do not cause specific problems, but they will if they break down.

LIFE EXPECTANCY. This is the number of years a person is expected to live. Figures can be the number of years of life expected from birth on but can also be the number of years of life expected after, for example, having reached the age of retirement.

LIFETIME INCOME. This is the income earned and accrued during a whole lifetime. The argument for using lifetime income when comparing different groups in a society is that this makes it possible to take different parts of an individual's life into consideration. That is, not only periods when income is earned, but also periods as a pensioner or undergoing education, are considered. Lifetime income can be measured in two ways.

The first, although not often used, is to follow a generation over its lifetime and in this way gather information about its total income. This makes it possible to compare the total lifetime income of different groups. It should in principle include earned income, interest income, and transfers from the public sector. It should be calculated at the same price level, and furthermore, one could argue that income tax and **social security** contributions should be deducted. The problem with this type of calculation is that, being ex-post, it is difficult to make a change in welfare policy which then counterbalancing the situation if, for example, the level is then too low.

The second way is to calculate a stylized income path for different groups in the labor market. It may or may not include their pension income, periods of unemployment, taxes paid, and expectation of future real income increases. Based on these calculations, it can be shown which groups over a lifetime are better off and which are worse off. This can then be used to make recommendations for social policy, that is, who are the most needy in relation to lifetime income. The concept's weakness is that it is a stylized calculation, and society changes over time. Groups that have been low-income earners may change position, and groups with high income may see their relative position decline.

LITHUANIA. This small Baltic country gained its independence from the Union of Soviet Socialist Republics (USSR) in 1990 and became a member of the **European Union** in 2004. The years since independence have been characterized by dramatic economic changes, and unemployment and poverty are the main social problems. Although some laws relating to social security originated earlier, all the current laws stem from the 1990s onwards. Unemployment was the first area to be covered, in 1919, and old age, disability sickness, and maternity were covered from 1925. Systems covering **family al-**

lowances (1990) and work **injury** (1991) were first introduced after independence. The system is based on **social insurance** to a very high degree, but for family allowances and medical care, it is a universal system. In this sense, the system combines elements from the **Scandinavian welfare state model** with those of the **conservative model**.

LONG-TERM CARE. This is care that is given over a long time especially for the elderly or those with long-lasting illnesses.

LORENZ CURVE. This tool illustrates the distribution in a given society by having the total number of people in a society on the x-axis in an accumulated form, then the total number with wealth or income on the y-axis—also in accumulated form. The resulting curve describes the degree of **equality** or **inequality**. If a straight line results, the situation is described as totally equal. If the line deviates then the size of the area of the curve inwards toward the straight line indicate the degree of inequality.

It is possible to use the Lorenz curve to compare the degree of inequality between different years in a single country and also between countries, as long as the lines drawn from the different years or countries do not intersect. Those closer to the straight line will have a more equal distribution compared than those father away. *See also* GINI COEFFICIENT.

– M –

MALTHUS, THOMAS R. (1766–1834). Malthus was a British economist whose main contribution was his *Essay on the Principle of Population As It Affects the Future Improvement of Society*. His thesis was that it would not be possible to produce enough food for an ever-growing population that was mainly restrained by war and poverty. He therefore suggested that wages should only be at a subsistence level to reduce the **demographic** pressure, assuming that with a low level of income the working classes were less prepared to have more children. His ideas have had a strong impact on many **conservative** approaches to welfare state ideology, which extend his theory to stating that the level of benefits should not be very high.

MARGINALIZATION. This is the state of not participating in mainstream society. Those who are not participating in certain mainstream activities are considered to be marginalized. They can be so in various ways, such as not participating in voting, cultural events, local activities in schools, and day care institutions. Marginalization can be permanent or temporary. It is temporary when for a while some (e.g., those in prison or hospitalized) are not able to participate actively, but when they leave these institutions, they may be able to participate and may even be easily reintegrated into society. For others, a temporary marginalization may lead to permanent marginalization by reducing contact and the ability to function with other persons.

Marginalization in the labor market has been seen as a core problem in many countries because welfare systems are highly dependent on people having jobs, and their **social security** coverage is low if they don't have them. Furthermore, the lack of a job apparently makes contacts with others unstable for many persons and also reduces their economic ability to participate in various activities. Working persons seem to be more integrated in society, which implies a need for labor market policy as a way of reducing marginalization. *See also* GENDER; INSERTION; INTEGRATION; RACISM; SEGREGATION; SOCIAL EXCLUSION.

MARKET. This is the arena for the exchange of goods and services. It is characterized by the supply and demand of goods and services. The exchange of goods and services is based on the price given full information and knowledge of the quality thereof.

The **labor market** is a specific type of market in which the demand and supply of labor have consequences for the levels of both wages and **unemployment**. This is a very varied market, which in most countries varies in terms of geography, qualifications, age of workers, and types of jobs available.

The delivery of goods and services to specific groups in the population will either be provided by the market, if **market failure** occurs, perhaps be provided by the state. If both fail to produce the **civil society** is left with the responsibility. Markets have strong and weak elements. Markets with goods produced by a large number of suppliers and with many demanding the goods seem to be the most efficient at delivering at a reasonable price. Monopolies, on the other hand, result in higher prices and perhaps also lower quality. This is why in most market economies the state has enacted rules to ensure competition in the market.

Weighting the level of responsibility to provide services among the market, the state, and civil society often results in a dichotomy between effectiveness and equity in the **welfare state**.

MARKET FAILURE. This is a common term for the situation when the **market**, left to itself, does not generate an efficient output of goods and services. A common example is pollution, where the cost of pollution is not reflected in market prices. Different types of market failures occur: lack of production of certain goods; monopolies, including natural monopolies; disequilibria (**unemployment**, inflation, balance of payment deficits); and information problems.

Market failure has been a core argument for public sector intervention in the economy. Most accept some types of public intervention, such as defense, police, foreign policy, and administration of common rules for society's functioning. However, there is greater disagreement about the need for social programs and real **welfare state** intervention.

Different types of market failure are often connected with imperfect competition. In welfare state analysis, it is especially in connection with a lack of supply of certain goods and disequilibria in the economy that the question of market failure arises. There may be a lack of supply of certain goods needed by handicapped groups because their demand is too low for production to generate a profit; in this situation, if the goods were produced, very few handicapped people would be able to buy them.

Disequilibria have several consequences in relation to **distribution** and the structure of society. One is that unforeseen price **inflation** redistributes wealth between those with and those without fixed assets. Another is **unemployment**. High unemployment in a market economy creates income and other problems for many families and a need for public intervention to reduce unemployment.

Market failure has therefore directly and indirectly been a central reason for the development of the welfare state in many countries, to counterbalance the consequences of market forces that, if left to themselves, could create serious problems for individuals and families.

Some argue that even if one accepts the idea of market failures, they have a less harmful effect on society's overall level of welfare than **government failure**. This cannot be decided at a theoretical level, but needs to be resolved by empirical analysis of the specific area in question.

MARKETIZATION. This is a process in several, mainly European, countries, in which elements from the market way of functioning are used in the production of welfare service. This can be done privatizing public production of a social service or by letting private companies play a role in the production of social services. The private impact can assume various forms, and the producers can have different degrees of freedom. At one end of the scale, this can be a fully free right to provide services under market conditions, with full competition, including prices determined by the market. At the other end, it can be giving the right to produce the service based on a fixed set of prices from the public sector and with a specified set of conditions to fulfill relating to quantity and quality. Sometimes marketization refers to the use of market type mechanisms within the public sector itself when providing services, for example, competition between various providers. *See also* PRIVATIZATION.

MARSHALL, T. H. (1893–1982). Marshall was a sociologist who taught at London School of Economics from 1925 to 1956 and was professor there from 1944. Marshall's contribution to welfare state analysis was to distinguish between different types of rights and how they were connected. His notion of **citizenship** has been a cornerstone of many analyses of why and how one could and can distinguish between welfare states.

Marshall introduced the distinction between civil, political, and social rights. He stressed that in early society only civil rights were developed, then in the nineteenth century in many countries political rights followed, but it was only in the twentieth century that the right to income or transfers was established. Many **welfare state** models do not use citizenship as the basic criterion for being eligible for benefit but rather participation in the labor market.

Marshall also worked on an analysis of welfare state policies in the **United Kingdom** between 1890 and 1945 to describe how social rights had been expanded. His vision of the welfare state was built on the conflicts among **democracy**, welfare, and **classes** in society.

MARX, KARL (1818–1883). Marx was born in Trier and studied at Bonn and Berlin. He wrote *The Communist Manifesto* in 1848 with Friedrich Engels. In 1849 he fled to London, where he spent the rest of his life. His main contribution is his historical analysis of society at that time, which included the inevitability of the **class** struggle that arises from the built-in conflict between workers and capital. This thesis was especially developed in *Das Kapital,* written in 1867.

Marx's analysis of social structures and conflicts in capitalist societies and their consequences has been used in many welfare state analyses to describe and explain the social conflicts within the welfare state. The development of the welfare state has also been interpreted in Marxist terms as a consequence of the ongoing struggle among different classes in society.

Marx's expectation that capitalist society would inevitably break down and be transformed into communist society is not supported by historical developments so far. Nevertheless, his analysis of the different classes' living standards and the consequences of capitalist production yields much useful information about the functioning of capitalist societies.

MARXISM. This ideology was built on **Karl Marx**'s ideas and his analysis of society. The main thesis is that internal **class** conflicts will occur continuously in society until there is a revolution in which the ruling class will disappear. Marxism has been a driving force behind many revolutions in Eastern Europe and in third world countries. It was the official ideology of the Union of Soviet Socialist Republics (USSR), the People's Republic of **China**, and many other countries, especially in **Eastern Europe**.

Presently, support for Marxism seems to be rather weak, although class analysis is still used in many types of analysis of the welfare state's development and of the degree of **inequality** in different countries. In addition to its use in **welfare state** analysis, the concept of class is still deeply rooted in interpretations of historical developments in numerous countries.

MATERNITY BENEFITS. These are benefits given in relation to the birth of a child. In most countries, these benefits are only given to the mother during a certain period when she can take care of the newborn child while receiving a public benefit. The duration and amount of the benefit vary between countries. In some countries, maternity benefits also exists for men in order to allow fathers to have closer contact with their children.

MEANS-TESTED BENEFIT. This is a benefit for which the individual is only eligible upon fulfilling certain income and wealth tests. As a result of being means-tested, certain groups are disqualified from the right to a benefit because they have too high a level of income or wealth. The specific criteria, a combination of income and wealth, differ in different countries.

Means tests can be so strict that very few people can receive the benefit, or they can help to ensure **legitimacy** in the welfare state by only giving benefits to those most in need. Means tests can also carry a degree of stigma, especially if the means test includes more than looking at objective criteria such as income or wealth. Means-tested benefits are especially used in the **liberal** and **conservative welfare states**.

MEDIAN VOTER. This is someone who is able to shift the majority from one group to another. In mathematics, the median is found exactly in the middle of the **distribution**.

In the analysis of the **welfare state** and **growth of the public sector** expenditure, the concept of the median voter has been important in trying to explain why, and how, it is possible to gain a majority. Therefore it may be important to support voters in the middle of the political spectrum, as they will be able to help form a majority. Changes in attitudes of the median voter can have a profound effect on overall decisions making. It is also argued that there may be an expansion of public expenditures in areas where the median voter has preferences.

MEASUREMENT OF INEQUALITY. This is part of the analysis of the degree of **equality** in a given society. The first problem that arises when measuring inequality is to decide which type of **inequality** is being investigated. Is it inequality of access to different types of goods and services, or is it inequality in relation to nonmonetary goods? Research has been focused on inequality in income and wealth, as this is possible to measure, whereas other types of inequalities require more qualitative data, which makes it difficult to get a comprehensive picture of the degree of inequality.

There are many tools for the measurement of inequality, such as Atkinson's index, Theil's entropy, the **Lorenz curve**, and the **Gini coefficient**. Pen's parade is a simple way of presenting inequality by showing from top to bottom the income of members of a society. The measurements all try to answer the question: What is the level of inequality in a specific country? They can have different ways of interpreting inequality, and this is the main reason for so many different forms of measurement.

The central question when using these indexes is how one should interpret the figures calculated and their relation to the numbers at the bottom of the income distribution. Should more weight be allotted to those at the bottom of the income distribution, and should there be a specific reduction in an index of inequality if those at the bottom are especially well taken care of? Another problem is how other changes within the income distribution should be calculated, and how they should be shown within the statistics. If the changes in income distribution, for example, are only within the top 20 percent but with a tendency toward a more even spread of resources, the question arises of whether this should then be reflected in the calculated index, or should only those with an income below the average income be taken into consideration? Answers to these questions involve making various **normative** decisions.

Most research measuring inequalities uses the Gini coefficient, which describes how far the distribution is from a hypothetical distribution in which each decile of the population has one-tenth of the income or wealth. Some of the problems in relation to measurement and interpretation of this are that the statistics do not necessarily tell the full story since there is a hidden economy, which includes gifts and bequests, public services, and so forth; and that the individuals may be at different points in their **life cycles**, which at least has consequences for an interpretation of whether they are in need or not. The impact of the size of the household, and in relation to this, which units are used when making the measurement, also raises questions about how to measure the degree of inequality.

An analysis of whether some persons are poor over their entire lives or for shorter periods is also used as a way of trying to analyze **poverty**. These types of analysis are more difficult because they require collecting data over a long period.

Nonetheless, analyzing a country or comparing countries over time by using the same statistics and information does produce valuable information about the development of inequality. Even if the data are not precise, they may provide hints about how to use the information in welfare state policies and the possible need for redistribution.

MEASUREMENT OF WELFARE. This measurement is one of the fundamental problems in **welfare economics**. Its starting point is the **individual**'s **utility** of different bundles of goods. The ability to describe total welfare in a society depends being able to add together the individual person's welfare functions. In theory, this is simple: just add all the individuals' utility curves together to get the society's total welfare.

Problems arise when trying to interpret the consequences of, or trying to find the exact value of, the individual's welfare. Although in principle we can just add these together, they are based on different bundles of goods and services, determined by the individual's income constraints. An individual might have chosen another bundle if his or her income constraint had been different and had presented him or her with other options. Therefore, by adding utility curves one indirectly assumes that the present **income distribution** is the acceptable income distribution in a given society. Furthermore, when adding the utilities it is necessary to compare different goods, which may have different functions for individuals. Some goods are basic **needs**, while others are luxury goods, and therefore reduction may be harsher for some (those with only basic needs covered) than for others if changes in distribution are made that require these groups to give up some of their resources. Therefore, value judgments are involved when making comparisons and adding together the information. The measurement of welfare is therefore highly **normative**, and information will be based on valuation in a specific time and specific historical context.

Using the information on individuals' utilities could also give rise to many different problems of interpretation. For example, should resources be taken away from a handicapped person if a healthy person can achieve higher welfare levels with these extra resources? Society's total welfare, measured as total utility, may be increased, but it will perhaps be at the expense of particularly vulnerable groups.

Finally, it is difficult to determine a specific figure when trying to measure value—should it be in money terms, level of satisfaction, or some other scale? Scale problems and decisions about which scale to use when measuring welfare are therefore also major problems.

MERIT GOODS. Merit goods refer to goods which, when left to the market, will be produced in insufficient amounts compared to what society would wish if it were to maximize its **welfare** function. The term was first defined by Richard Musgrave in 1959 in *The Theory of Public Finance*.

Musgrave used the example of luncheon tickets, which should ensure that children have meals with a high nutritional value. The market would do this by pricing the goods, and this would leave children from low-income families unable to buy the food. By having the state provide luncheon tickets, it should be possible to make sure that all children will get the food.

Today, a more common example is education. The market could provide education for payment, but fewer persons might enter education, which could therefore result in an overall reduction in the level of education. This could be because the individual's expectation of income after education, and thus the improvement in **human capital**, is less than society's expectation. Besides the economic arguments, it could be argued that **democracy** needs a well-educated population to make sure that all can participate in society's decision-making processes.

The debate about merit goods involves many **normative** judgments because of the difficulties in knowing and determining a society's welfare function. It is a political decision whether or not the welfare state should provide a specific good, to be decided by weighting whether a good has such a high value for society that it should be supplied even if, in principle, it could be provided by the market.

METHODOLOGICAL INDIVIDUALISM. This is the belief that the individual's evaluation should come first when making decisions. An individual's choice should thus have priority compared to societal wishes to intervene. This philosophy has consequences for many areas of the welfare state, as it implies less state intervention and therefore a higher reliance on market provision and market-based solutions. Some limits exist where the reference to the common good may imply a restriction of the individual's behavior. *See also* INDIVIDUALISM.

MEXICO. The development of **social security** programs in Mexico was slow compared to its big neighbor to the north, the **United States.** The explanation may be its relatively weak economic performance, slow economic growth, and a long period of political instability at the beginning of the twentieth century, which came to an end with the introduction of a new constitution in 1917, after which several reforms were made.

The first law covered industrial injury (1931) and was followed during World War II by laws concerning **pensions**, sickness, and maternity. **Unemployment benefits** and **family allowances** are only weakly developed, but there is a requirement that employers must pay dismissed workers an amount of money for a certain period.

Mexico's system is, in general, a **social insurance** system, so primarily those in the labor market are covered. Otherwise only specific persons are covered—and mainly on a voluntary basis. A relatively low level of benefits also limits the system.

MIGRATION. This is the movement and change of residence of an individual. Migration can be immigration (moving into a country) or emigration (moving out of a country). It can also be movement within a country, but it is mainly thought of as movements of citizens between different countries. Migration can be permanent or temporary. Temporary migration may occur because someone wishes to take up a job for a short period in another country, working two or three years abroad and then going back. Sometimes what is expected to be temporary migration turns out to be permanent.

Migration can be either voluntary or forced. Voluntary migration occurs when a person or **family** moves from one country to another of his or her own free will. Forced migration occures when a person or groups of persons are forced to move from one country to another. Voluntary migration can be induced by various causes. The major reason is large differences in the level of welfare (and differences in wages levels); movement is expected to improve the living conditions of those migrating from one country to another. Differences in unemployment rates, or lack of manpower in some countries compared to others, may be another reason for this type of movement. Increasing inequality between the rich and poor parts of the world may also be a reason for increased migration in the future. This likelihood has been part of the debate over how to best help poor countries achieve economic development, since economic development may reduce the migration from poor countries to rich countries.

The large movement of workers from the southern part of Europe and Turkey to the northern part of Europe in the late 1960s was due to a lack of manpower. Those who moved therefore had a chance to get a job and achieve a higher standard of living than in their home countries. Within the **European Union** (EU), there is now a right to free movement on the condition that the individual can find a job. Otherwise, and for third country nationals, it is difficult to enter an EU-country—except as a tourist. The same situation exists in the **United States** and many other countries. This makes it difficult to migrate to a country unless it is to take up a job that has arranged beforehand.

Involuntary migration is often connected with wars (both between countries and civil), making it necessary for many people to flee as refugees. International conventions state that the first safe country that a fugitive enters should take care of that individual. It may be difficult for countries that are neighbors to big conflicts to cope with increased migration, and therefore within the United Nations (UN) systems, most countries have agreed to accept a limited number of refugees each year.

A large influx of migrant workers or refugees may make it difficult to keep a society fully integrated and may also create greater domestic tensions, especially when the nation's economic circumstances are not good. Racism and xenophobia can result from large influxes of persons with a different cultural background. This seems to be one of the reasons for many countries imposing more stringent criteria concerning entry rights. The degree of tension naturally also depends on which measures are used when trying to integrate people into society.

Migration has been discussed in relation to its impact on welfare state delivery. If a large proportion of migrants require social transfers, then this may create problems for the welfare systems, depending to a large extent on the degree to which the migrants are able to enter the labor market. Although this has varied in different states, usually the first generation of migrants has more difficulty in entering the labor market. Therefore, they have a higher chance of being **socially excluded**. At the same time, the second generation of migrant workers and people who are being naturalized have a higher degree of affiliation with the labor market and are more integrated in societies. Integration may thus take several generations. Integration of migrants into the labor market is thus a formidable challenge facing the welfare states in the years to come.

On the other hand, migration can also have a positive influence on a country by generating a more multifaceted view and a greater understanding of other persons. The migrants' inspiration can become the source of new ideas and new production methods. Further migration can have a positive impact by reducing the **dependency ratio**, if the migrants are younger than the population on average.

Those countries from which the migrant workers come may also benefit in the form of remittances from those working abroad, which contribute positively to the inflow of foreign capital. This has been the case for many of those countries that in the 1960s and 1970s had a net migration to Europe. Furthermore, if those migrating make it possible for others to take over their jobs, that may reduce the overall unemployment in the home country.

In general it is not possible to know the precise effects of migration, and the impact at the micro- and macrolevels may be different— even if the economic and social consequences are substantial.

MINIMUM INCOME. This is the level of income necessary to avoid living in poverty, or the income needed to achieve a decent living standard. The level of the minimum income is to a large extent dependent on welfare in the country in question.

MORAL HAZARD. This risk arises when people's actions are influenced by a given structure of **incentives**. The term is often used in relation to insurance. Moral hazard exists, for example, when a person, after being insured against fire or theft, takes fewer precautions than before becoming insured. The individual will have less incentive—because of the insurance—to do something, and will in this respect have a **free ride** in relation to the insurance company. Moral hazard can also exist when a person is working less than expected at a workplace or can more easily accept the loss of his or her job because he or she will receive **unemployment benefit**.

In **welfare state** analysis, it has been argued that too high a public sector provision of, for example, **health care** makes people less careful about their own health. Furthermore, a system with too generous benefits has been used, especially in **public choice** theories, as an example of why people are less willing to take up jobs, relying on **sickness benefits**, and so forth. There does not seem to be firm evidence on a societal level that this is the case, but a thorough analysis would be difficult to make.

– N –

NATURAL RATE OF UNEMPLOYMENT. This is the rate of **unemployment** that a society eventually would move toward given the structure of the economy, the **labor market**, and related regulations. It is questionable what the level of the natural rate of unemployment actually is. One definition has been the rate of unemployment when the **inflation** rate is stable—sometimes referred to as the nonaccelerating inflation rate of unemployment (NAIRU). By relating unemployment to a stable inflation rate, it can vary greatly in different countries and will also change over time.

NEED. This is something an individual is lacking. It can be physical or psychological. It can be food and **housing** in order to survive but can also be social contacts with other people. **Basic needs** should normally be fulfilled before the individual expresses the need for loving and caring. Needs are individually bound, and the size is **normative**, which makes it difficult to decide which needs should be covered and which should not, because needs are seen as unlimited.

The **welfare state** primarily supplies basic needs such as food (or income to buy food) and housing; to a lesser degree it supplies loving and caring. In some welfare states, homes for the elderly, self-help groups, and support services for voluntary groups are established to reduce loneliness among specific vulnerable groups.

NEGATIVE INCOME TAX. This is a tax paid to those having an income below a certain defined level. It has been used to define a minimum income level that all members of society should have, and in this way it resembles a **means-tested** general benefit given to those with the lowest income in a society. It can be said to reduce the number of people living in **poverty** if the minimum is defined as the poverty line.

NETHERLANDS, THE. This is one of the mature European welfare states, which basically can be characterized as a mixture of the **continental** and **Scandinavian welfare state** models, as it has certain elements of and similarities to the **Bismarckian** model due to its combination of the universal system with insurance-based systems.

The Netherlands experienced slow and late industrial development. It was only in 1901 that a law on industrial injury was established, and in 1912, a change in the poor law was passed. During World War I, an **unemployment** system was developed, and only after the war (although The Netherlands was neutral during the war), new elements in the **social security** system were developed, that is, coverage in case of old age and **disability** in 1919 and **sickness** and **maternity** in 1931.

After World War II, although it was inspired by the **Bismarckian** model, The Netherlands turned to the **Beveridgian model** and gradually a more universal welfare state type emerged, which among other things included general **pensions**. During the 1960s, The Netherlands, like many other welfare states in Europe, experienced very rapid development and expansion of its welfare system.

With respect to old age, it is a universal system in which an individual may pay into a supplementary pension system above the state-supported level. The sickness and maternity benefits are also mainly based on a universal approach, whereas industrial injury, **unemployment benefits**, and some of the medical benefits are mainly for those in the labor market. The Netherlands is one of the countries in the world where spending on social protection as a proportion of GDP is highest, although some retrenchments were made in the 1980s and 1990s.

NEW LEFT. This is the term for those who tried to redefine the n and goals of the **welfare state**. It argues in favor of a more just i-ety, but at the same also argues for a higher degree of individu e-sponsibility. *See also* THE THIRD WAY.

NEW PUBLIC MANAGEMENT (NPM). This is a specific of understanding how to manage and steer public sector adminis , especially focused on the use of **marketization** as part of n ment. Integrating competition within the public sector's deli of social services has also been part of this approach. The NPM can be seen as one of the strategies criticizing the public sector for being inefficient and the **bureaucracy** for mainly expressing self-interest in the development of the public sector. It is also to a large extent inspired by **public choice** theorists and emphasizes how to make the public sector more efficient and responsive to user needs.

NEW RIGHT. This term is commonly used to describe a specific way of thinking about the state's intervention in the economy that evolved in the 1980s. Many New Right thinkers have seen the **state**, and especially social programs, as economic problems, which should be reduced to create a better overall economic situation. The result would be a situation in which those living in poor conditions could get a job.

The New Right emerged in many countries as a response to growing budget deficits, which it was claimed crowded out private investments. The way to reduce budget deficits and continued increases in state debt is to reduce social welfare benefits, not raise tax levels. New Right theorists wanted a more flexible labor market that should enable wages to go up and down in line with demand and supply. Furthermore, they argued for a reduction in labor force protection because, for example, protection against dismissal could make the labor market too rigid.

New Right recommendations included placing greater emphasis on using monetary policy as a measure to cure **inflation** and stimulate economic development, and less, if any, emphasis on **fiscal policy**, which would in this context mainly consist of reductions in public sector expenditure. This way of thinking has been highly influential in many Western countries—especially the **United States** and **United Kingdom**. New Right theorists traditionally argue in favor of a **conservative** type of welfare state. *See also* FREEDOM; LIBERALISM; NEW LEFT; PUBLIC CHOICE.

NEW ZEALAND. The **social security** system and social policy in New Zealand are a mixture of models and ideas about the welfare state. Inspired by participation in the British Commonwealth, it has some similarities to the **Beveridgian** notion of a welfare state but also has a high reliance on the labor market as a provider of welfare, as well as strong **means-tested** programs.

The old age **pension** was the first **social security** law to be introduced (1898) in New Zealand, and industrial injury followed in 1908. Then came a long period during which no real initiatives seem to have been taken, but in the 1920s and 1930s, a whole series of new laws rapidly followed, starting with **family benefits** in 1926, **unemployment benefits** in 1930, **disability** pensions in 1936, and **sickness** and **maternity benefits** in 1938.

The system is based on a general way of financing the different contingencies, and in this respect it resembles the **Scandinavian welfare state** type. Only for industrial injury is there payment by employers. In many areas a strong income test is used to find out if the individual is eligible for a certain type of benefit.

In the late 1990s, New Zealand adopted a more **liberal** approach to welfare state delivery, with a high degree of retrenchment of the state's intervention in welfare state issues. The model began moving toward a much more liberal form of welfare state. At the beginning of the twenty-first century, more emphasis on welfare state intervention has returned.

NONCONTRIBUTORY BENEFIT. This is a benefit that requires fulfilling certain criteria in order to receive, it and it is often based upon a citizens rigth. The criterion for receiving benefits can include a **means test**, but the benefit can also be based on fulfilling certain other criteria (age or having children). **Child benefits** are an example of a noncontributory benefit in many countries.

NONGOVERNMENTAL ORGANIZATION (NGO). This is an institution or body that is not directly managed or steered by the public sector. Nongovernmental organizations include various voluntary organizations and the **voluntary sector**, including the **church**.

Nongovernmental organizations may receive economic support from the state to carry out their activities. The main criterion is that they are independent of the state apparatus. In cases where they receive economic support, full independence may be difficult to achieve. For voluntary organizations, the possibility of having public support may therefore be looked upon with mixed feelings. The positive aspect of state support is the enhanced possibility of carrying out activities; the negative aspect is **dependency** on the state apparatus.

The NGOs' influence has been increasing in most welfare states in the 1980s, after a long period when they only played a minor role. They can be effective because they are independent of the public sector and thereby have a better possibility of access to vulnerable groups that do not like contact with the public sector. The increasing role of the nongovernmental sector is one of the reasons for the debate about the connection among **state**, **market**, and **civil society**.

In several welfare states the NGOs' role has also included the ability to do voluntary work, which can include more personal contacts with, for example, lone elderly persons. It is difficult for the state to both finance and find labor for this kind of work. At the same time, NGOs also fulfill a need of many of those participating in the voluntary work, as it gives them some self-satisfaction.

NONPROFIT ORGANIZATIONS. These organizations deliver welfare that is often based on state financing, but without the purpose of creating a surplus for the organization. They are especially important in continental Europe. They resemble **NGOs** in some ways.

NON–TAKE-UP. This is when a person eligible for a benefit does not claim it. Reasons for non–take-up can be that the individual either does not know about the right to a benefit or feels stigmatized and is therefore not willing to ask for a benefit. Administrative rejections or administrative lack of precise knowledge of the individual's right can also explain non–take-up. In several welfare states, appeal systems exist to help individuals who do not feel that they have been given proper treatment in the administrative system. *See also* TAKE-UP RATE.

NORMATIVE ANALYSIS. This is an analysis based on value judgments about whether an outcome or policy is desirable or undesirable, and how to change things to achieve the best possible outcome. Normative analyses, in contrast to **positive analyses**, ask such questions as, What ought to be done? Normative analysis is especially prevalent in areas concerning **justice** and **equality,** as these involve many normative issues. But discussions about what constitutes a good society can also involve a normative analysis.

NORMATIVITY. This describes a **normative analysis** that is value based, that is, an analysis based on questions such as, What ought to be done? Normativity can be both conscious and unconscious. Within politics normativity can, for example, take the form of more or less explicit references to party ideology and aims. Normative approaches can sometimes be difficult to avoid due to the individuals' historical background. *See also* NORMS.

NORMS. These are rules or sets of rules that serve as common guidelines for individual or collective behavior and by means of which deviation can be punished. Formal norms can be sanctioned by legal actions, whereas informal norms involve other types of sanctions, such as being cast out from the group.

A social norm describes how individuals are expected to behave. Some norms can be broken without punishment, for example, bad behavior at a party. Friends, relatives, and employers may sanction other types of norms, and the law sanctions certain norms. The type of sanction can vary depending on the degree of deviation from the norm.

Norms can also vary among countries and welfare systems. Cheating the public system may be morally more acceptable in one system than in another. Norms can also influence the understanding of who is **deserving** and who is **undeserving**.

NORWAY. Norway belongs to the **Scandinavian welfare state** type and has a very universal welfare state, which in the 1980s and 1990s was paid for primarily by the country's oil income. Norway has also accumulated an oil fund that is expected to help finance the welfare state in the future, and for this reason, the **aging** of the population seems to be a minor problem in Norway compared to other European countries.

In many respects, the development of **social security** in Norway followed the pattern in the other parts of Northern Europe, although the coverage of old age and **disability** was relatively late (1936). The first law on **industrial injury** was passed in 1895, inspired by the German example, followed by a law on **unemployment benefits** in 1906 and laws on **sickness** and **maternity** in 1909. After World War II a law on **family allowances** was adopted, and other laws, which emphasized the state's considerable involvement in societal development and coverage, were extended, and new groups were taken into consideration.

The Norwegian system is a universal one, with a high degree of public support and general financing, although employers and employees pay a specific contribution to the state. These contributions, however, resemble general income tax in many respects. The considerable level of public involvement and general financing, combined with the universal access to welfare state support, indicate that Norway's system is a **Scandinavian welfare state** type.

NOZICK, ROBERT (1938–). Nozick has mainly been known for his book, *State, Anarchy and Utopia*, in which he argued for a minimal state. His is mainly an ultra-liberal approach to societal development. He has inspired the **New Right** and many **liberals** in their thinking about the welfare state and its development, for example, the need to reduce the welfare state where possible. His views include the belief that our entitlements can only be based on our own efforts and abilities. This requires individual responsibility and therefore less need for state intervention. It is thus a highly individualistic approach, expecting that when individuals do what they deem to be best, the whole society will also benefit.

– O –

OCCUPATIONAL WELFARE. This is welfare obtained through one's occupation, that is, from one's employer. It is sometimes labeled "fringe benefits" to distinguish it from traditional wage income. But occupational welfare is broader and can consist of different elements: **pensions, sickness benefits, health care** coverage, day care for children, **education,** and training. Part of occupational welfare is supported through the **tax** system.

Sometimes occupational welfare is in addition to the state's welfare; this is the case, for example, when the welfare state has a ceiling on economic support in case of sickness or unemployment and the employer pays something above this ceiling. Sometimes occupational welfare can be part of a **collective bargaining** agreement. In some countries' **welfare state** systems, occupational welfare financed through **social security** contributions is the most important element of the welfare state.

Occupational welfare was one of the three elements in the social division of welfare identified by Richard Titmuss (1968). The distribution of occupational welfare tends to create inequality against women and persons with a low income in the labor market. *See also* BISMARCKIAN MODEL; FISCAL WELFARE.

OLD AGE PENSION. *See* PENSION.

OPEN METHOD OF COORDINATION (OMC). This is a method developed in the **European Union** (EU) that attempts to develop a common understanding of a specific policy area and at the same time accept local and national decisions on how to reach a specific goal. The EU has used the OMC method in such diverse areas as macroeconomic policy, **employment** policy, **social inclusion, pension** reform, the information society, and research and innovation. The process varies, using either soft or hard measures to develop the area. In most areas a very soft method is used, with naming and shaming being the hardest sanction for countries not following the agreed overall goals.

The OMC uses four stages:

1. Fixing guidelines;
2. Establishing indicators;
3. Translating guidelines into national practice and regional pr c-tices; and
4. Monitoring, evaluating, and comparing as a mutual learn process.

The aim of the OMC method is to achieve agreement on comn u aims and goals in the various areas, especially where the compe n cies of the EU are weak, which is the case in most areas of social n labor market policy. The expectation is that agreeing on the go would and could help in attaining **convergence** among the EU cou tries and at the same time be the first step on the path toward a **I ropean Social Model.**

– P –

PARETO, VILFREDO (1848–1923). Born in Paris, Pareto ma many contributions to economics, sociology, and political science, though he was trained as an engineer. Within political science, Pare was especially famous for his work on elites and his acceptance authoritarian regimes. In economic science his main contribution w what has become known as the Pareto principle. In accordance w this principle, redistribution should be continued as long as one p son's situation can be made better without making other persons' sit uations worse. This is called a Pareto improvement. This criterion can, on the one hand, be seen as a way of using overall resources in such a way that societal welfare is maximized and can thus serve as an argument for optimizing scarce resources. On the other hand, it is a conservative criterion in the sense that the existing distribution can not be changed by using this criterion and a very uneven distribution would thus be continued if this were the starting point.

PAY-AS-YOU-GO SYSTEM (PAYG). This is mainly used to describe a specific type of **financing** of **pension** systems. In this system, the expenditure on pensions is financed as a direct public sector expen diture and is therefore not part of the current public or private sector saving in a country. In a pay-as-you-go system, the present generation pays the pension to the pensioner, with the expectation that the next generation will do the same for it.

There are advantages and disadvantages to this type of system. The advantages are that it is possible to make immediate payment of pensions to the pensioners, and the decisions about changes in level of pensions can be implemented directly. Seen from the pensioner's point of view, a pay-as-you-go system can eliminate the risk of **inflation** if the system has an indexation of benefits built in. Such a system can be a way of guaranteeing all pensioners in a society a minimum standard of living and thereby fulfill one of the goals of a welfare state.

The primary disadvantage is that it does not in itself raise resources. The system must be financed from current taxes, duties, or contributions. If financed out of taxes and duties, it may have a negative impact on the labor market because it creates disincentives to work. If financed out of social security contributions, it may have a negative effect on competitiveness due to its impact on costs. Finally, it may create a negative **incentive** for people to save for pension purposes if they are guaranteed a decent living standard as pensioners.

The balance between minimum standards and decent living standards and redistribution in society and the possible negative impact on savings and work due to different ways of financing pensions is the central issue for political systems when deciding whether to use such a system and how to implement it.

Many welfare states have moved toward a combined system, attempting both to have sufficient financing for the pensions and to guarantee a minimum income for those who have not been able to save for pension purposes.

PENSION. A pension is a periodic payment of income from the state or another source to people who are above a certain age or fulfill specific criteria. Pensions and pension systems differ among the welfare states.

The pension system can include both an old age pension (the individual is entitled to a pension when reaching a certain age) and an **invalidity** pension (an individual is entitled to a pension when certain contingencies occur and the possibility of supporting oneself is not possible). Some countries also provide pensions for those who for various reasons, such as psychological causes or social events (e.g., a deserted or divorced wife without prior work experience), are no longer able to take care of themselves. The right to a pension can be based on various criteria, such as **citizenship**, **employment** (collective agreement or statutory), or private insurance. A citizen can have the right to a universal state pension, or the right can be based on fulfilling certain criteria.

Pensions are often presented as a tier system. The first tier consists of the public pension, the second tier of the occupational pension, and the third tier of the purely private pension. What this mix is depends on the structure of the particular welfare state. However, most countries use all these elements in order to cope with varied expectations about the living standard after retirement; various positions in the labor market, including specific options for the self-employed and coverage for those with only a weak affiliation with the labor market; and variations in society's willingness to support the elderly.

The benefit varies in different situations. In a citizenship model, it is either a flat rate or **means-tested**. Employment-related and private insurance pensions will typically depend on the individual's previous contributions to the system.

The citizenship model will typically involve a **pay-as-you-go system** (either paid by general taxes and duties or earmarked contributions), whereas employment and private-related systems will be **funded systems**. The public, through certain tax benefits, may support the private system indirectly.

Pension systems were developed to cope with the increasing number of elderly who had no income after leaving the labor market and who were therefore not able to take care of themselves. In many welfare states, the elderly have traditionally been looked after by their children and other relatives.

The first pension systems were designed for specific groups in the labor market to give them incentives to continue to work and with clear awareness that their specific working conditions involved very high risks of suffering industrial injury and therefore not being able to support the **family** any longer. This was especially important at a time when the system depended on the male **breadwinner** model.

In **France**, a right to pensions in cases of **invalidity** was created for seamen in 1797. This was in response to the growing number of seamen without any income due to invalidity resulting from their work. In 1844, **Belgium** followed with an obligatory invalidity and old age pension for seamen. In 1854, an invalidity pension for mineworkers was introduced in **Austria**. In 1861, **Italy** established such a system.

More generally, old age pensions were introduced in the late nineteenth century. In **Denmark** this was done in 1891, followed by Italy in 1898, and **Germany** in 1899. Most countries established general pension insurance between 1900 and 1940.

In the past 10 to 15 years, a combination of state universal pension and funded system has been developed in many countries. To some extent, this has been a response to the growing problem of a higher proportion of society consisting of elderly persons. This has sparked a discussion about **dependency ratios**, that is, how many people will have to be paid for by those working in the labor market.

With the average life expectancy increasing over the past 30 to 40 years and a falling birthrate, the proportion of elderly in the population as compared to those of working age has been growing. It remains to be seen if this is a problem, and that will depend on, among other things, the general economic growth. In several countries, the age of retirement has been increased as a way of coping with the number of years for which pensions will have to be paid.

The generosity of public pensions varies among the welfare states, and in general, they are most generous in the universal welfare states. Besides pensions, many elderly receive other forms of support, which means that comparing only the level of pensions would result in an incorrect impression of the living standard for pensioners in various welfare states.

In most countries, pensions are among those benefits that are most strongly supported by the electorate. There are two reasons: the elderly are seen as **deserving**, and most people expect to need a pension themselves when they reach the age of retirement. *See also* DEFINED BENEFIT PLAN; DEFINED CONTRIBUTION PLAN; EARNINGS-RELATED BENEFITS; FLAT-RATE PENSION; GENDER.

PERSONAL SOCIAL SERVICES. These are services individuals receive from the **welfare state** outside the scope of **health, housing, education**, and **social security**. They can take the form of home help for the elderly, homes for the elderly, housing for the **homeless,** or day care for children, etc. They can also include **social work** for an individual person. They are directed at both groups and individuals. Personal social services are **benefits in-kind** instead of **benefits in cash.** The importance of personal social services varies among the different welfare state models. The more universal models have more of this built into the system than those models that rely more on the market or families. Recent experiences have shown that even in state-financed systems delivery through the market has been more profound, including the use of various types of **vouchers.** Measuring quality in personal social services is difficult due to the extent of individual **needs** to be covered.

PLURALISM. This is a political philosophy emphasizing the need for different groups in society to be actively engaged in and have the ability to participate in society's development. It is felt that different groups being actively involved will keep **democracy** alive by not leaving the decision making solely to a limited power elite. In pluralist thinking, power will be not only in the hands of the state but also held by different groups in society, which can be **churches, nongovernmental organizations,** and so forth. This can also be a value position arguing for diversity and inclusion of many different actors in the decision-making process.

Critics of pluralist thinking argue that in reality there is **inequality** in access to the decision-making process, due to social segregation and differences in economic and political **capabilities.** This is further accentuated by the fact that access to the media plays an increasing role in decision making, and thus those who have access to or own the media will be better able to participate in the democracy.

POLAND. Despite its close connection with **Germany** and **Austria,** Poland was a latecomer to the development of **social security** programs. In 1889 an injury insurance system was introduced in a part of Poland that at that time was occupied by Austria.

The slower rate of industrial development in Poland seems to explain why this was so, combined with the fact that Poland has been occupied by other countries several times. It was only after World War I that it again became an independent country. After independence, laws were adopted covering **sickness** and **maternity** in 1920, **unemployment** in 1924, and **old age** and **disability** in 1927. After World War II, the system was strongly influenced by the Union of Soviet Socialist Republics (USSR), and thus there was considerable state responsibility for the support, including among other things a commitment to employment for all.

The system in Poland relies heavily on wage-related benefits, without a clear connection between what has been paid in and the benefits to be received.

After the changes in Eastern Europe in the 1980s, the system has also been changed, and one of the main problems has been how to finance these changes. This includes how to ensure the purchasing power of those receiving benefits from the state, as well as how to administer the system. It is still highly centralized and influenced by the labor market partners, primarily trade unions. This seems to be a consequence of the fact that the changes in the 1980s began with an uprising of workers, who then started a new movement (Solidarity).

Family allowances, which are means-tested, and health care are now a universal system, but the bulk of support is a social insurance-based system, although in most areas with some state guarantee. In 1999, a two-tier pension system was enacted in which the first tier's obligatory payment to a pension fund is coupled in the second tier with individual accounts. The system today thus greatly resembles a continental **conservative** welfare state **model**. *See also* EASTERN EUROPEAN WELFARE STATE MODEL.

POLARIZATION. This is the widening of social and economic differences between groups of people in society, for example, between social classes and between men and women. With increasing **inequality** in some countries, it is argued that there is also increased polarization, which can then cause an increase in crime. Polarization due to ethnic differences has also been witnessed in several welfare states.

POOR LAWS. This is a common term for policies that aim to relieve individuals from **poverty** and destitution. The first law was the Poor

Law of 1388, enacted in the **United Kingdom**. It established that the
local area was responsible for providing assistance to individuals.
    This law was changed in 1834 to make it more general and estab-
lish a more common level of support all around the country. At the
same time, workhouses were established, in which those needing
benefits had to work. But the conditions in these were such that only
a few applied for benefits.
    In many countries, poor laws distinguished between the deserving
and undeserving poor. They made it relatively easy to receive assistance, albeit with a few, hard conditions when one was deserving (although the benefits were low), but the undeserving in the UK were
often forced to work hard in workhouses. The expectation was that
this would reduce the number of individual's applying for assistance.
    Poor laws were later developed into **social assistance** schemes be-
cause after the Industrial Revolution poor laws were no longer able
to cover the new risks, and it was seen as too harsh to require that
those in need labor in workhouses. Yet the legacy of the poor laws
system can still be witnessed in many countries.

PORTUGAL. Portugal's system belongs to what has been labeled the
Southern European welfare state model. It is based on the **family**
and family structure, although participation in the labor market and
coverage thereafter was in its historical development and is still important.
    In 1913, a law covering **industrial injury** was passed, followed in
1935 by laws on **pensions** and **sickness** and **maternity**, and in 1942
a law on **family allowances** was enacted. Only after the so-called
Flower Revolution in 1974 was a law on **unemployment benefits**
passed. The long period of dictatorship and fascist rule from 1932 to
1974 and the poor economic situation are major reasons for the very
late development of social policy.
    Following the transition from dictatorship to democracy after the
revolution, a rapid development of the social system took place in
the 1980s and 1990s. During this period, Portugal was the country
in the **European Union** with the fastest growth in public sector expenditures for **social policy**.
    The main element of the policy is still participation in the labor
market. **Pensions** are the exception; those not covered by the labor

market are covered by a state subsidy for a minimum pension. The pensions are very low and are means-tested. The system is thus still relatively ungenerous, although Portugal has to fulfill a EU recommendation for a guaranteed minimum income for all citizens.

POSITIVE ANALYSIS. This describes a situation in completely objective terms, without any **normative** judgments. Positive analysis answers questions such as: What is the scale of **unemployment**? What will happen if x, y, or z happens? These are central questions for the analysis. This is in contrast to normative analysis. Positive analysis can thus help decision-makers find out what may be the most effective policy, for example, in active labor market policy.

POSITIVE DISCRIMINATION. This is discrimination not against, but in favor of, certain disadvantaged groups. It may consider, for example, how to help women and excluded minorities. Positive discrimination can thus help to ensure that weaker groups get a better position in society than would otherwise be the case. *See also* AFFIRMATIVE ACTION.

POST-FORDISM. This refers to the production system that followed the mass production system first introduced by Henry Ford. The post-Fordist production types are characterized by flexibility in the labor market, production, and regulation. Post-Fordist systems, it could be argued, are also characterized by less protection of the workers due to the higher degree of flexibility in the labor market and therefore jobs are less secure. This has raised the issue of **flexicurity**.

POVERTY. This is an old concept in social policy and welfare state analysis. Many of the original social policy measures were aimed at helping the poor. At that time and still today, the concept seems to encompass both **deserving** and undeserving people living in poverty. The deserving were the decent poor who had been residing in an area and tried as best they could to take care of themselves. They were incapable of doing so because of, for example, mental or physical **disabilities**. On the other hand, the undeserving were those supposedly living in poverty because they were shiftless and lazy.

The first attempt to measure poverty was the research done by B. Seebohm **Rowntree**. He only tried to analyze the absolute level of poverty by focusing on food and therefore did not include problems that—at least in contemporary societies—should also be considered, such as access to services and **integration** in society.

The European Commission has in line with those original thoughts presented poverty as when individuals or families have so limited resources that they are excluded from the minimum acceptable way of life of the Member State in which they live. By this poverty is not only an economic aspect, although central, but also refers to the whole debate about social inclusion or social exclusion.

However, poverty is a concept with many different definitions, some of which have led to a focus on **equality** instead. The two main types of poverty are absolute and relative.

Absolute poverty refers to the situation in which the individual (or **family**) does not have access to a certain level of goods and services. An absolute poverty line is therefore defined by a certain basket of goods multiplied by the prices of those goods. It could be supplemented by a certain percentage to cover items not included in the basket (e.g., nonfood items) or for inefficiency when buying goods.

Relative poverty takes into account the relative wealth of society and therefore refers to what is deemed a decent standard of living. A relative poverty line could therefore be, a certain percentage of the average income in a society. The **European Union** commission, for example, uses 60 percent of median income per person after tax as its relative poverty line. In this example the size of the family is taken into consideration. The use of relative poverty lines indicates that a person who in a given society is poor may not be so when compared to the living standards of other countries.

The advantage of using a relative line is that it is stable over time and provides a better possibility of comparing poverty levels among countries. Still, many problems arise when attempting to compare the level of poverty in a given year, including the choice of poverty line, family size, the difference between savers and spenders, purchasing power parities between countries, and the impact of the public sector. Some people, for example, may be living in poverty when only taking their income as a point of reference, but due to **benefits in-kind** from the public sector they have a decent standard of living. These problems with measurement show that data should be interpreted with caution.

Two explanations of poverty that are frequently referred to are the structural and the industrial.

The structural explanation takes the personal situation as a starting point, for example, the fact that some people are born poor or born to become poor. This type of explanations also points to **unemployment** and **segmentation** of the labor market as having an impact on poverty and its level. **Inflation** is also included as a factor, and those analyzing poverty from a structural point of view recommend as policy action creating jobs and income guarantees for those who are not covered.

The industrial explanation looks at the supply side of the labor market and changes in industrial structures. Furthermore, it examines **human capital** and how this can have an impact on the individual's chances of living in poverty. The industrial explanation suggests education and industrial policy combined with labor market flexibility as the main measures to combat poverty.

Many different suggestions have been made to reduce poverty, but the choice is a **normative** one. In recent years a movement has arisen that reduces emphasis on poverty and reinforces emphasis on **social exclusion**. This is because social exclusion and looking at the more vulnerable in society provide a broader focus, and it seems to be less **stigmatizing** to talk about the "socially excluded" than about those living in "poverty." *See also* POVERTY TRAP.

POVERTY TRAP. This term refers to the situation in which people living in **poverty** have no or only a limited chance of improving their economic position. This will be the case if an increase in income fully reduces the benefits received from the state. The poverty trap in most cases is not only the result of a reduction in social benefits, but of a combination of changes in benefits and taxes and contributions to be paid out of increased income. The poor will therefore have difficulty in improving their situation without having a very big increase in their wage income so that they can both enjoy a higher disposable net income and cope with the reduction in social benefits.

PRESSURE GROUPS. These are organized groups of people with the purpose of achieving certain goals. In welfare state analysis they are mainly seen as groups that put pressure on the political decision makers to expand certain areas of the public sector. Some pressure groups want better conditions for the unemployed, some for the disabled, etc. It has been argued that the existence of pressure groups has had an impact on the **growth of the public sector**.

Even if in theory it seems natural that pressure groups have an impact on the growth of the public sector, this is not really supported by empirical evidence, at least not when looking at developments on the macrolevel. Yet it would be naive to ignore the possible impact of pressure groups, because even though they only promote one or a few issues, which in relation to total expenditures may seem small, if many small changes in an upward direction are made, there will be an overall higher level of public sector spending.

At the same time, pressure groups may be driven by a specific knowledge of need in certain areas because, for example, one of their family members needs specific treatment. Pressure groups can thus be a way of providing inputs into political decision making. Many persons active in pressure groups are also active in NGOs and are doing voluntary work. *See also* INTEREST GROUPS.

PREVENTION. This is the process or act of preventing something from happening or reducing the risk of some social event becoming worse. In social policy, prevention is discussed to determine whether or not something can be avoided. If a preventive measure is taken, then curative measures do not have to be taken. Finally, prevention can involve less damage and less pressure on public sector expenditure.

Prevention can include good working conditions, which reduce work accidents; and good education and programs, which reduce the possibility of **social exclusion** and **poverty**. Prevention can be early health checks that make it possible to find out if people are at risk of being sick at an early stage, instead of when they fall ill. Prevention can also be used to avoid negative **social inheritance** by being aware of the impact of different types of continuous need for public support and helping children, especially, have better lives.

Prevention can be justified on the grounds that it is better to prevent than repair and that it may be cheaper to prevent damage at an early stage than at a later stage. On the other hand, prevention may also be costly, because it involves use of money to make the necessary search for those who may, if certain conditions persist, be the victims of a social event.

PRIMARY CARE. This is a form of **health care** that does not require that individuals go to a hospital to be treated for illness. Primary care includes general practitioners as well as district nurses and small clinics outside the hospital system. The distinction may sometimes not be clear, but the main distinguishing factor is how health care is provided. Primary care is often cheaper than care at a later stage because the problem is treated earlier. In many countries general practitioners also do the first screening for the need for treatment at a hospital.

PRIVATIZATION. This is the takeover of a publicly provided and delivered good or service by the market. The **New Right** has been one of the most outspoken proponents of privatization of the public sector. The argument has been that without clear profit goals in the public sector, public production leads to inefficient delivery, whereas private provision would optimize resource allocation. It has further been argued that privatization is a major prerequisite for lowering taxes and duties.

Arguments against privatization include the fact that this can result in **market failure** and that there may be a hindrance to some people getting the good if it is in the hands of a profit-maximizing private company.

Despite the prevalent rhetoric in many countries, privatization has mainly been carried out on a large scale in the **United Kingdom**. Most other **welfare states** have changed parts of the delivery system but maintained a considerable public sector involvement, directly or indirectly. **Marketization** has also been interpreted as a kind of privatization, but marketization uses elements from market systems, among which is competition between providers, to increase the pressure on producers to deliver more efficiently. Sometimes this is combined with the use of **vouchers**.

The use of private and public delivery combined with variations in **financing** indicates that the distinction between public and private delivery in relation to welfare state services may become less useful in the future. *See also* NEW RIGHT.

PROGRESSIVE TAXATION. This is a method whereby level of taxes paid results in a more **equal** distribution, because those with higher income pay more. Progressive taxation is most often connected to the income **tax** system but can also be applied to value added taxes and other duties if they are imposed in such a way that those with higher income pay both absolutely and relatively more than those with lower income. *See also* PROPORTIONAL TAXATION.

PROPORTIONAL TAXATION. This is a method whe y the taxes paid as a fraction of income remain constant as income es. Thus, if the level is 30 percent, then everyone will pay that prop on in taxes regardless of the size of income. However, proportiona ation may involve at least some degree of progression if it is co ed with a threshold before paying tax. *See also* PROGRESSIVE ATION.

PUBLIC CHOICE. This term can be defined as done by D is Mueller (2003) as "the economic study of non-market decision making, or simply the application of economics to political science" (Muller, Dennis (2003): Public Choice, III, page 1). The assumption of this concept is that the individual is a rational **utility** maximizer. James Buchanan (1988) wrote that it "essentially takes the tools and methods approach that have been developed to quite sophisticated analytical levels in economic theory and applies these tools and methods to the political or governmental sectors, to politics, to the public economy."

Public choice theory is concerned with the **growth of the public sector** and the **welfare state**. This growth has often been seen as a consequence of the impact of the **bureaucracy** and **pressure groups** on the decision-making process. The public choice theorist's argument is that although each individual decision may be rational, the overall result is irrational and leads to an over-expansion of the public sector because there is an asymmetry between those paying for the expenditures and those receiving the benefits. Those receiving will be few and those paying many. Therefore, pressure from the few will lead to higher expenditures than would otherwise exist. Furthermore, the possibility of forming coalitions and gaining a majority, according to public choice theory, leads to a higher level of expenditure than would otherwise be expected.

Public choice theorists have especially criticized the lack of a market mechanism within the public sector and have analyzed preference aggregation, party competition, **interest groups**, and **bureaucracy**. They also question the concept of **market failure**, pointing out that nonmarket failure (government-failure) will also occur. Their criticisms include that it is difficult to define and measure the output of the public sector, including the lack of a profit goal. The public sector often resembles a monopoly, with its consequences for prices and production, and furthermore, there is no clear connection between costs and revenues. Public choice theory has compared the public sector with the Leviathan monster from the Bible, arguing that the public sector would swallow up the private sector.

In the 1980s and 1990s, the development of the welfare state in many countries was influenced by the public choice theory argument about the consequences for the private sector of a growing public sector. The argument has been used to exert pressure on decision makers to reduce the growth of the public sector. *See also* NEW RIGHT.

PUBLIC GOODS. These are defined as those goods that one person's use of does not diminish another person's use of. They can be consumed collectively (e.g., fire brigade, military, foreign policy) or individually (e.g., air, beaches, parks, roads).

In welfare state analysis, public goods have been used as an argument for state intervention because in many areas there will not be a market to deal with the delivery of public goods. Among the characteristics of public goods is that it is not possible to establish a price because one person's use of the good does not reduce another person's use of the good. Therefore a public good cannot be sold on the market. **Health care** can be sold on the market, but a public system is necessary because otherwise not everyone would have access to necessary treatment. When everyone has access to a service, it is a public good, because one person's use of it does not reduce others' possibility of using it—except in some rare circumstances such as transplantation, where a lack of donors may reduce others' possibility of using that specific good.

Historically, many systems developed as a response to the fact that the market, left to itself, did not provide sufficient care. Therefore, state systems in the areas of industrial injuries, **social assistance**, and **unemployment benefits**, among others, were developed even if they were not, in a strict sense, public goods.

Most writers on these issues, including **Adam Smith**, agree that the public sector should provide public goods, but they disagree about what exactly can be defined as public goods. Borderline cases have been discussed, such as where the market may provide goods, but consumers do not have the possibility of paying for them. This is often the case for people with handicaps. Another instance is where the goods supplied by the public sector make it possible for many persons to have access to certain remedies. Because different persons can use these over time, they resemble a public good, without being so in the definition's purest sense. A related concept is **merit goods**.

Public goods may change over time, as is the case, for example, with lighthouses. Even when they change over time, analysis shows that some goods will not be provided by the market and therefore can only be provided by state intervention. This has been the reason for public sector intervention in specific areas.

In the wake of the debate on the impact of **globalization**, it has been argued that global public goods also exist in relation to environmental issues, security, and financial market stability. Understood in this way, public goods can be seen at the local, regional, national, supranational, and global levels.

PUBLIC WELFARE. This is welfare delivered by the public sector. Public welfare was one of the three ways in which, according to **Richard Titmuss**, welfare could be delivered. It includes most of the elements often studied in the analysis of welfare states, among them care of dependent persons and other services and transfers in kind and cash. Public welfare is often most dominant in the **Scandinavian welfare states**; it is less prevalent in, for example, the **Southern European welfare state model**. Public welfare is relatively well described in international statistics, **occupational** and **fiscal welfare** less so. *See also* SOCIAL DIVISION OF WELFARE.

– Q –

QUALITATIVE ANALYSIS. This is a method of analysis that is not based on precise quantitative measurement. Methods used include interviews, which try to get information on a specific subject from the informant. The interviews can be conducted in a variety of ways. Observation of behavior and case-based analysis can also be used.

QUASI-MARKETS. A quasi-market is one that is neither fully private nor fully public in its provision of goods. It is a system of delivering goods and services that takes elements from a "normal" market and combines them with public sector intervention. These markets also differ in that providers do not necessarily have a profit motive, and consumers do not necessarily have money power but rather power in the form of **vouchers** or rights to treatment or choice between various providers.

The development of quasi-markets has been seen as a way of breaking the state monopoly without fully reducing the possibility of state intervention. They can combine more effective provision of goods and services with equal access. However, whether or not this is the case depends on the concrete example and structure of the quasi-markets. Equal access and **equality** seem possible to achieve in the area of hospitals, whereas they seem less likely to occur in primary **education**.

– R –

RACISM. This is discrimination against another racial group in a society, which can be on the grounds of race, religion, or **ethnicity**. Direct discrimination is outright exclusion of certain racial groups from participation in, among other things, the labor market or the educational system. Indirect discrimination is nonlegislative exclusion from participation in certain social activities, for example, an employer avoiding employing people of a specific race. Racism can be difficult to measure and evaluate except in the clearest cases; for example, employers may argue that they have simply employed the most qualified persons. With the increase in **migration** between countries different types of racism and/or discrimination against persons who come from other countries have increased in several countries. *See also* MARGINALIZATION; SOCIAL EXCLUSION.

RATIONAL CHOICE THEORY. This is a theory recognizing the individual's behavior when taking part in collective activity in order to obtain a certain goal. Rational choice theory is based on an economic understanding of **rationality**. Thus rational choice is usually understood as a conscious and consistent choice, which maximizes the decision maker's utility. In contradiction to traditional economic theory, however, it focuses not on the individual alone, but on individuals acting collectively. Rational choice theory is used in economic, social, and political analyses, such as those focusing on family consumption patterns or voting behavior. *See also* PUBLIC CHOICE.

RATIONALITY. In its basic form, rationality is an argument based on reason or logic, that is, conclusions, positions, or beliefs reached on the basis of conscious and consistent reasoning or logic.

The understanding of rationality differs greatly within the social sciences. Within traditional economic theory, an individual behaving rationally is on the basis of a conscious and consistent logic to maximize his or her benefit. This understanding of rationality can be termed *goal-oriented rationality*. In sociology, the German **Max Weber** distinguished between four types of rationality, each characterized by a specific form of action (behavior):

1. Goal-oriented action, which, as mentioned, is identical to the common economic understanding of rationality and rational behavior. Furthermore, Weber added, it is perhaps the most dominant form of rationality in modern Western societies. It is part-and-parcel of capitalistic markets and bureaucratic organizations.

2. Value-oriented action, where the individual acts on the basis of belief in a certain way of judging the action's inherent value, that is, evaluating actions on grounds of ethics. Value-oriented action, like goal-oriented action, is an individual form of rationality. The judgments are made by individuals but on grounds of socialization and interaction with other human beings.

3. Affectual action, that is, action based on feelings.

4. Traditional action, that is, action based on identification with customs and traditions. It is a counterpoises to types 2 and 3. This is traditional (i.e., premodern) rationality threatened with

erosion by types 2 and 3. Despite this tendency to erosion, traditional action is vital in theory as well as in practice. It is a tool to explain, among other things, the social actions of human beings, **solidarity**, and **community**.

Some economic theorists argue that rational behavior can include nonegoistic traits such as sympathy and thus make possible an individual or collective distribution of wealth from the rich to the poor.

It has been argued that individuals cannot choose on a one-dimensional scale, making a ranking of choices impossible—and possibly implying the existence of what has been labeled "rational fools." Even if this is so, rationality is still a core concept in many economic welfare state analyses.

Finally, it must be noted that individual rational choice does not necessarily imply a societal optimal outcome. This is due to the existence of **market failure**, where an individual's decision may be rational for the individual person but may at the same time create disadvantages for other persons, for example, pollution. See also RATIONAL CHOICE THEORY.

RAWLS, JOHN (1921–). Rawls is an American philosopher whose main contribution has been his widely used and discussed book, *A Theory of Justice,* published in 1972, in which he outlined and discussed many of the central concepts relevant to the analysis of distribution, such as **equality** and **justice**—and significantly, which principles should be used when defining and interpreting these concepts.

Rawls's starting point is that, in all societies, it is possible to agree on some basic principles. These will be agreed on before one knows his or her situation in the given society, which is decided behind the "veil of ignorance." This leads to the maximin principle, according to which the individual will describe at least what is a minimum acceptable living standard and acceptable distribution in a society. In the modern welfare state, one could argue that this principle lies indirectly behind decisions about benefits for handicapped or disabled persons, because nobody knows whether or not he or she will become disabled.

Rawls defines two basic principles (1972, 302):

First principle: Each person is to have an equal right to the most extensive total system of equal basic liberties compatible with a similar system of liberty for all.

Second principle: Social and economic inequalities are to be arranged so that they are both: (a) to the greatest benefit of the least advantaged, consistent with the just savings principle; and (b) attached to offices and positions open to all under conditions of fair equality of opportunity.

These principles indirectly imply that liberty comes before equality, and in this sense, Rawls's way of thinking seems to be in line with the **liberal** position on welfare state analysis.

Criticism of Rawls's theory has focused on the conflict between liberty and equality but also on the theory's indirect acceptance of an unjust distribution. One reason the distribution of income in Rawls's theory may end as being very unequal is that most individuals behind the veil of ignorance may expect to be those with the highest income. In this case, they will not redistribute a lot to those unfortunate ones who end up being poor. Differences in risk aversion will make it very difficult to get the preferences for the individuals to converge, making it impossible to come to any conclusion about what a just distribution is. Despite these criticisms, Rawls's book has made an outstanding contribution to the debate about what justice is, which is a central part of the analysis of the welfare state and welfare societies' development.

Rawls's understanding of justice may also be regarded as a reason why in most welfare states the support for **health care**, including hospitals, is often higher than for other welfare measures, as most people do not know whether or not they are going to need treatment, so they will prefer to have a really good system.

REFLEXIVITY. This describes a situation in which each individual is confronted in the postmodern society with a variety of **risks**. Each individual will then have to constantly reflect on the impact of these risks, and make choices based thereon not only in relation to daily life but also concerning longer term decisions, for example, living standards in retirement.

REPLACEMENT RATES. These rates result from the calculation of benefits for a receiver of different kinds of benefits as a percentage of wages. They are often calculated in relation to the **average production worker**. The level of replacement rates can be compared between countries and is often used as an indicator of the generosity of the various **welfare states**.

RESIDENTIAL CARE. This is care of persons that takes place in some kind of residential area. It can be homes for the elderly, certain handicapped groups or certain groups not well-integrated into society. Universal welfare states seem to have more public residential care, whereas in other welfare state types residential care is less developed and more emphasis is placed on the role of the **family**.

RESIDUAL WELFARE STATE. This is a state characterized by the individual only receiving benefits if all other possible support has been exhausted. It is, in this sense, connected with the concept of **subsidiarity**. In a residual welfare state, support will only be provided as a safety net for those who otherwise would not be able to take care of themselves and where the **family** is also not able to do so.

In this model, private and market-based solutions are preferred to state solutions. The majority of countries that employ it are in **Southern Europe**. However, even here it must be borne in mind that no country follows the typical pattern exactly. Many countries developing welfare states will for economic reasons often have to start with a more residual approach and then gradually move toward a more universal one with a higher level of coverage. Thus a country having a residual welfare system does not have to maintain it in the long run.

RETRENCHMENT. This concept tries to describe the possible cutbacks and changes in **welfare states**, mainly due to financial pressure, **demographic** changes, and in the late 1980s and early 1990s, persistently high levels of unemployment. In most countries, the relatively high support for welfare state programs has made it very difficult to change popular welfare state initiatives. Historical developments in spending do not indicate that retrenchment on the overall level has taken place. This does not imply that certain areas have not been changed. Still, many systems today have the same structure as when they were started.

RIGHTS. This is what the individual/**family** has in certain situations, as defined in each welfare state. The rights may be based on **citizenship** but may also be based on previous contributions. They may depend on whether a certain **contingency** arises, for example, **unemployment**, sickness, maternity, or retirement, but may also depend on income and wealth, that is, being **means-tested**.

How rights gives rise to benefits varies from one welfare state to another and depends to a very large extent on the historical structure and development of the welfare state. In insurance-based systems, rights are often defined in the social insurance system, but they can have the same effects and implications as those defined in more state-organized systems. *See also* ENTITLEMENTS.

RISK SOCIETY. This concept stems from Ulrik Bech's book of the same name, published in 1986. It argues that in modern societies new types of risk arise, which the individual will have to try to cope with. This also implies a need for many to try to find ways of ensuring a higher degree of safety in relation to economic and other issues.

ROWNTREE, B. SEEBOHM (1871–1954). Rowntree, a social scientist from the United Kingdom, was the first to try to measure **poverty** by finding out what the necessary goods were for a **family** to have in order to cover its basic **needs**. In his study (1901) on poverty, conducted in York, England, in 1899, he based his views of the level of expenditure on "the necessary nutrients at the lowest cost possible." At that time, this mainly meant bread and items used to make porridge, and so forth. On top of this, he added an amount for clothes, **housing**, and heating. All in all, this could be described as the necessary basket of goods in order to survive.

The method is in many ways problematic, as it is difficult to assess what is necessary for a family, but it represented an attempt to measure poverty based on needs instead of what (especially later on) have been seen as the main methods—percentages of average or median income.

RUSSIA. This country is the largest part of the former Union of Soviet Socialist Republics (USSR). It can therefore be difficult to establish when the first laws were enacted, as some of them come from the period of the USSR and some from pre-Soviet times when the country also was called Russia. Most of the laws have been amended since the dissolution of the USSR.

The first law in relation to old age **pensions** was established in 1922, but in Russia, occupational work-injury was established as the first area to be covered in 1903, followed by **sickness** and **maternity** in 1912, with **family allowances** as the last part in 1944.

The present-day system is very largely a **social insurance** system, although with a high degree of mandatory elements with a combination of financing from employers and the state. **Family allowance** is, as in most countries, a universal system financed out of general taxation. The level of benefits is in general relatively low due to the economic problems the country is facing.

– S –

SAFETY NET. This refers to the last level of various types of support that ensure a decent standard of living and also for integrating people into society. The safety net may consist of various levels of economic and other types of support, and the holes in the net may be of differing sizes, implying that in some countries the risk of falling through the safety net is greater than in other countries.

SAVINGS. This is the portion of a person's earned income that is not spent during a year. Savings can, in principle, be both negative and positive. Negative savings mean that the individual has spent more than he or she has earned and therefore needed to take out a loan or reduce accrued wealth. Positive savings mean that not all the income has been spent.

Most people have negative savings when they are young (during their **education**, when they are establishing a **family**), then positive savings until retirement, when the savings again turn negative (using up the money one cannot take along).

In relation to welfare state analysis, savings have been important in connection with **pensions**, because many put money aside during their years in the labor market in order to have a good pension. The relationship between welfare spending and incentives to save is often debated. One argument is that if the welfare state provides too high benefits, then people will not have **incentives** to save. It is also argued that the same result will occur as the consequence of a high level of income tax, including taxes on interest income. On the other hand, it is argued that the individual's preferences are very diverse and that therefore the impact on savings of various type of welfare benefits and taxes is apparently not very high.

SCANDINAVIAN WELFARE STATE MODEL. This model is characterized by an all-encompassing nature and high reliance on state intervention in society. It also involves less reliance on the market as the main provider of **social security**. Access to, and **rights** to, social security benefits are mainly a consequence of being a citizen of the country one is living in. The model also involves more, and a higher, use of general **taxes** and duties as a way of financing the welfare state. Its greater reliance on state intervention indirectly implies less scope for involvement from voluntary organizations, **church**es, and labor market partners. The levels of benefit in this model have in general been seen as very generous compared to other countries.

Historically, the Scandinavian welfare state model was built as a compromise between the different **classes** in society and was seen as a possible way of combining capitalist and socialist development by maintaining a reasonably high degree of **equality**, stability in the labor market, and a free market economy.

In the late 1980s and early 1990s, the Scandinavian welfare state model came under pressure due to the more open economies in the world, increasing international competition, and changes in the economic and political systems of Eastern Europe. Some movement toward a more continental model, with more emphasis on social insurance, has thus occurred, although only to a limited degree.

The model still has the characteristics of universality and high coverage, although increasing emphasis is placed on **voluntary** organizations and self-help groups and, at the same time, pressure to have public sector expenditure reduced. The emphasis on full employment and a high degree of equality can also still be seen in the Scandinavian welfare states. Comparing the welfare states in Scandinavia with other countries shows that they still are a more distinct welfare state type, despite the fact that in some areas there has been some **convergence** with other European countries.

SCHUMPETARIAN WORKFARE STATE. This model is named after the Austrian-born U.S. economist Joseph Schumpeter (1883–1950). It marks the transition in the welfare state from being general and all-encompassing to a focus primarily in the labor market and rights in accordance with work. A Schumpetarian workfare state focuses on ways to strengthen the competitiveness of the economy, including a higher degree of flexibility in the labor market. Consequently, welfare state policies in a Schumpetarian welfare state support flexibility and improved competitiveness more than creating jobs and **equality**, as in the **Beveridgian** and **Keynesian** interpretations of the **welfare state**.

The reason this type of welfare state has arisen is growing international competition and specialization and the need for increased innovation. The focus is on labor market policy, which increases flexibility and indirectly reduces pressure on public sector expenditures because of a constantly higher level of employment. It includes a shift from a Fordist to a **post-Fordist** production mode. The Schumpetarian workfare state has many similarities to **liberal**, neoliberal, and neocorporatist ways of thinking about the relationship between state and market, including public sector involvement in **social policy**.

It can be argued that emphasis on work as a condition for receiving benefits is not new, since ever since the time of the **poor laws** it has been in most cases a requirement for receiving benefits. In most unemployment benefit systems, it has also always been a precondition for receiving unemployment benefits that the individual is actively seeking a job.

SCROUNGERPHOBIA. This fear is part of the occasionally hysterical debate about "scroungers," persons who are cheating the **social security** system. In the **United States**, scroungers are known as "chiselers." This term also indirectly includes the distinction between the **deserving** and undeserving, but the debate is primarily about whether persons who do not have a right to receive a benefit nevertheless do so, for example, persons who have a job but receive **social assistance**. The debate about scroungers in the welfare system has in some countries been used as an argument for reducing the level of benefits.

SEGMENTED LABOR MARKET. This term describes a systemati-
zation and concept of the labor market as consisting of not just one
market, but several. In the theory of segmentation, this means that at
least two separate markets exist. One market is the core labor market,
where the jobs are secure, with high wages and possibilities of promotion. They require a certain level of skill (either through education
or job training). Persons working in the core labor market run very
little risk of being **unemployed**.

The second market—the periphery—is characterized by jobs with
low wage levels, which are often unstable and insecure, and workers
have a small possibility of promotion. Those in the second market
therefore have a higher risk of being unemployed for shorter or
longer periods and therefore implicitly have a greater need for public
support. Those at the periphery in many countries are the young,
women, migrant workers, and the unskilled, and more recently elderly workers are also at risk of becoming unemployed.

Segmentation of the labor market suggests that if persons are to be
more permanently integrated into society, they should have the possibility of access to the core labor market. It is here that **social security** also seems to be higher.

SEGREGATION. This refers to the division in society of different
groups or persons. Segregation may be in different **housing** areas,
among different groups in the labor market, and so on. Segregation
also implies **marginalization**. The processes and causes of segregation may derive from different types of policies or be a result of
market forces. Segregation may have an impact on **social inheritance**, and it may also be influential in **stigmatization**. Furthermore, more segregated societies seem to have a higher risk of
crime. Segregation may also occur due to more free choice about,
for example, education.

SELECTIVISM. This is a type of social policy emphasizing and making a selective **targeting** of benefits—either in-kind or **in cash** —to
those mostly in need. A selective approach implies a **normative**
choice between different groups in society and deciding who will be
supported and who will not.

SELF-EMPLOYMENT. The self-employed are persons who, at their own risk and investment, run a company or deliver certain services. They have a different status in **social security** systems, as keeping control of their previous work records, income, and so forth, is more difficult. Still, being self-employed is also a way of having a job in the labor market, and the trend has been to try to build up systems that can also cope with the specific problems of the self-employed by, for example, making unemployment-benefit systems also for the self-employed, at least in some countries. Self-employed persons also, to a higher degree in the nonuniversal welfare states, have to find ways to ensure that they have saved money for pensions.

SEN, AMARTYA (1933–). Amartya Sen, professor of economics and philosophy at Harvard University until 1998 and since then professor at Cambridge University in the **United Kingdom**, has contributed widely to the debate and discussion on **equality** and **inequality** and social choice, and has been awarded several honors, especially the Nobel Prize in Economics in 1998. He has written several books, which not only try to examine equality from traditional economic viewpoints but also include normative elements and the political decision-making process. His writings have been influenced by his Indian origin, including important contributions on **poverty** and famine. He has analyzed questions of rational behavior and how **rationality** and **social choice** can interact. He can thus be labeled a **social choice** theorist.

SICKNESS BENEFIT. This benefit is provided when the specific contingency of sickness occurs. It is organized and structured differently in different countries. In some, it comes within the public sector **social security**; in others, it is related to being a member of, and having paid into, a private sickness insurance fund. Some systems have waiting periods before individuals are able to receive the benefit (one or more days). The benefits are typically a percentage of previous income, with a ceiling. In some countries, collective agreements have built in a higher benefit from the first day of sickness. In some systems, the principles of the sickness benefit system are also used in calculating the level of **maternity** and paternity leave.

SICKNESS INSURANCE. This is a way of guaranteeing people income during a period of illness. In many countries, this is done not by the public sector but by private insurance companies. The agreements may be generated by individual insurance, but frequently it is part of the collective system, or the state makes it obligatory that the individual (employer/employee) must pay into an insurance company.

Individual sickness insurance can be provided for all citizens except the chronically ill. Insurance companies estimate and calculate the risk and thereby decide the level of a premium with no risk of **moral hazard** or **adverse selection** because they have the chance of asking for the previous health records before granting an insurance policy. If this is done, however, it will cause problems for persons with bad health, as they may have difficulty getting insured. This is less of a problem if sickness insurance is made obligatory by the state or if the individual belongs to an employer's group plan. *See also* HEALTH INSURANCE.

SLOVAKIA. This is a country in Central Europe that was established on January 1, 1993, after a referendum. It has approximately 5.5 million inhabitants. Previously Slovakia was part of what is now the Czech Republic. Slovakia's welfare system was thus to a high degree developed as part of the old communist type of system.

Industrial injury was the first area to be covered, in 1887, followed by **sickness** and **maternity** in 1888. In 1906, **pensions** for salaried employees were established, followed by pensions for wage earners in general in 1924. **Family allowances** were adopted in 1945.

To a large extent the present system is an obligatory social insurance system, except for family allowance, which is a universal system. In the pension system, the insured pay part of the costs, the employers approximately one-fifth, and the state around one-third. The level of benefits is in general rather low.

SLOVENIA. This is a small country in Central Europe with a population of around 2.5 million. Slovenia became independent in 1991 after breaking away from the former republic of Yugoslavia. Most of the first laws date back to when it was part of Yugoslavia. **Pension, sickness, maternity**, and **industrial injury** benefits were all established in 1922, followed by **unemployment** benefits in 1927 and **family allowances** in 1949.

Before independence, the system was based on work for all. Slovenia presently has a stable economy and also benefits that try to ensure a guaranteed minimum income for all citizens. The pension system is a social insurance system, with the contributions mainly from the insurers, but also from employers and with the state providing a guarantee in case of deficit. The principles are the same in the other parts of the social security system, with the exception of the family allowance, which is state financed.

SMITH, ADAM (1723–1790). Smith was a Scottish philosopher and economist during the Scottish Enlightenment. He studied at Glasgow University and later went to Edinburgh to teach. Between 1751 and 1763, he held a chair in moral philosophy at Glasgow University. His contribution to economic theory has been a foundation for many **liberal** thinkers and advocates of a free market economy. It is mainly found in *Inquiry into Nature and Causes of the Wealth of Nations*, published in 1776. His reputation as a philosopher was mainly established by *The Theory of Moral Sentiments,* published in 1759.

Smith's main contribution was that he believed that decision making by many individuals would be complementary and that most would act in their own self-interest. This has led to research and further analysis by many other authors of the conflict between state and society.

Even though Smith was a firm believer in the market, in *The Wealth of Nations* he advocated that certain duties be preserved by the state. Among others, the state should attend to defense, **justice**, and foreign policy. But he also said that, "The third and last duty of the sovereign or commonwealth is that of erecting and maintaining those public institutions and those public works, which it never can be for the interest of any individual, or small number of individuals, to erect and maintain because the profit could never repay the expenses" (1970, 211). This is, in fact, still at the core of present discussions and problems in relation to welfare state analysis and part of the argument concerning **market failure**, as well as an argument for state intervention.

SOCIAL ASSISTANCE. This is the main way of distributing state benefits that are not based on previous contributions. It is therefore paid out of general **taxes** and duties. Eligibility criteria differ from country to country, but they are frequently based on the principle that other types of help are no longer available and, in addition, on a **means test**. In most countries, social assistance is received by those who are not eligible for **unemployment** or **sickness benefits** or different types of **pensions**. It is thus the last part of the social **safety net**.

SOCIAL CAPITAL. This refers to forces in society that can be used for active involvement in societal activities. Social capital is thus often measured by looking at the membership of and active participation in various organizations, including voluntary organizations.

Social capital can be seen as elements that are also important for the **third way** politics in welfare development, for they are a manner of integrating forces in the civil society in societal development. To some degree, social capital thus also expresses the **solidarity** in a society and, at least in a broad interpretation, the society's cohesive forces.

Social capital was made famous by Robert Putnam's book *Bowling Alone*, where the expression "bowling alone" indicated a change in American society from a time where people used to engage in activities together, whereas now an increasing number do such activities alone.

SOCIAL CHANGE. This refers to the changes taking place in the abilities and possibilities of individuals in different societies over time. Social change and the different ways this has developed in various countries have had an impact on the way **welfare states** have been built.

Knowledge of social change may be used to explain differences in political outcomes under different social and cultural conditions. In **Germany**, social change in the nineteenth century resulted in new **social security** systems with a considerable reliance on the labor market.

The way social change occurs is based on political, administrative, and economic conditions in different countries. The way changes are transmitted will have a different impact on and consequences for the way the welfare state is structured and changed.

SOCIAL CHOICE THEORY. This theory examines how different individuals' value judgments will have an impact on societal development; it focuses on the maximizing of welfare in a given society. This has mainly been done by using strict formal axioms to describe what the outcome of different choices would be in a given society. Included in this theory, moreover, is how individual **rationality** has an impact on society's many decisions, and in turn how social considerations can have an impact on the rationality of the individual.

Social choice theory is closely connected to **welfare economics**. It also gave rise to **public choice** theory. Social choice theory research includes many of the questions about **justice, equality,** and **distribution** involved in finding a social welfare function.

SOCIAL COHESION. This is a term for the degree of **social inclusion** in different countries and their ability to ensure political and social stability. Social cohesion in a more sociological sense relates to the ability to develop connections and relations between members of a given society and can also be used in relation to the debate on **social capital**.

SOCIAL CONTROL. This is the process by which some people and their behavior are controlled by others or by **norms**. Social control can be used to get people to act in ways that society or specific groups want them to. In relation to social policy, social control may mandate that an individual can only receive social security benefits if the person does what he or she is told to by the authorities. This can consist of engaging in **community** work, getting an education, or just going to a specific place each morning. Social control then involves a reduction of the individual person's freedom, but it is the price the individual will have to pay to receive public support.

Social control through norms may vary over time, and for the individual, it may have the consequence that it is difficult to know how to act. In welfare models that emphasize **family** help, the norms may implicitly apply pressure toward fulfilling the norms of the family structure.

SOCIAL DEMOCRATIC WELFARE MODEL. This model has a universal character and is primarily state financed. **Citizenship** is the key factor when deciding who is eligible for a certain benefit. It resembles in many ways the **Scandinavian welfare state model**.

SOCIAL DIMENSION. Social Dimension refers to social aspects of societal development. This refers especially to a debate within the **European Union** (EU) in which this was the other side of the coin to free movement of capital and labor. The higher mobility of capital and labor was expected to increase the use of market forces, which could therefore create greater inequalities within and between the EU countries. The social dimension can thus indirectly be seen as the price capital in Europe paid to have a freer and more open market. However, it can also be seen as a wish to keep competition in working conditions and social policy from dominating European economic and social development.

There are two positions in Europe in the debate on the social dimension. One is that a social dimension would go against the whole notion of an internal market. The other is that the social dimension was the best way of avoiding social dumping on a European scale.

The Social Charter, negotiated in 1989, was therefore only agreed to by 11 out of the then 12 member states, the **United Kingdom** deciding to opt out. The Social Charter covers freedom of movement, employment and remuneration, improvement of living and working conditions, social protection, freedom of association and collective bargaining, vocational training, equal treatment for men and women, information, consultation and participation for workers, health protection and safety at the workplace, protection of children and adolescents, elderly persons, and the handicapped.

Its prescriptions are general and not binding, but it was followed up and included in the Maastricht Treaty, with the United Kingdom still rejecting it, but the new member states (**Sweden, Finland**, and **Austria**) accepted it. In May 1997, the United Kingdom accepted the social dimension after the Labour Party under Tony Blair won the general election. It was later included in the EU Amsterdam Treaty, and all the 10 new member states since 2004 have also accepted a social dimension, as it was also part of the Nice Treaty. This will involve some change in **social policy**, mainly to improve the lowest possible level of social protection within the European Union.

The social dimension is thus not very precise and does not involve binding elements for the individual countries, but on the other hand, it does show that a more uniform **social security** system may develop in the future on a European level. The social dimension of European development is sometimes also referred to as the ability to create a social Europe.

SOCIAL DIVISION OF WELFARE. This term describes a concept proposed by Richard **Titmuss** in *Essays on the Welfare State* in 1958. He distinguished among the following three levels of welfare: public, fiscal, and occupational. These three levels refer to different ways of delivering and financing welfare.

Public welfare refers to the welfare supplied and financed by direct state intervention. It is this that most statistics on social expenditure show, and cross-national comparisons often have this as the starting point for the way in which the different countries' systems are connected.

Fiscal welfare refers to what is directly or indirectly provided for by the tax system. This may take the form of tax allowances and tax relief (*see* TAX EXPENDITURES). Fiscal welfare has an impact on public sector income by reducing it when giving these specific allowances.

Occupational welfare is the benefits and services provided by employers in the private market. These range from being fully voluntary to being a part of collective bargaining in the labor market, where the employers (as part of an agreement) have also promised to pay all or part of some **social security** expenditure. Finally, occupational welfare can be decided by the state, but the financing and implementation will be an obligatory duty for employers.

These three levels do not exhaust the ways welfare can be delivered, and they can be interwoven. One example is that many of the **pensions** provided in the occupational welfare systems are indirectly supported by tax relief, which is fiscal welfare, and they are also often supported by a direct public provision of a basic level of pension.

This concept is useful for pointing to different routes and ways to social security.

SOCIAL EXCLUSION. This term describes a situation in which individuals in a society are not included in one or more aspects of society's life or do not participate in societal activities. In the literature, there does not seem to be one agreed upon definition of what social exclusion is. Basically, it seems to be the opposite of **integration** in society.

Different definitions have encompassed different aspects of the concept. Some have emphasized the relation with the labor market, whereas others have taken a broader approach. The **European Union**'s observatory on social exclusion defined it as the absence of "a certain basic standard of living and to participation in the major social and occupational opportunities in society." In this way, a person subject to social exclusion can be seen as not having the same rights as other citizens in the given society.

Social exclusion can be in relation to one or more aspects of societal life but can also encompass a broader interpretation of the individual's position in society. This means that the individual can be excluded from the labor market and participation in cultural activities or not be integrated in local life, and so forth.

The term was first developed in **France**. In the mid-1970s, it was used to describe groups or persons not covered by the traditional **social security** system. They were thus excluded from certain social protection systems. Under such a definition, those excluded will change over time as the social security system changes. The term's origin also seems to stress the relationship between individuals in society and society's structure. Finally, it emphasizes the role of societal processes rather than considering this to be a necessarily permanent situation.

The term seems to have evolved from a broader concept, which was used to encompass the broader societal structure and development, rather than the narrower focus of concepts such as **equality**, **poverty**, and **justice**.

As the term seems to be the antonym of integration, many policies with the aim of reducing social exclusion have focused on what could integrate people into society. As many welfare state systems are based on labor market participation, research into social exclusion has primarily examined how labor market measures could help integrate people into society. As a result, many ways of discussing social exclusion have been narrowed down to the consequences of **unemployment** and of not being part of the labor market's core force. This is a too-limited version of the concept that does not integrate other types of social exclusion, for example, the elderly who do not want to be alone but are feeling lonely and in this sense are excluded from social life.

Although the term has different connotations, and there is no single way of defining it, it has influenced the debate about welfare state policies. Researchers have concentrated on analyzing the situation of those who are **marginalized**, and not only those living off traditional income transfers. This approach emphasizes that income transfers are only one part of the welfare states' policy for a better functioning of society. *See also* SOCIAL INCLUSION.

SOCIAL INCLUSION. This is the opposite of **social exclusion**, but is often referred to as a set of policies with the explicit aim of getting individuals or groups of persons included in society through different types of polices and initiatives. **Active labor market policy** is often looked upon as one measure that can be used to include people in society. However, this only counters one type of inclusion, that is, in the labor market, and not more generally the need to be included in the society in a broader sense. In several welfare states, various types of programs both in the public and voluntary sectors try to help integrate people who are otherwise on the margins of society. *See also* SOCIAL INTEGRATION.

SOCIAL INDICATORS. These are measures of welfare and **social change** in various countries. This is a relatively new concept, which originated in the early 1950s and gradually developed in many Western countries because, among other things, it was expected that it would produce new types of information, which were not previously collected by traditional economic measurements. In 1954, a United Nations (UN) report on International Definition and Measurement of Standards and Levels of Living was published and gave rise to regular collection of data, followed by an Organization for Economic Cooperation and Development (OECD) agreement in 1973 on 24 areas of fundamental social concern. Today, it is used to a more limited extent, mainly due to problems with the definition. However, the OECD publishes social indicators, including many of the elements mentioned below. Still, in many areas only few data at a comparative level are available.

Social indicators have been developed by a process of defining welfare areas that may be of interest and then finding components that, in general, are able to describe the chosen areas. The social indicators thus reflect how different groups in society have access to certain services or the average life expectancy. The indicators not only include components that can be measured in terms of money but also try to encompass a broader version of society's impact on individuals and their position. This is the reason, for example, for including information on life expectancy, infant mortality rate, and so forth.

Unlike economic indicators, social indicators include nonmonetary aspects. Researchers have focused on areas such as **health, demography, education, housing**, safety, **employment** and work safety, recreation, consumption possibilities, and democratic participation.

Reports on social indicators have been a part of the general trend of publishing and making material available in order to analyze living standards in various countries. They not only reflect the economic and material perspectives but also include a nonmaterial insight into daily living standards.

SOCIAL INHERITANCE. This refers to a situation in which children end up in similar sorts of jobs or problems as their parents. It is especially the negative type of social inheritance that is of interest in relation to social policy, that is, when the same families receive social assistance generation after generation. It needs to be made clear that this is not the case for all children and that many children have a higher level of education than their parents. At the same time, it may be important for a society to be aware of how negative social inheritance can be reduced by, for example, improving **education** and ensuring education for all in the society.

SOCIAL INSURANCE. This is a system in which the individual, in the event of a certain contingency, can receive a benefit without a **means-test**, but must fulfill the criteria for receiving the benefit, for example by being sick or unemployed but actively looking for a job. Social insurance is typically publicly organized, and membership can be compulsory but may also be voluntary. The compulsory nature of the system means that it is not possible for those offering the insurance to analyze individual risk. A social insurance system will therefore tend to be more equal than private insurance systems. The social insurance will often be paid by those insured, but support from the state may be possible, often in the form of a guarantee in case of deficits. Social insurance systems are often used in the more **continental welfare states**. *See also* HEALTH INSURANCE.

SOCIAL INTEGRATION. Social **integration** refers to whether the individual is an integrated part of society's way of functioning and includes both economic and noneconomic aspects. It also refers to policies with the aim of integrating people into a society. *See also* SOCIAL INCLUSION.

SOCIAL MOVEMENTS. These are a variety of groups or persons who have in common one or more specific topics they want to pursue in society. Historically, they have been involved in different areas and have different views about which solution to find. The socialist movement is just one example.

Today social movements are of interest in the way they point to and can have an impact on welfare state policies. This can be done by creating pressure for changes in social structures or societal policies aimed at the weaker groups in society. An impact on welfare state policies can also be the way in which they influence and form self-help groups to support each other. Social movements have in recent times also included various groups wanting changes in environmental policy or social integration. *See also* INTEREST GROUPS; PRESSURE GROUPS; TRADE UNIONS.

SOCIAL NETWORKS. This term describes the individual's way of having contact with other persons in society. The network may include families or friends but can also be social workers and their clients.

Social networks are seen as playing a central role in reducing **marginalization** and feelings of loneliness in the welfare state. The expectation is that social networks can reduce the pressure on the welfare state because they can support the individual and reduce the need for **benefits in-kind** or **in cash**.

Supporting social networks can be a way of increasing cohesion in a society. It can also be a way of reducing the need for public economic support in various areas, including the risk of crime. However, it is debatable whether state-supported networks have the same impact as the more voluntarily created networks. *See also* INTEGRATION.

SOCIAL POLICY. This type of policy is traditionally included in the **welfare state**. It can be restricted to a very narrow area—for example, only the Ministry of Social Security—but will often be understood in a broader context, including the core areas of the welfare state such as **social security, education, health care**, and **housing**. Social policy is often investigated by integrating various disciplines in the analysis of how it has an impact, but this requires a very multidisciplinary approach.

SOCIAL RIGHTS. These are the **rights** that individuals have in a **social security** system. How these rights are acquired and maintained is a specific element in the **welfare state** systems of various countries. The whole issue of social rights is often also connected to **A. Marshall**'s discussion of citizen rights.

SOCIAL SECURITY. This is the set of policies established to compensate for the economic consequences of a specific social **contingency**. Social security as a concept has been codified by International Labour Organisations (ILO) Convention No. 102 (1952). It covers nine areas, including medical care and benefits in relation to **sickness, unemployment**, old age, **industrial injury, family, maternity, invalidity**, and widowhood. It has also been described in EU Regulation 1408/71.

Industrial injury—which was one of the first social contingencies to be covered in most countries—is still also the area that is most developed worldwide. The other types are developed and implemented differently around the world. They will also differ in relation to eligibility and level of benefits.

Social security is a narrower concept than **social policy**, as it does not include services and different types of policies with the intention of reducing the problems—that is, **preventive** measures. It also does not include measures and initiatives to avoid **poverty** and **social exclusion**. Still, social security does include many of the central elements in the welfare state policies of many countries, in particular

pensions, which are very central and account for a large proportion of spending in many countries.

SOCIAL WELFARE. This concept can be approached from different angles. From a statistical perspective, social welfare is measured by examining real income and its distribution among groups or persons. The other approach considers social welfare as the aggregate of the individual's utilities, which are a function of his or her access to various goods and services.

Social welfare is a way of trying to evaluate a society's welfare by taking both production and distribution into consideration. Most of the analyses involve **normative** judgments and **interpersonal comparisons**, which often makes the concept quite difficult to use as a basis for making recommendations. Still, making judgments based on different measures of **inequality**, and from this providing a description of social welfare, is a way of informing about society's welfare.

SOCIAL WELFARE FUNCTION. This is the sum of the individual **utilities** in a given society. From this definition, it implicitly follows that if the utility of one person is increased, then society's total utility is increased. It can fulfill different criteria by emphasizing different elements, for example, the distribution between different persons in society.

This is mainly a theoretical concept, which can be used to discuss the implications of different types of activities and intervention. It is not possible empirically to find a society's welfare function, as it requires that we possess full information about all individuals' welfare and utility, and that all individuals will be able to establish an order among various alternatives. (*See also* ARROW'S IMPOSSIBILITY THEOREM.)

Analytically, the principle is useful as a reminder that establishing priorities among scarce resources is necessary.

SOCIAL WELFARE POLICY. This type of policy emerged out of the development of the welfare state in many countries after World War II and the rapid expansion of the public sector. It was—and still is— a policy in many countries with the general aim of making improvements in living standards for those in **need**, and it was originally and still is mainly achieved by state intervention. Economic demand management was expected to be the policy that would ensure full employment and continuous growth to finance the development of the **welfare state**.

During the economic crisis in the Western world after the first and second oil shocks in the 1980s, social welfare policy was increasingly questioned from different perspectives—both right and left. The Left criticized it for helping and maintaining the capitalist **class**, the Right for harming the dynamics of production. This led to suggestions for reducing the level of welfare, often presented as arguments about **retrenchment** but also about **privatization**.

Today, it seems that the period of very rapid growth is over in the most mature welfare states but that there is still considerable state involvement in social and welfare policies in many countries. Furthermore, it seems that we are witnessing **convergent** trends in social welfare. *See also* NEW LEFT; NEW RIGHT.

SOCIAL WORK. This is work done by field workers and those in the administration dealing with social problems. A social worker is a person who, as a representative of a statutory or nonstatutory body, delivers different types of social services (income and in-kind) and advice to individuals.

Mainly persons having undergone a specific education perform the work, and on this basis, they know the social systems and how to communicate with the people concerned. They should also have a psychological understanding of processes and reasons for changes. Social workers are often the front line workers in social policy and thus the first contact the user of the system meets. Some forms of social work are also labeled **street-level bureaucracy**.

SOCIALIZATION. This is the process by which people are integrated into society, either by learning or adaptation of **norms**, rules, and values in a specific society. Socialization often takes place within the **family** and the **educational** system. *See also* INTEGRATION.

SOLIDARITY. In its most general sense, solidarity is unity resulting from common interests or feelings. It is a collective responsibility between people who are dependent upon or related to each other; it can describe the population of the nation state, the workers in a specific trade union, employees in a specific firm, people in a given **community**, members of an organization, and so on.

Solidarity is a central element of the **welfare state**. The willingness to contribute to the provision of a welfare state through taxes and duties can be seen as one type of solidarity. The macrosolidarity, that is, the overall agreement of solidarity, may be different from microsolidarity, that is, the individual's willingness to support families, friends, and/or the local area.

The degree of solidarity and interrelated level of welfare services differs among the welfare states. Different types of welfare states may have different levels of the abstract formalized form of solidarity mentioned above.

Emile Durkheim distinguished between two types of solidarity, mechanical and organic solidarity. These types refer to different commitments within the different states and models. Solidarity as a prime mover for development of welfare states emerged more recently mainly in the twentieth century.

Solidarity in the sense of willingness to pay for welfare state activities, especially for the most vulnerable, seems to exist more generally in all welfare states. The willingness to pay for welfare state activities seems to be dependent to a certain degree on the **legitimacy** of the welfare state. The willingness to pay for and accept activities has often been highest in relation to **pensions** and **health care**.

SOUTH AFRICA. South Africa's system was historically influenced by the system in the **United Kingdom**, but its development was relatively late due to the fact that it was a colony. Furthermore, the long period of apartheid dampened the development of social programs. Some of the programs, when developed, actually excluded Asian, colored, and black employees. This was the case for **family allowances**, introduced in 1947.

The welfare state started with the introduction of the **industrial injury** law in 1914 and was followed by old age **pensions** in 1928. **Unemployment benefits** were available from 1937. The government mainly pays for the system, although with some contributions

from the insured and employers for unemployment   nefits and industrial injury.
This system has very low coverage and a strict me   s test for eligibility for a benefit. The breakdown of apartheid h   changed this,
but in the long run, change will depend on economi   nditions. The
relatively weak economic position of South Africa, w   so many living in poverty, makes it more difficult to develop a w   e state. This
explains why it still has a more rudimentary coverage   th a high reliance on the **family**.

SOUTHERN EUROPEAN WELFARE STATE MO1   . The South-

ern European welfare state model is also sometimes   red to as the
Latin Rim model. It is a rudimentary welfare state   to its limited
coverage of citizens in many areas.

It is highly influenced by the Catholic way of thinking and is therefore also often connected with the **subsidiarity** principle. This implies that the state's intervention in the field is rather limited and that
the state primarily takes over only as the last resort.

The more influential role of the **church** in Southern Europe may
also explain why the development of welfare state systems started
later. This was partly due to greater reliance on the **family** structure,
partly because needy people could get some help from the church.
This reduced the scope of and need for public sector involvement.

Southern European countries (here referring mainly to **Greece**,
Italy, **Spain**, and **Portugal**) have what some would call a more du-
alistic welfare state model. This is so because coverage, to a large extent, depends on having a job. Those without a job or those having a
job in the **hidden economy** will therefore not be covered unless the
family steps in. On the other hand, the **health care** sector is mainly
universal and for all citizens regardless of **class** and status in society.
The consequence is that a particular segment of the population in
these countries is highly protected, whereas the rest are almost not
covered.

In the area of **pensions**, the system is in general well developed,
and it is therefore not just a rudimentary system. However, the core
areas in **social security** are only developed to a very limited degree,
and with a compensation level below the levels in other European

countries. This can in part be explained by lower economic possibilities.

Finally, this model has been connected with the clientelism principle, under which the possibility of receiving a social benefit will depend on support for a specific political party. This has been the case, for example, in Italy, especially in the southern part. It also exists in the other Southern European welfare state types but due to long periods under dictatorships it has not been developed to the same degree.

SPAIN. Spain's social policy development has been influenced strongly by civil war in the 1930s and the long period of dictatorship until the mid-1970s. As did other European countries, it introduced quite early a law on **industrial injury**, in 1900. But it was only after World War I that laws covering old age (**pension**) and **unemployment benefits** followed (both in 1919), then in 1929 **sickness** and **maternity benefits**, and finally in 1938 **family allowances**, were introduced.

The system belongs to the **Southern European welfare state model**, with a large proportion of the system financed by contributions. In relation to family allowances, a more general scheme has been developed.

Spain expanded its social policy in the 1980s and 1990s but still keeps the core of the old system intact. The gap in spending on social policy between Spain and northern Europe is still considerable, although a lot of catching up has taken place, making it **converge** with other welfare states in Europe.

STATE, MARKET, AND CIVIL SOCIETY. This refers to the interaction and division of responsibilities in **welfare states** among three different actors: the state, the **market**, and the **civil society**. States have certain responsibilities in areas not taken care of by the market or civil society because of **market failure** or due to a wish to provide a higher degree of **equality**. The market delivers certain goods and services in areas where it is possible to create market conditions. The civil society delivers other types of activities.

The balance among state, market, and civil society varies among welfare states and welfare state types. The balance has changed over time, creating a different welfare mix in various countries. It will presumably also continuing changing in the future.

Within the triangle of state, market, and civil society, one can also distinguish between formal and informal provisions and for-profit and nonprofit activities. There are no clear-cut divisions among them—overlaps exist and will presumably continue to do so—but as a way of thinking about different elements of providers and services in the welfare state the formal/informal and for-profit/nonprofit distinctions among the actors are useful.

The division of responsibility varies among welfare state types. The responsibility of the family is higher in the residual model, the market in the liberal model, and the state in the social democratic model.

STATUTORY RETIREMENT AGE. In several welfare states, the age when the right to a state **pension** is available. The form of retirement is different from the average age of retirement, which is often lower by using, for example, **early retirement** benefits.

STIGMATIZATION. This refers to the phenomenon when individuals feel that they are looked negatively upon when receiving social benefits from the welfare state. This may reduce the individual's willingness to take up a benefit due to the negative psychological implications of receiving it.

Stigmatization may derive from having to ask for a benefit, the risk that others see one is receiving a benefit, or a feeling that one is no longer able to take care of himself or herself. These elements may give rise to a sense of stigma, which can then contribute to **social exclusion**. Stigmatization may be different for different persons and can also depend on the prevailing **norms** in the individual's surroundings.

STREET-LEVEL BUREAUCRACY. This term refers to those persons who are in direct contact with the clients within the **social security** system. They often have discretionary power to make decisions about whether or not an individual will receive a benefit, and in some countries, about the size of the benefit.

The power of street-level bureaucrats in some countries has led to criticism of their work. This is because a client who is not able to communicate well with the bureaucrat may have difficulty receiving the benefits he or she has a right to.

On the other hand, it has been argued that by having street-level bureaucrats with discretionary power it is possible to take a more holistic view of the clients' problems and help to solve them. The ability to take a holistic view is greater when there is leeway for decisions than when the benefits are fixed. *See also* SOCIAL WORK.

SUBSIDIARITY. This is a concept that originated from Catholic thinking in the twentieth century. Definitions today often quote Pope Pius XI in *Quadragesimo Anno* (1931): "It is wrong to withdraw from the individual and to commit to the community at large what private enterprise and endeavor can accomplish." Furthermore, it was stated in the *Quadragesimo* that what can be done at a lower level should not be taken over by the higher level. This implies that a welfare state model building on this principle will be very **individualistic** and decentralized. The individualistic approach is indicated in the sentence on withdrawing from the individual. The decentralized approach is based on the idea that any intervention should be undertaken at the lowest possible level.

It can be argued that the individual level includes the **family**, which can be the firm ground upon which social policy is built. This has been a cornerstone of welfare state models such as the **Southern European welfare state model** and also in many Catholic countries.

The concept of subsidiarity has also influenced social policy in the **European Union** (EU) and the process for European integration. In the Maastricht Treaty, subsidiarity was directly stated in article 3b: "In areas which do not fall within its extensive competence, the Community shall take action, in accordance with the principle of subsidiarity, only if and in so far as the objectives of the proposed action cannot be sufficiently achieved by the Member States and can, therefore, by reason of the scale or effort, be better achieved by the community." Following the discussion at the Edinburgh summit of the concept of subsidiarity, this is understood to mean that the EU must be able to show that the action is necessary. Furthermore, it must add value to the community that action is taken on a higher level than that of the nation states, regional, or local authorities. Subsidiarity has since been integrated in all treaties in the European Union. It is naturally sometimes difficult to evaluate whether or not added value exists.

In the **United States**, the Constitution also—indirectly—uses the concept of subsidiarity by stating that the federal government should only step in if intervention cannot be undertaken in the different states or by the people themselves.

In **Germany**, it is also stated that the Länder (Germany's regional units) should implement as much of EU regulations as possible rather than having the federal government impose them.

The concept has therefore had a clear impact on the way welfare states have developed and been structured in many countries, by proposing the sharing of competencies among different levels of society. It has also been used as an argument for rolling back the state's influence in society and reducing welfare state spending by leaving a larger proportion of the activities to local and individual spending. The degree of centralization and decentralization varies markedly among welfare states, including a large diversity due to the existence of local differences. Differences in services may be greater than those in direct economic support.

SUBSIDIES. These are support intended to reduce the price the consumer would otherwise have to pay for a good. They can, for example, be used to reduce the price of goods that are assumed to be very important for people with a low income. Subsidies can therefore be a way of trying to alleviate **poverty**. They have been used in many countries as a way of reducing the costs of basic **needs** for a **family**. Subsidies to ensure cheap housing, cheap bread, and heating are elements that, especially in former Eastern European countries, reduced the need for social assistance. Subsidies can in this way be an alternative to other types of income transfers. Subsidies can also be a way, like **taxes** and duties, to provide **incentives** for the individual or family to spend more money on a specific good than on another good. With the increase in health problems due to growing obesity, the use of subsidies for, for example, vegetables may be a way addressing the problem.

SUPPLEMENTARY PENSIONS. These pensions are received in addition to the basic pension provided by the welfare state. Supplementary pensions may be either voluntary, to specific targeted groups, or based on **occupational welfare**. They can also be supported indirectly through the tax system (*see* **tax expenditures**). In many countries, supplementary pensions have been developed in order to have a broader variety of **pensions** and a possibility of a higher savings rate for people who need more than the level that the welfare state is able to cope with given its economic and demographic situation. Supplementary pensions have thus become an important pillar in the pension systems of several countries and have broadened them from being mainly **pay-as-you-go** to **funded** systems.

SURVIVORS. These are the people who survive the death of a relative. In several **welfare states**, there have historically been survivors **pensions** for women when their husbands died, mainly because the societies were built around the male **breadwinner** model.

SWEDEN. Sweden is the **Scandinavian welfare state** type, with a very universal, all-encompassing system, even though in recent years it has been under economic pressure and **marketization** has come more widely into use. Basically the individual is covered as a citizen, although certain parts of the system rely on his or her being in the labor market.

Sweden developed its system early, with the introduction of a **sickness benefit** in 1891 and a law on **industrial injury** in 1901. A law covering old-age **pensions** followed in 1913; **unemployment benefits** followed in 1934 and in 1947 a law on **family allowances**.

The pension system, family allowances, and **health care** are all universal and are mainly paid through general **taxes** and duties, although some of the money comes from obligatory social security contributions. The social security contributions, however, have many resemblances to general taxes and duties. Unemployment benefits are based on membership in an unemployment benefit fund, which is the case for approximately two-thirds of the Swedish labor force.

The late development of unemployment benefits in Sweden may be a reason for the very **active labor market policy**, which is intended to get people back in the labor market as soon as possible.

Besides developing benefit systems after World War II, Sweden rapidly developed more comprehensive coverage in many service areas in the welfare state, including child care and care for the elderly.

In addition, the Swedish welfare state was decentralized, with many decisions—and related financing—dealt with at a local level. After a long period with rather few initiatives in social policy, when Sweden was ruled by **liberal** governments, the first Social Democratic government came to power in 1932, presumably as a consequence of rising **unemployment**. Welfare state development in Sweden has since been inspired by the rule of the Social-Democratic Party from 1932 until 1976. This was done in such a way that the farmers felt satisfied, and in many senses, the developments were built on a consensus among different **classes** in Sweden. The compromise implied a capitalist production structure but with state intervention and regulation to improve employment conditions and create a more equal society. The compromise and consensus strategy was also necessary, as the Social-Democratic Party did not have a majority in parliament. It has also been labeled an attempt to create "a people's home," implying that after political **democracy** was established the time had come for social democracy, by building a welfare state with emphasis on the rights of citizens. Only with the breakdown of the coalition between the middle class and the labor movement did the Swedish model run into problems.

Sweden has been inspired by **Bismarckian, Beveridgian,** and **Keynesian** ways of managing the economy. This continues to have an impact on the structure of the system by maintaining financing through taxes and duties but also through social security contributions.

After World War II, in which Sweden was neutral, a rapid expansion of the welfare state took place. The ground had already been laid before the war. But with Swedish society becoming more affluent, many areas were extended and improved, in relation to both services and income transfers. Until the late 1980s, active labor market policy and a very broad and generous coverage were the main elements of the Swedish welfare state model. It has been further strengthened by a relatively large degree of stability in the labor market, despite the fact that since 1976 liberal and conservative governments have from time to time run Sweden.

The increase in international competition especially since the 1970s has made it difficult for Sweden to continue to support one of the largest public sectors and highest levels of taxes and duties in Europe. Thus it witnessed a series of **retrenchments** in the 1990s in several areas, and in some, there is now less emphasis on universality. Still, Sweden's is a very developed welfare state, with a high level of public spending on welfare, a high degree of equality, and a continued commitment to a full employment policy. However, the model does seem to have matured.

SWITZERLAND. This country has been neutral since the last century and has been outside the international political arena. It is based on highly independent cantons. The Swiss welfare system developed relatively late. **Industrial injury**, sickness, and **maternity benefits** were adopted in 1911. Unemployment insurance followed in 1924, **pensions** in 1946, and finally, **family allowances** in 1952. Some of the cantons had at that time already developed social programs including family allowances.

The structure is ased primarily on voluntary and compulsory insurance, with contributions from employers and employees. There is only very limited state support, although there is some support for old age pensions and sickness and maternity benefits. A continental **conservative type** of welfare state has emerged in Switzerland.

– T –

TAKE-UP RATE. This is the percentage of those eligible for benefits who actually receive them. A take-up rate of 100 percent means that all those who have a right to a certain benefit receive it. Reasons for non–take-up may be the feeling of **stigma** when receiving a benefit or lack of knowledge about the right to receive it. It is difficult to estimate take-up rates, as those eligible for a benefit but not claiming it may not be included in the statistics and also not be known to the public sector.

TARGETING. In **social policy**, this means directing benefits toward groups with specific needs. Targeting involves selection of who receive the benefit, and it can thereby be used to reduce the economic pressure on the **welfare state**. Very specific targeting can make it possible that certain groups will not be covered by the system, and thus the use of targeting can result in **marginalization** of these groups.

TAX EXPENDITURES. These are a way to give, redistribute or allocate resources in society. A government may use tax expenditures to have an impact on the distribution of welfare in a society. **Richard Titmuss** labeled tax expenditures **fiscal welfare**.

Tax expenditures are defined as a departure from the generally accepted or benchmark structure, which produces a favorable tax treatment. This can be for either individuals or certain groups in society.

Measuring and calculating tax expenditures is quite difficult. They can be calculated by the use of revenue forgone, revenue gained or the outlay equivalence method. Most empirical studies use revenue forgone, as this can be calculated by looking at the different favorable tax treatments and their impact on revenue. Both the revenue gained and outlay equivalence methods raise more problems and further questions, for example, in relation to the consequences of the dynamic changes in an economy.

Tax expenditures are not only used in the field of **social policy** or welfare state expenditure but also in broader areas. They have an impact on the welfare state distribution and redistribution of resources. By using tax expenditures, it is possible to give certain groups better conditions than others or provide incentives to promote savings/ investments and so on.

The advantage of tax expenditures in relation to social policy is the ability to reach targeted groups quite easily through the tax system. This can result in a high **take-up rate,** as all those qualified for the benefit will have easy access to it and do not have to make a special application and go through other formalities. Furthermore, tax expenditures can be targeted at those groups with the lowest income by, for example, giving a specific tax reduction to income groups below a certain ceiling.

The disadvantage of tax expenditures is that they are mainly based on income statistics, which may be inaccurate. Moreover, if the individual has to claim them when sending in tax returns, some will not receive them. Furthermore, they may hide the welfare state as information on the macro-level rarely is available. Because of their general characteristics, they mainly benefit the middle class and groups in society with a higher income level.

In many countries, it is not possible to get information on the size of tax expenditures, which makes it difficult to assess the distributional and social impact of their use. Tax expenditures often have an upside down effect, that is, mainly benefiting those with high incomes.

TAXES AND TAX BASE. Taxes are the legislated amount of private income, sales, or property the individual will have to pay to government, regional, or local authorities without any right to receive anything specific back. Taxes can in principle be imposed anywhere in the economic system.

The tax base is the value of everything subject to taxes. The base varies with the items defined as taxable and the valuation (or assessment) of those items. The trend has been to broaden the tax base as a way of reducing marginal taxes and duties, thereby reducing the possible **disincentives** arising from taxes and duties. *See also* INCENTIVES; TAX EXPENDITURES.

THIRD SECTOR. This is that part of society that lies outside the state and the market. Some prefer to describe the third sector as activities lying within the welfare triangle of **state, market, and civil society**. The third sector includes **voluntary organizations**, nonprofit organizations, private nonprofit organizations, philanthropic bodies, foundations of charities, charitable trusts, self-help groups, and other activities related to and between individuals outside the public and private sectors.

The size of the third sector can be very difficult to measure and can also vary between different types of welfare states. Still, in all welfare states, third sector activities are important elements in the society's total activities.

THE THIRD WAY. This is the welfare policy advocated especially by Tony Blair in the **United Kingdom**. The idea in third way politics has been to try to combine traditional social democracy with the challenges of a more **globalized** world. Elements in third way politics include activation and labor market policies in order to increase **equal-**

ity, **residual welfare**, social responsibility and individual obligations, **targeting** of benefits, and more effective government services. *See also* NEW LEFT.

THREE WORLDS OF WELFARE. This is the title of a book by Gøsta Esping-Andersen published in 1990 that continued research on comparative welfare state issues by and with the use of the concept of **decommodification** and divided welfare states into three different regime types (continental, **liberal**, and **social democratic**).

TITMUSS, RICHARD MORRIS (1907–1973). Titmuss was one of the key figures in research and writings on social policy in the twentieth century. He was from 1950 and until his death professor of social administration at the London School of Economics. He wrote on **poverty, social exclusion**, and **the welfare state** and was also the first to introduce the distinction among **public, fiscal**, and **occupational welfare**.

TRADE UNIONS. This is a collection of persons who have the same interests and either the same type of **education** or same type of jobs, who have come together to improve pay and conditions of work. In some countries, trade unions are divided along religious or political lines.

In many countries, trade unions have been a major factor, acting as **pressure groups** urging the development of a welfare state by emphasizing the need for coverage and support in case of specific contingencies, for example, **industrial injury**. The trade unions still play a role in many **social security** issues, and in many countries, they participate actively in shaping collective agreements, which have an impact on the level of wages and coverage for pensions and sickness.

Trade unions often play a central role in integrating the social partners in decision making and also participate in **tripartite** negotiations. Such social partnerships as a way of developing societies can be found in many welfare states. Trade unions are integrated in the development of labor market policy, including **active labor market policy** and other policies related to, for example, work and safety at the workplace.

TRIPARTITE. This describes participation by three parties in discussions and decision making, in relation especially to labor market policy, but in the most developed tripartite structures, for example, **corporatism**, also in relation to economic policy in a broader sense. The three parties participating are normally understood to be the state, the employers, and the employees. In corporatist states these three parties are central actors in relation to core elements of welfare policy.

TRUST. This concept has gained importance in analyzing welfare states in recent years, as there has been greater focus on trust in the delivery of welfare service and the relationship between provider and user in many countries. Trust in this connection is central to prevent **free rides** and to avoid, for example, when using **vouchers**, the service provider engaging in cream-skimming. Trust can vary and is a highly individual element. It is often stated that it takes a long time to build trust but that it can be lost in few seconds.

– U –

UKRAINE. This country was part of the former Union of Soviet Socialist Republics (USSR), but it been an independent country since 1991 and has around 50 million inhabitants. The country's welfare state policy was to a large extent developed in the former USSR with, until 1991, a strong emphasis on guaranteed work as a core of the welfare system.

The first social welfare legislation dates from 1912 and concerns **industrial injury, sickness**, and **maternity**. A law on **unemployment** followed in 1921 and one on **pensions** in 1922. In 1944, the **family allowance** system was adopted. All these laws have been reformulated and changed since independence. The system today is to a great degree a social insurance system, although providing universal coverage for family allowances and **health care**. Employers pay a large proportion of the cost through 37-percent taxes on payroll. Employees also pay a small percentages based on their earnings.

UNDERCLASS. *See* CLASS.

UNEMPLOYMENT. This is the state of being without a job but actively looking for work. Unemployed persons should be both able and willing to take up a vacant job. The unemployment rate describes the percentage of the labor force that is unemployed.

Different types of and explanations of unemployment exist, including classical unemployment, **Marxist** unemployment, and **Keynesian** unemployment. Some focus more on the reasons behind unemployment, which can be structural, voluntary, weather conditions, seasonal, technological, and the business cycle.

In **classical economic** theory, unemployment is explained by inadequate flexibility in real wages; that is, if the wages of those searching for a job were entirely flexible, full employment would prevail. In Keynesian economic theory, a lack of demand in the economy explains the level of unemployment; thus a change in the overall demand for labor would help ensure a balance between demand and supply. This could, for example, be achieved by public works, such as were used in many countries during the 1930s, including Franklin D. Roosevelt's New Deal in the **United States**. In Marxist theory, the explanation is that there is too low a profit level.

The different theories suggest various remedies to change the level of unemployment. In welfare states, the level of unemployment and the consequences for the individual and families have had an impact on the creation of unemployment schemes and policies to increase employment and hopefully also reduce unemployment. Unemployment has been seen as one of the major explanations of **poverty, inequality**, and **social exclusion** in many welfare states. This depends to a large degree on the level of **unemployment benefit** and the length of time unemployment benefits are available. In welfare states with low levels of unemployment benefits, the risk of poverty is greater, and at the same time the figures in relation to the level of unemployment may be misleading, as fewer people may register for unemployment benefits if the level is very low. *See also* HIDDEN ECONOMY; LABOR MARKET POLICY.

UNEMPLOYMENT BENEFIT. This is a benefit that can be received when the social **contingency** of **unemployment** occurs. Different countries have different systems for delivering, and various criteria for receiving, unemployment benefits. In most systems, the individual will have to be a member of an unemployment insurance fund, have paid contributions for a certain period, and be actively seeking a job while unemployed. Furthermore, the level of unemployment benefits is subject to a ceiling, and the time period to receive it is limited. It may also be **means-tested**, and it may vary for young educated people and those who have only been in the labor market for a few years. The systems may also vary from a **social insurance** system to a fully actuarial insurance system. The financing can vary from a purely individual system to a system in which employees, employers, and the state participate in financing it.

UNION OF SOVIET SOCIALIST REPUBLICS (USSR). *See* RUSSIA.

UNITED NATIONS (UN). This is one of the most important international organizations, established in 1945 with the purpose of helping to create and maintain peace, and further to encourage international cooperation and the ability to find solutions for economic, social, and cultural problems. Most countries in the world today are members of the UN.

The UN Nations has many important institutions, such as the **ILO**, the World Health Organization (WHO), UNICEF, and UNESCO. WHO helps especially poor countries with a food program and vaccinations for various diseases, whereas UNICEF deals with children's daily lives, and UNESCO with education. There is an economic and social council (ECOSOC), with the goal of improving living standards around the world, which promotes full **employment**.

In 2004 and 2005, the UN helped the victims of the tsunami in Southeast Asia through both a huge relief program and by coordinating the assistance from the many donor countries.

UNIVERSALISM. This is often interpreted as access to **social security** for all citizens of a given society as long as they fulfill certain criteria for eligibility for the specific benefit, for example, being sick, having had a work-related injury. or reaching a certain age. It often characterizes the **institutional** welfare state **model** and has been used primarily in the northern part of Europe.

The basic arguments for universalism are, first, that a society's development has resulted in individuals needing more help and that as societies developed (industrialization, more complex societies, etc.), it has been a collective responsibility to help those in need after these changes. Second, is the idea that all of us, as human beings, have basic rights.

A narrower definition of universalism is that rights only apply to persons who are in similar conditions and have the same rights. This principle can involve a distinction between those who through no fault of their own need help and those who, due to their own way of living, need help.

In many welfare states, the distinction between universalism and particularism has had an impact on the way systems were functioned. The more universal systems have been based on citizens' rights (*see also* T. H. MARSHALL), thereby reducing the scope for individual solutions. Even with universal rights some welfare systems are mainly guaranteeing a minimum protection, and those wishing a higher level of protection they will have to find individual solutions, for example, by taking out private insurance.

UNITED KINGDOM. The first elements of **social policy** in the United Kingdom were the **poor laws**. These changed in 1834 to take account of industrialization and the new **risk** that arose as a consequence thereof. Poor relief was at such a low level that the income was below that of those working in the factories. A workhouse test was introduced, which meant that individuals not able to support themselves could be put in a workhouse, where they received just enough food to survive.

In the period between 1830 and 1880, many **voluntary organizations** were established, with the aim of self-help. They included friendly societies, building societies, and **trade unions**. They tried to prevent people from falling into **poverty** and being forced into workhouses. The combination of continuous bad working and living conditions as a consequence of the Industrial Revolution and the growth of new political groups is a major explanation for the emergence of new initiatives in social policy legislation.

Industrial injury was the first area to be covered (1897), followed by a universal old age **pension** in 1908, unemployment and **sickness benefits** in 1911, and finally, in 1945, **family allowances.**

The changes from 1908 onward were brought about by a liberal government, elected in 1906, which was committed to a policy in which those who were poor or unemployed for good reasons would be covered to a certain degree. It seems obvious that the British government—although it did not use the insurance principle—was inspired by Otto Von **Bismarck**'s reform and in this way was trying to reduce social unrest.

Reforms were not undertaken during World War I, and only in relation to unemployment benefits was radical change made in the interwar period. A reform of 1934 was, in fact, an amalgamation of poor relief acts and the unemployment benefit system. This was forced through because the unemployment benefit systems were no longer able to pay for themselves and needed public support. Between the two wars a situation emerged in which voluntary groups played an important role in the whole system. At the same time, a very complicated system, which still did not cover all risks, had been developed.

Because of these changes and the social consciousness that developed during World War II, the **Beveridge** Commission was established. The Beveridge Report had a profound influence on British social policy. Furthermore, the ideas of John M. **Keynes** on economic demand management influenced the decision-making process.

The Beveridge Report pointed out that the system was "conducted by a complex of disconnected administrative organs, proceeding on different principles." The proposal for reform was to pool risks by individuals having access to a **social insurance** system through paying a flat-rate contribution and with a possibility of receiving a flat-rate benefit. This was the cornerstone of the Report's recommendations. The Report's main recommendation was implemented through a new National Insurance Act in 1946, National Insurance Injuries Act in 1946, and National Assistance Act in 1948. The levels of benefits were set very low, presumably lower than those envisaged by Beveridge. In 1948 a new national **health** service was introduced by act of Parliament. The general consensus supporting the reforms can be seen as one of the reasons why the system lasted nearly 35 years without any radical changes.

Still, more general systems and services developed and grew until the end of the 1970s, when the Conservative Party under Margaret

Thatcher took over. The system continued to build on flat-rate contributions and a low level of benefits. Gradually other elements were introduced. These included a state earnings related pension in 1975, which was a break from the tradition of flat-rate benefit. It was put on top of the flat-rate pension. Thatcher dismantled the scheme by making it possible to opt out, and it was replaced by private insurance—supported by tax grants.

The Thatcher era saw a tightening of eligibility conditions and periods when unemployment benefit could be received. **Means tests** for benefits were introduced in several areas—the Social Security Act of 1980 and the Social Security and Housing Benefit Act of 1982. There was greater reliance on the market for social provisions (either individually or as occupational systems), which to a certain degree could be supported by tax allowances. Finally, voluntary organizations were again playing a pivotal role in the social system. It was argued that more voluntary contributions could help the British system continue to give the dependent a decent living standard.

The British welfare state is therefore no longer as universal as was the intention of the Beveridge Report, and it has many characteristics that more closely resemble the **liberal** approach to the welfare state. In recent years, the United Kingdom has moved to what the Labour Party has called a **third way** in social policy. The third way, it is argued, is somewhere between the liberal approach and the more social democratic approach, emphasizing both the use of market forces and the state's social responsibility. Still, the British welfare state, compared to other welfare states, places less emphasis on direct delivery of care, especially for children, and is nearly a full private market solution.

UNITED STATES OF AMERICA. Generally the United States has been a latecomer in the development of **social security** and social policies, and even today it lags behind the European notion of what a welfare state is. The late development of federal systems does not mean that no social security had existed due to the federal structure of the United States. At the local level, several types of poor relief existed, which changed over time as economic conditions and possibilities changed. Some—mainly white veterans—also received state pensions, although not as part of a general pension system.

In the period after World War I, the strategy seems to have been to move away from the more European types of welfare state. To an even greater extent than the **Bismarckian** welfare state, America relied on **occupational welfare**, that is, company-related benefits and pension plans, which sometimes were supported by tax incentives. Still, the development of federal legislation was slow until 1935.

Workers compensation was introduced in several states. In 1915, approximately 30 percent of the workforce was covered. In general, **pensions** were introduced in 1935, and in the same year **unemployment benefits** were introduced as part of the New Deal. Sickness and **maternity benefits** were first introduced in 1965, and health insurance for the disabled in 1972.

The New Deal, the reforms implemented by Franklin D. Roosevelt in two rounds—1933–1935 and 1935–1939—were cornerstones of later U.S. welfare systems. The first round mainly focused on the creation of jobs in the aftermath of the collapse of the financial markets in 1929 and the Depression. The second round focused on social security and introduced new legislation, with a broader scope and perspective than had ever been witnessed before in the United States.

The New Deal included a federal state unemployment insurance program and a federal grant program to help dependent children, the blind, and the elderly. Matching grants for vocational rehabilitation, infant and maternal health, and aid to crippled children were introduced. Finally, it included the above-mentioned old age program.

These new initiatives were financed out of payroll taxation, and a large part of the programs relied on the individual states to follow up and undertake local initiatives.

In contrast to Western European welfare states, only very few and limited changes took place after World War II in the United States, and it can still be regarded as a laggard compared with Europe in relation to social policy. Part of the explanation is that there was no real pressure from trade unions, and the balance of power between federal and state authorities has made it difficult to implement general and more universal systems. Furthermore, the historically very individualistic approach in America emphasized a preference for solutions based on non-state organizations. The United States still does not have a comprehensive health care system.

Only in the 1960s, during the John F. Kennedy and Lyndon Johnson administrations, was there any intention to initiate new social programs, but only few and limited changes actually occurred.

The system today consists of two main areas—an insurance-based system and public assistance. The insurance system is for the employed and is therefore biased in favor of the middle class. Public assistance is targeted and **means-tested** so only the poorest can receive the benefits. Compared to Europe, there is very great reliance on private charity organizations to provide welfare in relation to children and health care. This means that there is a much broader scope for nongovernmental organizations and less impact from direct public provision. There does not seem to be any change underway in this respect, and it seems that the best chance for the poor is a flexible labor market policy and creation of new jobs in the service sector.

In general the model can be described as a **liberal** market-based system in which only those who have a job are covered. The rest of the population is only covered to a very limited extent and often only if they can afford to take out insurance. Therefore, the most vulnerable have a relatively low living standard because they have to rely upon Temporary Assistance for Needy Families, which eliminated individual entitlement and instead focused on work and personal responsibility. The law further limited the number of months for receiving social assistance over a lifetime to 60. The absence of any guaranteed minimum income explains why the U.S. model is sometimes described as a working poor model.

UTILITARIANISM. This is a theoretical framework within which society's overall aim is to maximize the total **utility** of the citizens. If total utility is the most important goal, resources have to be increased for one citizen even at the cost of another. A utilitarian will mainly argue for a free market, given that the individual is seen as the best one to know exactly what to choose in all areas, which can be done in the market under the condition that no **market failure** exists. In principle it is the individual's pleasure when using a resource that results in what is best for society.

Utilitarianism has been used to try to define a society's **welfare function** based on the addition of individual preferences. This concept can also be labeled **methodological individualism** due to its emphasis on the individual.

Utilitarianism would also prescribe intervention to increase **equality**, as this would be in line with the moral and political philosophy behind the theory, emphasizing that society should take into account and maximize all individuals' happiness; this despite that fact that subjective and normative elements are involved in such a procedure.

UTILITY. In **welfare economics**, utility describes the individual's satisfaction in having or consuming a specific combination of goods and services. In classical descriptions (Bentham, Mill), utility is defined as happiness and pleasure. According to **classical economists**, the individual will try to maximize his or her utility given the constraints, for example, of production possibilities, wealth, and income.

An individual's choice will be based on the highest utility level that can be achieved. It is not only absolute utility that is of interest. The marginal utility, which refers to the extra utility one person gets from an extra unit of a good, has been an influential concept in the debate on **justice** and **inequality**, indicating, for example, that a rich person will at some point have a decreasing utility from the consumption of extra units of a specific good. Society's overall welfare function—if measured as the total utility—could then be increased if redistribution from the rich to the poor took place.

The main problem with the concept of utility is the difficulty in measuring it. When it is not possible to measure utility in a way all can agree on, its use in concrete policy making is more difficult. Furthermore, the utilities one person derives from a good may be very different from what another derives from the same good due to very diverse preferences. This means that utility can be a very difficult concept to use systematically. *See also* UTILITARIANISM.

UTOPIA. This is an ideal state described by Thomas More (1478–1535) in a book published in 1516. The name is of a place that does not exist. In welfare state and philosophical discussions, Utopia is seen as an ideal that one could move toward but presumably never reach. At the same time, utopian approaches have been seen as a ways to formulate ideas and hypotheses that can be used in debates about the development of the **welfare state**, including discussion on how to balance rights and duties.

– V –

VERTICAL EQUITY. This term describes the consequences of redistribution from wealthier to poorer groups in society. This redistribution can be in terms of income, wealth, buying power, or access to different types of services. How this redistribution takes place does not influence the principle, but when measuring inequality, it may have an impact on whether the redistribution is first to those who have the lowest income or, for example, to someone at the top or to someone just below the middle in the income distribution. Both types of redistribution would be achieving a higher degree of vertical equity, but the overall change in the level of **inequality** would be different.

VOLUNTARY SECTOR. This is defined as those who are willing to perform functions in society for the benefit of people other than themselves and their closest relatives. The voluntary sector can be found in most **welfare states**, but it is more developed in some than others. Voluntary action is not only directly related to social policy, it is also related to the whole area of sports and leisure activities, especially for children and young persons in many countries.

The voluntary sector is based on — as the words say — voluntary activities by individuals but will often receive support from the welfare state. There is a conflict in being a voluntary organization yet receiving state support to carry out activities, since receiving state support may reduce the independence of the organization.

In the welfare state debate, the quality and ability of the voluntary sector to support the vulnerable has been questioned by those who think that individuals should not have the risk of becoming dependent on the charity and that there is a risk that discretionary judgment by those performing the voluntary work will not provide access to social benefits in a just way. Furthermore, voluntary work may have a tendency to concentrate in some very specific areas, leaving other areas of the welfare state with less support. In most welfare states, the voluntary sector supplements state involvement in welfare policies. *See also* NON-GOVERNMENTAL ORGANIZA-TIONS.

VOUCHERS. These are coupons that are connected with certain rights to buy a given service or good. Vouchers have been used, among other things, to provide lunches for school children. They are also a way to give citizens rights as consumers in relation to teaching, day care for children, and care for the elderly. The use of vouchers creates a possibility of creating something that resembles a market within the public sector in the welfare state. In the **United States**, for example, vouchers have been issued in the form of food stamps/cards giving the individual a right to get food. An argument for using vouchers has been that it is thereby known what the individual gets for the public economic support. Vouchers are also used in different welfare states as part of **marketization** of welfare services and as a way of creating more competition within the public sector. A risk with vouchers is that cream-skimming will occur and that a more segregated society will emerge.

– W –

WEBER, MAX (1864–1920). One of the most outstanding theorists of the twentieth century, Weber published works in many different fields of the social sciences (philosophy, theology, sociology, economics, and political science). With respect to welfare state analysis, his work is of particular interest in that it focuses on two elements: (a) **bureaucracy** and (b) the understanding of human behavior.

Bureaucracy in a Weberian sense is an effective administrative body that knows exactly what to do and will do it in the most efficient way. The reason for this efficiency can be seen in the clear rules and hierarchical order of the administrative system. Therefore all those employed will know what to do and when to do it. They act in a rational way, and the system will be rational and effective.

The understanding of human behavior refers to an analysis of how and to what degree individuals interact and has the intention of learning and understanding why they are acting as they are. Learning about individual behavior could then lead to understanding actions.

Weber's ideas have been challenged by some who have argued that his work on bureaucracy and political systems was a legitimization of fascism and a demand for a strong political leader. Others see Weber as a founder of modern sociology and claim that he merely wanted to develop an analytical way of looking at modern society that would be open to debate and better ways of understanding social processes.

Weber's research on the Protestant work ethic has been influential in the discussion about the organization of society and production. In this way, his ideas have influenced many scholars, who have tried to understand what is behind the welfare state and how it can be understood.

WELFARE ECONOMICS. This is a theory that is concerned with how to maximize society's welfare function and find ways to improve welfare in a society. Furthermore, it tries to analyze whether different types of intervention will increase or decrease society's welfare. It is often based on using the individual's value judgment of welfare as a condition for comparing different situations. Changes in the individual's welfare will always be seen as an improvement if one person's situation is improved without any other person's situation being worsened (the **Pareto** criteria).

This analysis is quite difficult in practice; therefore, other types of criteria have been developed. The Kaldor-Hicks compensation principle is one of the most famous. This states that it is still a welfare improvement if those gaining by the change can compensate the losers and still have a surplus.

Today, welfare economics is merely a broad term describing analysis of the welfare state and society by using economic theory based on rational behavior in various situations and involving various decisions in society.

WELFARE SOCIETY. This is a broader term than **welfare state**, as it includes wider and more elaborate viewpoints on democracy and non-monetary items. However, as the two concepts are frequently used interchangeably, in this book, the main presentation and discussion comes under the concept of welfare state. Welfare society can sometimes also be understood in a broader context by including **nongovernmental organizations**, **voluntary work**, **occupational welfare**, and the welfare created in *the* **families**. The concept thereby emphasizes that welfare is produced not only by the state but also to a large extent by other actors in various societies.

WELFARE STATE. This term has been defined in various ways over time, and there is still no consensus about what a welfare state is. According to Flora et al., the term was introduced by Archbishop Temple in 1941 as an answer to the aggression and power of **Germany**. It could be argued that the rise of the welfare state after World War II—at least in the **United Kingdom**—was especially due to the vision of William **Beveridge** on administration and of John M. **Keynes** with regard to having a commitment to full **employment** and economic stability. Others claim that the term was coined by Alfred Zimmern of Oxford in 1934 but made more popular by Archbishop Temple *Citizen and Churchman* in 1940.

The concept may be seen as a contrast to the **laissez-faire** state and also a way to interpret the state's role in more than political terms. It develops the rights of individual citizens as part of the state's role in society. Again, it may further be seen as a contrast to a power state.

Different definitions of *welfare state* can be found in various dictionaries:

- *Oxford English Dictionary* (1955): "A polity so organized that every member of the community is assured of his due maintenance with the most advantageous conditions possible for all."
- *Oxford Paperback Dictionary* (1988): "A country seeking to ensure the welfare of all its citizens by means of social services operated by the State."
- *Encyclopedia Americana* (1968): "A form of government in which the state assumes responsibility for minimum standards of living for every person."
- *International Encyclopedia of the Social Sciences* (1968): "The institutional outcome of the assumption by a society of legal and therefore formal and explicit responsibility of the basic well-being of all its members."

- *Encyclopedia Britannica* (1974): "A concept of government in which the state plays a key role in the protection of the economic and social welfare of its citizens."

All these definitions center on the way in which the state makes and develops **social security** for its citizens.

A definition often quoted comes from **Asa Briggs** (1969) : "A welfare state is a state in which organized power is deliberately used in an effort to modify the play of market forces." This definition emphasizes the questions of how and why a welfare state intervenes in society. Deliberate intervention is a core problem when discussing welfare state issues. It is often interpreted as state intervention, but state intervention is sometimes not, at least deliberately, used to modify the play of market forces, although the intervention will have an impact. An example is education, which does not directly aim at intervention in the market. However, it may, in the long run, have an impact on the market forces' ability to work.

Asa Briggs suggested that the modification of the market should take place in at least three ways:

- by guaranteeing minimum income
- by the narrowing of insecurity
- by all citizens having a right to the best standards available

The last point refers to what in the welfare state debate has been labeled **universalism** versus selectivism. An instrument that should guarantee all citizens—within certain defined limits—rights is a universal principle, which could mean that many states will not be regarded as welfare states.

Still, even if this is agreed upon as being a good definition of a welfare state, there is and will be many problems in measuring it. When is a state deliberately trying to modify the play of market forces? Is it when stating rhetorically that it is doing so, or is it when we can see direct intervention in the economy? Or should we examine the laws passed in the legislature, which have an impact on the individual firms? Or should we be more interested in the way the financing of the state has an impact on individual households, firms, or markets? The Briggs definition is therefore mainly a starting point for a discussion of what a welfare state is.

Economists focus on the economic impact of the state on society, political scientists focus on the decision-making process, and sociologists focus on who has responsibility for the individual in society. Social policy and social workers focus more on how society is organized and how the interaction between social workers and society and the client should be.

From different theoretical perspectives, it is still difficult to find out when we are really dealing with a welfare state. How great should the state's involvement in society be before we can talk about a welfare state? What will we include in our measurement of the welfare state? The reason for asking these types of questions is clearly that some of the state's expenditures do not belong to expenditures in the area of a welfare state. This is the case, for example, with expenditures on military service, foreign policy, and at least part of the administration. Expenditures on internal security, control of mergers, and other legal areas would normally also be outside the scope of a welfare state. This gives rise to further problems about how to analyze the concept and which expenditures should be included when analyzing it.

Should we focus on expenditures from the Department of Social Security, or should we take a broader view, including the Department of Labor or Department of Housing, and how should we draw the boundaries? There are no straightforward answers to these questions. They will to a large extent depend on the purpose of the analysis. Furthermore, it is often not enough to just examine legal intervention and the legal rules, as economic rules in the tax system may have an impact and, moreover, collective bargaining either directly or indirectly supported by the government could have an impact on the welfare state.

Using OECD, International Monetary Fund (IME), EUROSTAT, or other central statistical sources is another way to describe the size of the welfare state that may yield different results, and therefore it is necessary to be aware of, and investigate how, these entities have defined different areas before using the data for an interpretation of the welfare state's development. In addition, the data may be skewed, as they do not include **tax expenditures**, which means that those parts of the welfare state that are provided for by the tax system are not reflected in the figures used for analytical purposes.

These difficulties in analyzing the nature of the welfare state also indicate why the literature has been so full of attempts to find typologies able to describe different types of welfare state, such as the **Beveridgian** Model, **Bismarckian** model, **Confucian** model, **Conservative** model, **Liberal** model, **Scandinavian welfare state** model, **Social Democratic** model, and **Southern European welfare state** model. This large variety of models indicates why the welfare state is so difficult to describe and define.

The measurement of the welfare state often focuses on the level expenditure as a proportion of Gross Domestic Product, the way welfare state is financed, and the organization of the welfare (private/public delivery). But this is not sufficient; one also has to amine the welfare state in its historical context. This due to that both the historical reasons for the development of different and welfare state and chosen strategies differs, and the solutions quently chosen will therefore also presumably differ despite convergence also has taken place

The introduction in many countries of programs that can be seen as forerunners to welfare state programs is related to the political and economic situation in those countries. In **Germany**, for example, the intention of Bismarck's programs was to reduce, or eliminate, unrest in the working population by introducing **social insurance** programs. In other countries, the introduction of welfare state programs was a response to the changing needs for protection in the population in the wake of the Industrial Revolution.

The new needs had first and foremost to do with the fact that due to the Industrial Revolution many workers were not covered in case of accidents and sickness, and families when they moved to the cities were dependent on the income of one person. This created a need for new types of organization and structures in society. In many countries the state was involved in fulfilling these needs, because the market, left to itself, did not provide these types of security.

Along with the first kinds of protection (accidents and sickness) there was an increased need for support in relation to **pensions**, education, **housing**, and spouses. Furthermore, the systems gradually developed support for people living in **poverty**, income supplements for low- income earners, housing benefits, and so on.

Today the welfare state can be found in many different forms, from the all-encompassing "cradle to the grave" to a more minimalist system in which only a minor part is provided by the public sector and the rest by the private sector. They differ in the way they are financed, from universal tax systems to systems mainly based on individual contributions and private insurance. The variety is also in systems, where the emphasis varies from being on specific contingencies to being on the living standards for individuals and from systems in which a large part consists of income support and mainly public income transfers to systems that to a large extent rely on transfers in-kind or provision of care, for example, in the form of care for the elderly by providing homes for them.

In Europe, a slight tendency toward **convergence** seems to be taking place through the emphasis on certain minimum standards to be provided by the state. In addition, occupational benefits or private sources will supplement that support. This has a historical connection with the continental model but is a more mixed model in which universal entitlement and universal delivery are also included.

History indicates that welfare states often have taken a long time to develop and mature, and even then changes may be continuously taking place. These changes can involve **retrenchment**, but they may also be coverage of new areas, improving levels of benefits, and so on. No clear trends can be perceived when analyzing different welfare states' development, and even looking at a few years may be misleading, as a change can be of a temporary nature. Some of the changes are related to the general economic climate, but in some countries, the **aging of societies** also has had an impact on welfare state development in the past 10 to 15 years and may perhaps do so in the coming years as well.

Still, the main issue in most countries in relation to welfare states is the ability to guarantee basic economic security and also protect individuals and families from various types of market failures.

The following definition is based on analysis of the various regimes and approaches to welfare:

> By a welfare state is understood a institutionalized system where the actors the state, market and civil society interact in various relations with the purpose of maximizing society's welfare function and where the degree of public involvement is sufficiently high to be able to coun-

teract the consequences of market-failure, including ensuring a guaranteed minimum income. Greve (2002)

WELFARE STATE TRIANGLE. This term refers to the relationship among the **state**, **market**, and **civil society**, and how they interact with each other.

WORKFARE. This term describes welfare systems with a high emphasis on people receiving welfare benefits, for example, **social assistance** and **unemployment benefits**, fulfilling certain work requirements. It can be debated how much this differs from the early **poor laws**, and it can also be debated whether this is therefore actually new. For some, workfare has a negative connotation of putting pressure on individuals to work even if they are not able to; for others, the positive connotation lies in the attempt to integrate or reintegrate persons into the labor market.

How to Find Additional Information

This appendix provides more ideas about where to look for further information about the welfare state and its development in different countries. It includes references to some recent articles in the field.

One of the best places to search for information is in a particular country's national statistics and legislation, as the collectors of these data will have the best access to information. Often this is not possible because of language barriers or because one is mainly interested in a specific subject that is related to the situation and development in a particular country. Depending on the country, several organizations collect and publish data of a comparative nature.

The U.S. Department of Health and Human Services produces, in addition to specific information on the welfare system in the United States, a publication containing an overview of social security programs throughout the world. This is a very comprehensive book that deals with the institutional structure of programs and systems in different countries. It is created in collaboration with the International Social Security Association (ISSA), which consists of administrative representatives from most of the countries in the world.

The ISSA and many other international organizations regularly publish information and research papers dealing with social security and its development. One of the most important of these is the Organization for Economic Cooperation and Development (OECD). In 1996, for example, the OECD published the report *Ageing in OECD Countries: A Critical Policy Challenge*, in Social Policy Studies series. The OECD studies focus mainly on economic impacts and consequences. They analyze OECD member states, which include European countries plus the United States, Canada, Japan, Australia, New Zealand, and Mexico. Furthermore, the OECD publishes regular studies on national development in individual countries. It issues an annual report, *Employment*

Outlook, which provides information about developments in the labor markets such as social systems, including unemployment, benefits, and leave schemes.

Other important international bodies that concentrate on more specific issues are the World Health Organization (WHO) and the International Labour Organization (ILO). Both focus on health care and the labor market. The ILO, for example, publishes a yearbook of labor statistics.

The World Bank and the International Monetary Fund (IMF) also analyze social problems, but their main interests are economic. Nevertheless, the World Bank has been interested in problems connected with changes in demography and the impact on macroeconomic development. The IMF publishes information on public sector expenditure, including expenditures on social security and welfare state programs.

Regional bodies such as the Organization of American States (OAS) and the European Union (EU) also generate reports covering the welfare state. The EU regularly publishes information on social security systems, such as its overview of community provisions on social security. Within the EU, the Mutual Information System on Social Security (MISSOC) regularly provides information in a comparable manner on the core elements in the social protection systems within the 15 European member states. These reports, like those of the U.S. Department of Health and Human Services, are mainly institutional descriptions. However, this information can be supplemented with data from Eurostat, which is concerned with, among other topics, social security, migration, and the labor market, and can also provide statistics on development in European countries. Most data are based on macrolevel statistics, but sometimes more micro-based data can be found.

The EU has several observatories as well. Their subjects and focus vary. In recent years, there have been observatories on social exclusion, family, children, equal treatment, and employment. Reports from these observatories often provide good background because they are based on information from national rapporteurs.

Finally, the Luxembourg Income Study (LIS) consists of microdata collected from household surveys in several countries. Data may be requested directly from the LIS.

Most of these institutions have a presence on the World Wide Web, and many of their Web sites are listed at the end of this appendix. The listings are useful for getting an idea about whom to contact and where an organization is located. The Web sites can be accessed directly.

In order to stay current with publications in the field, a database search is highly recommended. The Social Science Citation index is one of the best resources, but many other databases exist, and some also have direct access to the articles and books, in some cases, especially journals, full text. For some of the databases access is free of charge, but for others there is a fee.

Following are overviews of important journals and of useful websites that contain information on welfare state issues.

IMPORTANT JOURNALS IN THE FIELD OF THE WELFARE STATE AND WELFARE STATE ANALYSIS

Some of the main journals in the field are listed below. These journals provide regular and updated information on welfare state developme t many from a comparative perspective, enabling the reader to get so e of the most recent information for as many countries as possible.

Administration & Society
Administration in Social Work
Adult Education Research in the Nordic Countries
Ageing and Society
American Historical Review
American Journal of Sociology
American Political Science Review
American Sociological Review
Analysis of Social Issues and Public Policy
Annual Review of Sociology
Asian Journal of Economics and Social Studies
Australian Journal of Social Issues
Benefits
Brookings Review
Comparative Journal of Social Issues
Comparative Political Studies
Contemporary Crises: Crime, Law, Social Policy
Critical Review
Critical Social Policy
Current Sociology
East-West Journal of Social Policy

Economic History Review
European History Quarterly
European Journal of Industrial Relations
European Journal of Political Economy
European Journal of Political Research
European Journal of Public Health
European Journal of Social Security
European Journal of Women's Studies
European Review of Economic History
History of European Ideas
International Journal of Health Services
International Journal of Sociology and Social Policy
International Labour Review
International Social Science Journal
Journal of Ageing and Health
Journal of Common Market Studies
Journal of Economic History
Journal of Economic Literature
Journal of Economic Theory
Journal of European Social Policy
Journal of Family History
Journal of Income Distribution
Journal of Law and Social Policy
Journal of Medicine and Philosophy
Journal of Policy Modeling
Journal of Political Economy
Journal of Politics
Journal of Social Policy
Journal of Social Work Education
Journal of Sociology and Social Welfare
Labor History
Labour Market and Social Policy (Occasional Papers from the OECD)
Philosophy of the Social Sciences
Policy and Politics
Policy Review
Politics & Society
Public Administration
Public Finance Quarterly

Quarterly Journal of Economics
Review of Economics and Statistics
Review of Income and Wealth
Scandinavian Journal of Economics
Scandinavian Journal of Social Welfare
Scandinavian Political Studies
Social Epistemology
Social Indicator Research
Social Philosophy and Policy
Social Policy
Social Policy & Administration
Social Policy Review
Social Policy Studies (OECD)
Social Problems
Social Science Information
Social Work
Sociological Inquiry
Sociology
Work, Employment and Society
World Politics

USEFUL WEB SITE ADDRESSES

The following important and useful Web sites are sources of updated and new information on welfare state policies. They are for the most part sites that have international information.

In addition to these Web sites, many countries have sites in English, making it possible for people not familiar with the national language to get information from the government's perspective. These national Web sites often spread the information on welfare state issues over a variety of ministries, such as the Ministry for Social Security, Ministry for Labor, and the Ministry of Health Care (and they will often be on different Web sites). They have normaly a lot of relevant information on national welfar systems, but as the administrative structure varies from country to country so will the information available. The variations in institutional structures of these agencies indicate that no uniform structure or system can be expected.

Some information must be sought at the websites of the social insurance companies. Many international organizations also provide important information on welfare state issues. Several nongovernmental orgainzations (NGOs) have information on welfare state policies on their Web sites.

Web sites frequently change URLs or even disappear; therefore some of the addresses listed below may not be current.

The List

British Academy Portal, http://www.britac.ac.uk/portal/. This is the British Academy's directory of online resources, which include several in the social sciences.

Centre for the Analysis of Social Policy, www.bath.ac.uk/casp. This center is a part of the University of Bath; it aims to draw together and develop the considerable range of research work underway in this field.

Centre for European Policy Studies, www.ceps.be. This is an independent policy research institute in Belgium covering research on European policy, including aspects of welfare state analysis.

Council of Europe, www.coe.int. This body consists of representatives from all European countries. Useful information and commentary on social cohesion and social policy can be found on the website.

EDIRC, www.edirc.repec.org. EDIRC provides information on more than 8,000 institutions in more than 200 countries that are doing economic research, on subjects of interest for welfare state analysis such as financing and social and labor market policy.

European Centre for Social Welfare Policy and Research, www.euro.centre.org. This is an international center for social research, policy, information, and training. It is an intergovernmental organization focused on social welfare and is affiliated with the United Nations.

European Foundation for the Improvement of Living and Working Conditions, www.eurofound.ie. This is a European agency established in Ireland by the European Council to work in specialized areas of EU policy. Its main area of research and analysis is living and working conditions in Europe.

European Institute of Social Security, www.eiss.be. This is an international organization with researchers and administrators from most European countries interested in the field of **social security**. The Web site contains information on publications and conferences as well as valuable links to social security institutions in many European countries.

European Social Welfare Information Network, www.eswin.net. This Web site provides information on social policy and other related welfare state issues, primarily in Central European countries. It has many links to international research in these areas.

European Union (EU), Europa.eu.int. The EU has formulated several policies that have an impact on welfare state development in its member states. Information on these policies can be found on the Web site, as well as data on and analysis of developments in, for example, labor market policy and social inclusion.

EUROSTAT, www.europa.eu.int/comm/eurostat. Eurostat's home page provides up-to-date statistical information on social and labor market issues in the EU- member states.

International Council on Social Welfare (ICSW), www.icsw.org. This agency consists of a range of national and international member organizations that are interested in social welfare, social justice, and social development. The development aspects are central for the oranizations work.

International and Comparative Social Policy Group (ICSP), www.sheffield.ac.uk/socst/ICSP. This Web site contains information primarily on comparative social policy issues but also has links to international organizations—both governmental and nongovernmental—and activist groups in the field.

International Labour Organization (ILO), www.ilo.org. This Web site focuses primarily on labor market issues, including safety at work, but also has information on social protection and human rights.

Mannheim Centre for European Social Research, www.mzes.uni-mannheim.de. This Web site covers comparative tendencies and developments in social policy, mainly in European states, from the perspective of the increase in European integration.

Max Planck Institute for the Study of Societies, www.mpi-fg-koeln.mpg.de. This institutes in Germany is concerned with basic research in the social sciences related to welfare state development. The Web site has links to other German institutions in the field.

MOST Clearing House, www.unesco.org/most. MOST (Management of Social Transformations Program) is a research program designed by UNESCO to promote international comparative social science research, with particular emphasis on migration and international developments.

Observatorium für die Entwicklung der Sozialen Dienste in Europa, www.soziale-dienste-in-europa.de. This German-based observatory follows the development of social services in Europe. It shows trends and perspectives in development processes in the area of social services in Europe.

Organisation for Economic Co-operation and Development (OECD), www.oecd.org. The OECD consists mainly of the more affluent countries of the world. There is a great deal of detailed information on social and labor market policy on the website. The site is especially useful not only because many detailed analyses in a comparative perspective are presented, but also because it provides access to data on core issues of social and labor market expenditures, changes in demography, and other aspects of life.

The OECD also publishes numerous reports, some of which can be ordered online and or downloaded. Among these publications the most important provide information annually on labor market and educational issues.

Social Science Research Council, www.ssrc.org. This international association is devoted to the advancement of interdisciplinary research in the social sciences, especially in the following areas: HIV/AIDS as a global challenge, children and armed conflict, economic growth, development and inequality, global security and cooperation, international migration, and democracy and the public sphere.

Social Work Access Network, cosw.sc.edu. This Web site from the University of South Carolina includes research prmarily related to social work but also covers children and families, as well as research on access to social work.

United Nations Institute for Research into Social Development (UNRISD), www.unrisd.org. This is an autonomous institution mainly focusing on social aspects of development, but the Web site also includes a variety of information and analysis on social policy, migration, and other aspects of societal development.

World Health Organisation (WHO), www.who.org. This is a specialized **organizationwithin the United Nations.** As its name indicates, this special organization of the UN focuses mainly on health and health care around the world.

Bibliography

The following lists of books and articles on the welfare state do not tend to be exhaustive, although they encompass as many different thors and viewpoints as possible. More specific and detailed des tions of the subjects referred to in this dictionary can be found in works cited in the 28 topic sections. More can also be found on the bate about the welfare state, welfare state models, and their histo developments. The literature supplements the dictionary for those no want more detailed descriptions and more discussion of and elaboration on theoretical elements of the welfare state debate.

In the appendix are references to other sources of information, covering data on individual countries or groups of countries about such topics as spending in various areas, institutional structures, and persons unemployed.

It is difficult to point to just a few central books analyzing the welfare state and related concepts. Analysis and research on the welfare state have been and will presumably always be interdisciplinary and therefore will appear not only in books or articles dealing with welfare state issues in disciplines such as economics, sociology, political science, law, and history, but also in works that combine approaches. Nevertheless, several important topics can be highlighted, and the topics covered here integrate the various core areas so that the debates and knowledge on concepts, theories, and individual countries will supplement the entries in the dictionary.

Central to a description of the historical development of many welfare states are the works of Peter Flora, including Peter Flora, ed., *Growth to Limits: The Western European Welfare States Since World War II,* . volumes 1–4 (Berlin: De Gruyter, 1986); Peter Flora and A. Heidenheimer, eds., *The Developments of Welfare States in Europe and America* (London: Transaction Books, 1981); and G. Rimlinger, *Welfare*

Policy and Industrialization in Europe, America and Russia (New York: Wiley, 1971). A good overview of important historical contributions to welfare state analysis is in Christopher Pierson and Francis Castles, eds., *The Welfare State Reader* (Oxford: Polity Press, 2000). These works can be used to compare the various welfare states and the way they have developed.

Books of central importance for a historical understanding of the origins of and changes in the welfare state are *Social Insurance and Allied Services,* by Sir William Beveridge ("The Beveridge Report") (London: HMSO, 1942); John Maynard Keynes, *The General Theory of Employment, Interest and Money* (London: Macmillan, 1933); and Richard Titmuss, *Essays on the Welfare State* (London: Allen & Unwin, 1958).

Understanding and presentation of the classical elements of welfare economics, including theoretical aspects, can be found in J. R. Hicks, "The Foundation of Welfare Economics," *Economic Journal* 49 (1939): 696–712; Kenneth J. Arrow, *Social Choice and Individual Values* (New York: Wiley, 1951); Amartya K. Sen, *Collective Choice and Social Welfare* (San Francisco: Holden-Day, 1970); Amartya Sen, *Choice, Welfare and Measurement* (Cambridge, Mass.: MIT Press, 1982).

The debate about and analysis of different types of welfare state models are covered in Gøsta Esping-Andersen, *The Three Worlds of Welfare Capitalism* (Oxford: Polity Press, 1990). For an overview, see Peter Abrahamson, "The Welfare Modelling Business," Social Policy & Administration 33, no. 4, 1999: 394–415.

The standard works about financing of the welfare state and public sector economics are by Richard A. Musgrave, *The Theory of Public Finance* (New York, McGraw-Hill, 1959) and Paul A. Samuelson, "Pure Theory of Public Expenditure," *Review of Economics and Statistics* 36 (1954): 387–89.

Central works on poverty are Seebohm Rowntree, *Poverty: A Study of Town Life* (London: Macmillan, 1901); Seebohm Rowntree, *Poverty and Progress* (London: Longmans, 1941); and Seebohm Rowntree and G. R. Lavers, *Poverty and the Welfare State* (London: Longmans, 1951).

Discussion of the crisis of the welfare state can be found in James O'Connor, *The Fiscal Crisis of the State* (New York: St. Martin's Press, 1973) and Ramesh Mishra, *The Welfare State in Crisis: Social Thought and Social Change* (Brighton: Wheatsheaf Books, 1984). Several older books that have been central to historical understanding and research in the area are also included in the bibliography.

The bibliography covers the central areas of the analysis of the welfare state and its historical development. Developing this organizational structure has not been an easy task, as many books could be placed under more than one category. Each work has been included only once, so difficult decisions had to be made about where to put those works that could fall under more than one topic. Each subject area in the bibliography may provide a starting point for further reading, and by using the books presented here—and also the literature listed in these books—a full picture of the welfare state can be obtained. Furthermore, using databases for searches has become easier, so it should be possible for a reader to find more information about any particular topic.

The literature on the welfare state is expanding rapidly, including many new journals. The central journals in the area have been listed in the appendix to help the reader carry out a more focused search for new and updated information. The journals will often cover many of the areas for which literature has been listed in this bibliography.

The organization of the bibliography is as follows:

I. GENERAL HISTORY OF THE
WELFARE STATE'S DEVELOPMENT

Baldwin, Peter. *The Politics of Social Solidarity*. Cambridge: Cambridge University Press, 1990.

Beveridge, William. *Full Employment in a Free Society*. London: Allen & Unwin, 1944.

———. *The Pillars of Security*. London: Allen & Unwin, 1943.

———. *Social Insurance and Allied Services*. Report by Lord William Beveridge. London: His Majesty's Stationery Office, 1942.

Birch, R. C. *The Shaping of the Welfare State*. London: Longman, 1974.

Briggs, Asa. "The Welfare State in Historical Perspective." In *The Welfare State*, edited by C. Schottland. New York, Harper and Row, 1969, pp. 29-45.

Bruce, M. *The Coming of the Welfare State*. London: Batsford, 1961.

Clarke, J. "The Problem of the State after the Welfare State." *Social Policy Review* 8 (1996): 13–39.

Dostaler, G., D. Ethier, and L. Lepage, eds. *Gunnar Myrdal and His Works*. Montreal: Harvest House, 1992.

Durkheim, E. *De la division du travail social*. Paris: Felix Alcan, 1893.

Evans, Eric J. *Social Policy 1830–1914: Individualism, Collectivism and the Origins of the Welfare State*. London: Routledge & Kegan Paul, 1978.

Flora, Peter, ed. *Growth to Limits: The Western European Welfare States Since World War II*. Vols. 1–4. Berlin: De Gruyter, 1986.

Flora, Peter, and A. Heidenheimer, eds. *The Developments of Welfare States in Europe and America*. London: Transaction Books, 1981.

Henriques, Ursula. *Before the Welfare State*. London: Longman, 1979.

McEvedy, C., and R. Jones. *Atlas of World Population History*. Harmondsworth, England: Penguin, 1978.

Roberts, D. *Victorian Origins of the Welfare State*. New York: Yale University Press, 1960.

Roof, M. *A Hundred Years of Family Welfare*. London: Michael Joseph, 1972.

Saville, J. "The Welfare State: An Historical Approach." *New Reasoner* 3 (1957).

Schottland, Charles I., ed. *The Welfare State: Selected Essays*. New York: Harper Torchbooks, 1967.

Thane, Pat. *The Foundations of the Welfare State*. London: Longman, 1982.

Titmuss, Richard. *The Irresponsible Society*. London: Allen & Unwin, 1960.

Williams, G. *The Coming of the Welfare State*. London: Allen & Unwin, 1967.

II. HISTORY OF THE WELFARE STATE AFTER WORLD WAR II

Ashford, Douglas *The Emergence of the Welfare State*. Oxford: Basil Blackwell, 1986.

Berkowitz, E., and K. McQuaid. *Creating the Welfare State: The Political Economy of Twentieth-Century Reform*. New York: Praeger, 1980.

Marshall, Thomas H. *Social Policy in the Twentieth Century*. London: Hutchinson Educational, 1975.

Myrdal, Gunnar. *Beyond the Welfare State*. London: Duckworth, 1958.

Palmer, Geoffrey, ed. *The Welfare State Today*. Wellington, New Zealand: Fourth Estate Books, 1977.

III. ECONOMICS AND THE WELFARE STATE

Arrow, Kenneth J. *Social Choice and Individual Values*. New York: Wiley, 1951.

Asimakopulos, A. et al. *Economic Theory, Welfare and the State: Essays in Honour of John C. Weldon*. Basingstoke, England: Macmillan, 1990.

Bardhan, Pranab, and John E. Roemer, eds. *Market Socialism: Current Debate*. New York: Oxford University Press, 1993.

Barr, Nicholas A. *The Economics of the Welfare State*. Oxford: Oxford University Press, 1998.

Baumol, William, and Charles Wilson. *Welfare Economics*. Cheltenham, England: Edward Elgar, 2001.

Boadway, Robin W., and Neil Bruce. *Welfare Economics*. London: Basil Blackwell, 1984.

Cairns, R. D., and C. Green, eds. *Economic Theory, Welfare and the State*. Basingstoke: Macmillan, 1990.

Gelauff, G. M. M. *Modelling Welfare State Reform*. Amsterdam: North-Holland, 1994.

Gough, Ian. *The Political Economy of the Welfare State*. London: Macmillan, 1979.

Harris, R. *Choice in Welfare*. London: Institute of Economic Affairs, 1971.

Harris, R., and A. Seldon. *Overruled on Welfare*. London: Institute of Economic Affairs, 1979.

Harsanyi, John. "Cardinal Individualist Ethics, and International Comparisons of Utility Economics and in the Theory of Risktaking." *Journal of Political Economy* 3 (1955): 309–21.

Hicks, Alexander M., and Thomas Janoski. *The Comparative Political Economy of the Welfare State*. Cambridge: Cambridge University Press, 1994.

Hicks, John R. "The Foundation of Welfare Economics." *Economic Journal* 49 (1939): 696–712.

Hills, J. *Changing Tax: How the Tax System Works and How to Change It*. London: Child Poverty Action Group, 1988.

Janoski, Thomas. *The Comparative Political Economy of the Welfare State*. Cambridge: Cambridge University Press, 1994.

Johansson, P. O. *An Introduction to Modern Welfare Economics*. Cambridge: Cambridge University Press, 1991.

Judge, K. *Rationing Social Services*. London: Heinemann, 1987.

Keynes, John Maynard. *Essays in Persuasion*. London: Macmillan, 1931.

———. *The General Theory of Employment, Interest and Money*. London: Macmillan, 1933.

———. "How to Pay for the War." A Radical Plan for the Chancellor of the Exchequer. London: Macmillan, 1940.

Le Grand, Julian, and Saul Estrin, eds, *Market Socialism*. Oxford: Clarendon, 1989.

Le Grand, Julian, and R. Robinson. *The Economics of Social Problems*. London: Macmillan, 1984.

———, eds. *Privatisation and the Welfare State*. London: Allen & Unwin, 1984.

Lindbeck, Assar. *The Selected Essays of Assar Lindbeck*. Vol. 1, *Macroeconomics and Economic Policy;* Vol. 2, *The Welfare State*. Aldershot, England: Edward Elgar, 1993.

Little, I. M. D. *A Critique of Welfare Economics*. 2d ed. Oxford: Clarendon Press, 1957.

McKenzie, G. W. *Measuring Economic Welfare: New Methods*. Cambridge: Cambridge University Press, 1983.

Ng, Y.-K. *Welfare Economics*. London: Macmillan, 1979.

Pierson, Christoffer. *Beyond the Welfare State? The New Political Economy of the Welfare State*. Cambridge: Polity Press, 1991.

Pigou, A. C. *The Economics of Welfare*. London: Macmillan, 1920.

———. *Wealth and Welfare*. London: Macmillan, 1912.

Rowley, C. K., and A. T. Peacock. *Welfare Economics: A Liberal Restatement.* Oxford: Martin Robertson, 1975.

Salannié, Bernard. *The Economics of Taxation.* Cambridge, Mass.: MIT Press. 2003.

Samuelson, Paul A. *Foundations of Economic Analysis.* Cambridge, Mass.: Harvard University Press, 1947.

Sen, Amartya K. *Collective Choice and Social Welfare.* San Francisco: Holden Day, 1970.

Sen, Amartya K., and B. Williams, eds. *Utilitarianism and Beyond.* Cambridge: Cambridge University Press, 1982.

Sinn, H. W. "A Theory of the Welfare State." *Scandinavian Journal of Economics* 97, no. 4 (1995): 495–526.

Smith, Adam. *The Wealth of Nations.* London: J.M. Den & Sons, Everymans Library, 1970.

Sugden, Robert. *The Economics of Rights, Welfare and Co-operation.* Oxford: Blackwell, 1986.

IV. IDEOLOGY AND THE WELFARE STATE

Abel-Smith, Brian. *"Whose Welfare State?"* In *Conviction*, edited by Norma Mackenzie. London: MacGibbon Kee, 1959.

Alber, J. "Continuities and Changes in the Idea of the Welfare State." *Politics and Society* 16, no. 4 (1988): 451–457.

Bean, P., J. Ferris, and D. Whynes, eds. *In Defence of Welfare.* London: Tavistock, 1985.

Borchert, J. "Welfare-State Retrenchment—Playing the National Card." *Critical Review* 10, no. 1 (1996): 63–94.

Bradshaw, Jonathan. "A Taxonomy of Social Need." *New Society* 496 (March 30): 640–43.

Brown, Martin K. *Remaking the Welfare State.* Philadelphia: Temple University Press, 1988.

Bulmer, Martin, Jane Lewis, and David Piachaud, eds. *The Goals of Social Policy.* London: Unwin Hyman, 1989.

Castles, Francis G. *The Working Class and Welfare.* Wellington, New Zealand: Allen & Unwin, 1985.

Cutler, Antony, et al. *Keynes, Beveridge and Beyond.* London: Routledge & Kegan Paul, 1986.

Deacon, Alan. *Perspectives on Welfare. Ideas, Ideologies and Policy Debates.* Buckingham, England: Open University Press, 2002.

Douglas, J. D. *The Myth of the Welfare State.* Brunswick, N.J.: Transaction Books, 1989.

Doyal, L., and Ian Gough. "A Theory of Human Needs." *Critical Social Policy* 10 (Summer, 1990): 6–33.

Esping-Andersen, Gøsta, and R. Friedland. "Class Coalitions in the Making of West European Economics." *Political Power and Social Theory* 3 (1982): 1-52.

Evers, Adablert, et al. *The Changing Face of Welfare*. Aldershot, England: Gower, 1987.

Freeman, Roger A. *The Wayward Welfare State*. Stanford, Calif.: Hoover Institution Press, 1981.

Friedman, Milton. *Capitalism and Freedom*. Chicago: University of Chicago Press, 1962.

Furniss, Norman, ed. *Futures for the Welfare State*. Bloomington: Indiana University Press, 1986.

Furniss, Norman, and T. Tilton. *The Case for the Welfare State*. Bloomington: Indiana University Press, 1979.

Giddens, Anthony. *The Third Way. The Renewal of Social Democracy*. Oxford: Polity Press, 1998.

George, V., and P. Wilding. *Welfare and Ideology*. Hemel Hempstead, England: Harvester Wheatsheaf, 1994).

Gilbert, N. *Capitalism and the Welfare State*. New Haven, Conn.: Yale University Press, 1983.

Ginsburg, N. *Class, Capital and Social Policy*. London: Macmillan, 1979.

Glennerster, Howard. *The Future of the Welfare State*. London: Heinemann, 1983.

Glennerster, Howard, and James Midgley, eds. *The Radical Right and the Welfare State. An International Assessment*. Hemel Hempstead, UK: Harvester Wheatsheaf, 1991.

Golding, P., and S. Middleton. *Images of Welfare*. Oxford: Martin Robertson, 1982.

Goodin, Robert. *Reasons for Welfare*. Princeton, N.J.: University of Princeton Press, 1988.

Hall, P., H. Land, R. Parker, and A. Webb. *Change, Choice and Conflict in Social Policy*. London: Heinemann, 1975.

Hills, John. *The Future of Welfare: A Guide to the Debate*. York, England: Joseph Rowntree Foundation, 1993.

Johnson, Norman. *Reconstructing the Welfare State*. Hemel Hempstead, UK: Harvester Wheatsheaf, 1990.

———. *The Welfare State in Transition: The Theory and Practice of Welfare Pluralism*. Hemel Hempstead, UK: Harvester Wheatsheaf, 1987.

Jordan, B. *Rethinking the Welfare State*. Oxford: Blackwell, 1987.

Kim, Sung Ho. *Max Weber's Politics of Civil Society*. Cambridge: Cambridge University Press, 2004.

Klein, R., and M. O'Higgins, eds. *The Future of the Welfare State*. Oxford: Basil Blackwell, 1985.

Marshall, Thomas H. *The Right to Welfare and Other Essays*. London: Heinemann, 1981.

Murray, Charles. *Losing Ground*. New York: Basic Books, 1984.

Nozick, Robert. *Anarchy, State and Utopia*. Oxford: Basil Blackwell, 1974.

Offe, Claus. "Advanced Capitalism and the Welfare State." *Politics and Society* 4 (1972).

———. *Disorganized Capitalism*. Cambridge, Mass.: MIT Press, 1985.

Pinker, R. *The Idea of Welfare*. London: Heinemann, 1979.

Pierson, Paul. *The New Politics of the Welfare State*. Oxford: Oxford University Press, 2001.

Pius XI Quadragesimo Anno. *Papal Encyclical*. Vatican City, 1931.

Robson, W. *Welfare State and Welfare Society*. London: Allen & Unwin, 1976.

Room, Graham. *The Sociology of Welfare*. Oxford: Blackwell, 1979.

Sen, Amartya K. "Rational Fools." *Philosophy and Public Affairs* 6 (1977): 317–44.

Sleeman, J. F. *The Welfare State: Its Aims, Benefits and Costs*. London: Allen & Unwin, 1973.

Spicker, Paul. *Principles of Social Welfare: An Introduction to Thinking about the Welfare State*. London: Routledge, 1988.

———. "The Principle of Subsidiarity and the Social Policy of the European Community." *Journal of European Social Policy* 1 (1991): 3–14.

———. *Social Policy. Themes and Approaches*. Hemel Hempstead, UK: Harvester Wheatsheaf, 1995.

Taylor-Gooby, Peter. *Social Change, Social Welfare and Social Science*. New York: Harvester Wheatsheaf, 1991.

Taylor-Gooby, Peter, and J. Dale. *Social Theory and Social Change*. London: Longman, 1981.

Taylor-Gooby, Peter, and Stafan Svallfors. *The End of the Welfare State? Responses to state Retrenchment*. London: Routledge, 1999.

Therborn, Gøran. "Karl Marx Returning: The Welfare State and Neo-Marxist, Corporatist and Statist Theories." *International Political Science Review* 7, no. 2 (1986): 131–164.

Titmuss, Richard M. *The Gift Relationship*. London: Allen & Unwin, 1971.

———. *The Philosophy of Welfare*. London: Allen & Unwin, 1987.

Urry, John. *The Anatomy of Capitalist Societies, the Economy, Civil Society and the State*. London: Macmillan, 1981.

Walker, Alan. *Social Planning*. Oxford: Blackwell, 1984.

Webb, A., and G. Wistow. *Planning, Need and Scarcity*. London: Allen & Unwin, 1986.

Wilensky, Harold, and C. Lebeaux. *Industrial Society and Social Welfare*. New York: Russell Sage, 1958.

V. TYPOLOGIES OF THE WELFARE STATE

Arts, Will, and John Gelissen. "Three Worlds of Welfare Capitalism or More?" *Journal of European Social Policy* 12, no. 2 (2002): 137–58.

Castles, Francis. *The Future of the Welfare State*. Oxford: Oxford University Press, 2004.

Castles, Francis, and Deborah Mitchell. *Three Worlds of Welfare Capitalism or Four? Public Policy Programme*. Canberra: The Australian National University, 1990.

Esping-Andersen, Gøsta. *The Three Worlds of Welfare Capitalism*. Oxford: Polity Press, 1990.

——, ed. *Welfare States in Transition: National Adaptions in Global Economies*, London, Sage, 1996.

Greve, Bent. *Vouchers—nye styrings—og leveringsmåder i velfærdsstaten. (New ways of steering and managing in the welfare state)*. København, DJØF's forlag, 2002.

Kolberg, J. E. *The Study of Welfare-State Regimes*. Armonk, N.Y.: M. E. Sharpe, 1990.

Leibfried, Stephan. *Towards a European Welfare State? On Integrating Poverty Regimes in the European Community*. Bremen, Germany: University Bremen, ZeS—Arbeitspapier Nr. 2/91.

Room, Graham, ed. *Towards a European Welfare State?* Bristol, England: School for Advanced Urban Studies, 1991.

Sainsbury, Diana. "Analysing Welfare State Variations: The Merits and Limitations of Models Based on the Residual-Institutional Distinction." *Scandinavian Political Studies* 14 (1991): 1.

VI. POVERTY AND INEQUALITY

Abel-Smith, Brian, and Peter Townsend. *The Poor and the Poorest*. London: Bell, 1965.

Abrahamson, Peter. "Poverty and Welfare in Denmark." *Scandinavian Journal of Social Welfare* 1 (1992): 1.

——. "Welfare and Poverty in Europe of the 1990s: Social Progress or Social Dumping?" *International Journal of Health Services* 21 (1991): 2.

Alcock, Pete, et al. *Welfare and Wellbeing. Richard Titmuss's Contribution to Social Policy*. Bristol, England: Policy Press, 2001.

Atkinson, A. B. "Horizontal Equity and the Distribution of the Tax Burden." In *The Economics of Taxation,* edited by H. J. Aaron and M. J. Boskin. Washington, D.C.: Brookings Institution, 1980.

———. "Income Distribution and Social Change Revisited." *Journal of Social Policy* 4, pt. 1 (1975): 57–68.

———. "On the Measurement of Inequality." *Journal of Economic Theory* 2 (1970): 244–63.

———. *Poverty and Social Security.* London: Harvester Wheatsheaf, 1989.

Atkinson, A. B., B. Cantillon, E. Marlier, and B. Nolan, *Social Indicators: The EU and Social Inclusion.* Oxford: Oxford University Press, 2002.

Blackorby, C., and D. Donaldson. "Measures of Inequality and Their Meaning in Terms of Social Welfare." *Journal of Economic Theory* 18 (1978): 59–80.

Bradshaw, Jonathan, and Alan Deacon. *Reserved for the Poor.* Oxford: Martin Robertson, 1984.

Bryson, Luis. *Welfare and the State: Who Benefits?* London: Macmillan, 1992.

Deacon, Alan. *In Search of Scrounger.* London: Bell, 1976.

———. "The Scrounging Controversy." *Social and Economic Administration* 12, no. 2 (1978): 120–132.

Friedmann, J. "Rethinking Poverty—Empowerment and Citizen Rights." *International Social Science Review* 48, no. 2. (1996): 161+.

Joseph, Sir K., and J. Sumption. *Equality.* London: John Murray, 1979.

Kangas, Olli, and Joakin Palme. "Does Social Policy Matter? Poverty Cycles in OECD Countries." *International Journal of Health Services* 30, no. 2 (2000): 335–52.

Korpi, Walther. "Social Policy and Distributional Conflict in the Capitalist Democracies." *West European Politics* 3 (1980): 296–316.

Le Grand, J. *The Strategy of Equality.* London: Allen & Unwin, 1982.

Millar, Jane. *Poverty and the Lone-Parent: The Challenge to Social Policy.* Aldershot, England: Avebury, 1989.

Novak, T. *Poverty and Social Security.* London: Pluto, 1984.

———. *Poverty and the State.* Milton Keynes, England: Open University Press, 1988.

Rodgers, B. *The Battle Against Poverty.* Vol. 1, *From Pauperism to Human Rights;* Vol. 2, *Toward a Welfare State.* London, Routledge, 1969.

Rowntree, B. S. *Poverty: A Study of Town Life.* London: Macmillan, 1901.

———. *Poverty and Progress.* London: Longman, 1941.

Rowntree, B. S., and G. R. Lavers. *Poverty and the Welfare State.* London: Longman, 1951.

Saunders, Peter. *Welfare and Inequality.* Cambridge: Cambridge University Press, 1994.

Sen, Amartya. *Choice, Welfare and Measurement.* Cambridge, Mass.: MIT Press, 1982.

——. *Commodities and Capabilities*, Amsterdam: North-Holland, 1985.

——. *Inequality Reexamined*. Oxford: Clarendon Press, 1992.

——. *On Economic Inequality*. Oxford: Clarendon Press, 1973.

——. *Poverty and Famines*, Oxford: Clarendon Press, 1981.

Sinfield, Adrian, ed. *Poverty, Inequality and Justice*. Edinburgh: New Waverly Papers, 1993.

Smeeding, Tim, M. O'Higgins, and Lee Rainwater, eds. *Poverty, Inequality and Income Distribution in Comparative Perspective*. Hemel Hempstead, UK: Harvester Wheatsheaf, 1990.

Tawney, R. M. *Equality*. London: Allen & Unwin, 1931.

Titmuss, Richard. *Income Distribution and Social Change*. London: Allen & Unwin, 1962.

Townsend, Peter. *The International Analysis of Poverty*. London: Harvester Wheatsheaf, 1993.

——, ed. *The Concept of Poverty*, London: Heinemann, 1970.

Towsend, Peter, and David Gordon. *Breadline Europe: The Measurement of Poverty*. Bristol: Policy Press, 2000.

Walker, R., R. Lawson, and P. Townsend. *Responses to Poverty: Lessons from Europe*. London: Heinemann, 1984.

Weale, A. *Equality and Social Policy*. London: Routledge & Kegan Paul, 1978.

Webb, A. L. *Income Redistribution and the Welfare State*. London: Allen & Unwin, 1971.

VII. LIBERTY AND JUSTICE

Berlin, Sir I. *Four Essays on Liberty*. London: Oxford University Press, 1969.

Brian, B. A. *Treatise on Social Justice*. London: Harvester Wheatsheaf, 1989.

Campbell, T. *Justice*. London: Macmillan, 1988.

Glyn, A., and D. Miliband, eds. *Paying for Equality—The Economic Cost of Social Injustice*. London: IPPR/Rivers Oram Press, 1994.

Hamlin, A. *Ethics, Economics and the State*. Brighton, England: Harvester Wheatsheaf, 1986.

Hayek, Friedrik. *The Constitution of Liberty*. London: Routledge & Kegan Paul, 1960.

——. *The Mirage of Social Justice*. London: Routledge & Kegan Paul, 1976.

Hindess, Barry. *Freedom, Equality and the Market: Arguments on Social Policy*. London: Tavistock, 1987.

Le Grand, Julian. *Equity and Choice*. Bristol: University of Bristol/Harper-Collins Academic, 1990.

Le Grand, Julian, and Robert Goodin. *Not Only the Poor: The Middle Class and the Welfare State*. London: Allen & Unwin, 1987.

Millar, D. *Social Justice*. Oxford: Clarendon Press, 1976.
Rawls, John. *A Theory of Justice*. Oxford: Clarendon Press, 1972.
Walzer, M. *Spheres of Justice*. Oxford: Martin Robertson, 1983.

VIII. UNITED KINGDOM

Atkinson, Anthony B. *Incomes and the Welfare State: Essays on Brita   ι
   Europe*. Cambridge: Cambridge University Press, 1996.
Castles, F., and Pierson, C. "A New Convergence—Recent Policy D el
   ments in the United Kingdom, Australia and New Zealand." *Policy ι l
   itics* 24, no. 3 (1996): 233–45.
Finlayson, Geoffrey. *Citizen, State and Social Welfare in Britain 1830–*
   Oxford: Clarendon Press, 1994.
Gregg, Pauline. *The Welfare State: An Economic and Social History of
   Britain from 1945 to the Present Day*. Amherst, University of Massach
   Press, 1967.
Mommsen, W. J., ed. *The Emergence of the Welfare State in Britain and
   many: 1850–1950*. London: Croom and Helm, 1983.
Peacock, Alan, and Jack Wiseman. *The Growth of Public Expenditure ι he
   UK*. Oxford: Oxford University Press, 1961.
Pedersen, S. *Family, Dependence and the Origins of the Welfare State—
   Britain and France 1914–1945*. Cambridge: Cambridge University Press,
   1993.
Timmins, Nicholas. *The Five Giants: A Biography of the Welfare State*. Lon-
   don: HarperCollins, 1995.
Walker, Robert, and Michael Wiseman. *The Welfare We Want?: The British
   Challenge for American Reform*. Bristol: Policy, 2003.

IX. GERMANY

Mommsen, W. J., ed. *The Emergence of the Welfare State in Britain and Germany: 1850–1950*. London: Croom Helm, 1983.

X. UNITED STATES

Axinn, J., and H. Levin. *Social Welfare: A History of the American Response to
   Need*. New York: Dodd, Mead, 1975.
Blank, R., and R. Haskins *The New World of Welfare,* Washington, D.C.: Brook-
   ings Institution Press, 2001.

Levine, Daniel. *Poverty and Society: The Growth of the American Welfare State in International Comparison.* New Brunswick, N.J.: Rutgers University Press, 1988.

Marmor, T. R., T. L. Mashaw, and P. L. Harvey. *America's Misunderstood Welfare State.* New York: Basic Books, 1990.

Myrdal, Gunnar, et al. *An American Dilemma: The Negro Problem and Modern Democracy.* London: Harper & Row, 1962.

Patterson, J. *The Welfare State in America.* Durham, England: British Association of American Studies, 1981.

Peck, J. *Workfare States.* New York: Guildford Press, 2001.

Quadagno, Jill. *The Transformation of Old Age Security: Class and Politics in the American Welfare State.* Chicago: University of Chicago Press, 1988.

Solow, Robert. *Work and Welfare.* Princeton, N.J.: Princeton University Press, 1998.

Trattner, Walter I. *From Poor Law to Welfare State: A History of Social Welfare in America.* New York: Free Press, 1979.

Weil, Alan, and Kenneth Finegold, eds. *Welfare Reform: The Next Act*, Washington, D.C.: Urban Institute Press, 2002.

Weir, M., A. S. Orloff, and T. Skocpol. *The Politics of Social Policy in the United States.* Princeton, N.J.: Princeton University Press, 1988.

XI. SCANDINAVIAN COUNTRIES

Allardt, Erik. *Having, Loving and Being: Welfare in the Nordic Countries.* Lund: Sweden Lund Universitetsforlag, 1975.

Blomqvist, Paula. "Privatization of Swedish Welfare Services." *Social Policy & Administration* 38, no. 2 (2004): 139–56.

Castles, Francis G. *The Social Democratic Image of Society: A Study in the Achievements and Origins of Scandinavian Social Democracy in Comparative Perspective.* London: Routledge & Kegan Paul, 1978.

Cox, Robert. "Why Scandinavian Welfare States Remain Distinct." *Social Policy & Administration* 38, no. 2 (2004): 204–19.

Eriksen, R., E. J. Hansen, S. Ringen, and H. Usitalo, eds. *The Scandinavian Model: Welfare States and Welfare Research.* Armonk, N.Y.: M. E. Sharpe, 1987.

Greve, Bent. "Denmark: Universal or Not so Universal Welfare State." *Social Policy & Administration* 38, no. 2 (2004): 156–69.

Greve, Bent, ed. *The Scandinavian Model in a Period of Change.* Basingstoke, England: Macmillan, 1996.

Hansen, Erik Jørgen, ed. *Welfare Trends in the Scandinavian Countries.* Armonk, N.Y.: M. E. Sharpe, 1993.

Kautto, Mikko, et al. *Nordic Social Policy: Changing Welfare States.* London: Routledge, 1999.

———. *Nordic Welfare States in the European Context.* London, Routledge, 2001.

Kosonen, Pekko. "Flexibilization and the Alternatives of the Nordic Welfare States." In *The Politics of Flexibility: Restructuring States and Industry in Britain, Germany and Scandinavia,* edited by Bob Jessop et al. Aldershot, England: Edward Elgar, 1991.

Olsson, Sven Erik. *Social-Policy and Welfare-State in Sweden.* Stockholm: Arkiv, 1990.

Olson Hort, Sven Erik. "*Welfare Policy in Sweden.*" In *Scandinavia in a New Europe,* edited by Thomas P. Boje and Sven E. Olsson Hort. Oslo: Scandinavian University Press, 1993.

Palme, Joakim, et al. "Welfare Trends in Sweden: Balancing the Books for the 1990s." *Journal of European Social Policy* 12, no. 4 (2002): 29–46.

Sipilä, Jorma: *Social Care Services: The Key to the Scandinavian Welfare Model.* Alsderhot, England: Avebury, 1997.

Zetterberg, Hans L. *Before and Beyond the Welfare State: Three Lectures.* Stockholm: City University Press, 1995.

XII. OTHER COUNTRIES

Aspalter, C., ed. *Discovering the Welfare State in East Asia.* Westport, Conn.: Praeger, 2002.

———. *Welfare Capitalism around the World.* Times Academic Press. Hong Kong: Casa Verde Publication, 2003.

Deacon, Bob, et al. *The New Eastern Europe: Social Policy, Present and Future.* London: Sage, 1992.

Dimitri, A., Ileana Neamtu Sotiropoulos, and Maya Stoyanova. "The Trajectory of Post-communist Welfare State Development: The Cases of Bulgaria and Romania." *Social Policy & Administration* 37, no. 6 (2003): 656–73.

Dixon, J., and R. P. Scheurell, eds. *Social Welfare in Developed Market Countries.* London: Routledge & Kegan Paul, 1989.

George, V., and N. Manning. *Socialism, Social Welfare and the the Union of Soviet Socialist Republics (USSR).* London: Routledge & Kegan Paul, 1980.

Goodman, R., G. White, and H. J. Kwon, eds. *The East Asian Welfare Model. Welfare Orientatlism and the State.* London, Routledge, 1998.

Gough, Ian, et al. *Insecurity and Welfare Regimes in Asia, Africa and Latin America.* Cambridge: Cambridge University Press, 2004.

Lee Min-kvan. *Chinese Occupational Welfare in Market Transition: Beyond the Iron Rice Bowl.* New York: St. Martins Press, Palgrave Publishers, 2000.

Lee, P., and C. Raban. *Welfare Theory and Social Policy: Reform or Revolution,* London: Sage, 1988.

Madison, B. *Social Welfare and the Union of Soviet Socialist Republics (USSR).* Stanford, Calif.: Stanford University Press, 1968.

Matsaganis, Manos, Maurizio Ferrera, Luis Capucha, and Luis Moreno.: "Mending Nets in South: Anti Poverty Policies in Greece, Italy, Portugal and Spain." *Social Policy & Administration* 37, no. 6 (2003): 639–55.

McAuley, A. *Economic Welfare in the Union of Soviet Socialist Republics (USSR).* London: Allen & Unwin, 1979.

Peterson, W. C. *The Welfare State in France.* Nebraska, University of Nebraska, 1960.

Pfaller, A., I. Gough, and G. Therborn, eds. *Can the Welfare State Compete? A Comparative Study of Five Advanced Capitalist Countries.* Basingstoke, England: Macmillan, 1991.

Rhodes, Martin, ed. *Southern European Welfare States: Identity, problems and prospects for reform.* Southern European Society and Politics, 1, no. 3 (1996): 1–22.

Springer, B. *The Social Dimension of 1992: Europe Faces a New EC.* New York: Praeger, 1992.

Széman, Zsuzsa. "The Welfare Mix in Hungary as a New Phenomenon." *Social Policy & Society* 2 (2003): 101–8.

Tang, K. L., ed. *Social Welfare Development in Asia,* Dordrecht, Netherlands: Kluwer, 2000.

XIII. COMPARATIVE ANALYSIS OF THE WELFARE STATE

Bouget, Denis. "Convergence in Social Welfare Systems in Europe: From Goal to Reality." *Social Policy & Administration* 37, no. 6 (2003): 674–93.

Bradshaw, Jonathan, et al. *The Employment of Lone Parents: A Comparison of Policy in 20 Countries.* London: Family Policy Studies Centre, 1996.

———. *Support for Children: A Comparison of Arrangements in Fifteen Countries.* HMSO Research Report no. 21. London: Department of Social Security, 1993.

Bradshaw, Jonathan, Mary Daly, and Jane Lewis. "The Concept of Social Care and the Analysis of Contemporary Welfare States." *British Journal of Sociology* 51, no. 2 (2001): 281–98.

Faist, Thomas. *Ethnicisation and Racialisation of Welfare State Politics in Germany and the USA.* Bremen, Germany: Zentrum für Sozialpolitik, Universität Bremen, 1994.

Ferge, Zzusa, and Jon Kolberg, eds. *Social Policy in a Changing Europe.* Frankfurt: Campus Verlag, and Boulder, Colo.: Westview Press, 1992.

Friedmann, R., N. Gilbert, and M. Shere, eds. *Modern Welfare States: A Comparative View of Trends and Prospects.* Brighton, England: Harvester Wheatsheaf, 1987.

Gordon, M. *Social Security Policies in Industrial Countries: A Comparative Analysis.* Cambridge: Cambridge University Press, 1988.

Gough, Ian, A. Pfaller, and Gøran Therborn, eds. *Can the Welfare State Compete—A Comparative Study of Five Advanced Capitalist Countries.* London: Macmillan, 1991.

Greve, Bent. "Indication of Social Policy Convergence in Europe." *Social Policy & Administration* 30, no. 4 (1996): 348–67.

———. *Social Policy in Europe: Latest Evolution and Perspectives for the Future.* Copenhagen: Danish National Institute of Social Research, 1992.

Hantrais, L. *Social Policy in the European Union.* Houndsmills, England: Macmillan, 1995.

Higgins, J. *States of Welfare: Comparative Analysis in the Social Policy.* Oxford: Blackwell/Martin Robertson, 1981.

Johnson, Norman. *Mixed Economies of Welfare. A Comparative Perspective.* Hemel Hempstead: Prentice Hall, 1999.

Jones, Catherine. *New Perspectives on the Welfare State in Europe.* London: Routledge, 1993.

Kennett, Patricia. *Comparative Social Policy.* Buckingham, England: Open University Press, 2001.

Leibfried, S., and P. Pierson, eds. *European Social Policy: Between Fragmentation and Integration.* Washington, D.C.: The Brookings Institution 1995.

Millar, J., and A. Warman. *Family Obligations in Europe.* London: Family Policy Studies Centre, 1996.

Mishra, Ramesh. *The Welfare State in Capitalist Society: Politics of Retrenchment and Maintenance in Europe, North America and Australia.* Hemel Hempstead: Harvester Wheatsheaf, 1990.

Oyen, Else, ed. *Comparing Welfare States and their Futures.* London: Gower, 1986.

Rimlinger, G. *Welfare Policy and Industrialization in Europe, America and Russia.* New York: Wiley, 1971.

Rose, R., and R. Shiratori. *The Welfare State East and West.* Oxford: Oxford University Press, 1986.

Spicker, Paul. "Social Policy in a Federal Europe." *Social Policy & Administration* 30, no. 4 (1996): 293–304.

Taylor-Gooby, Peter. "Introduction: Open Markets versus Welfare Citizenship: Conflicting Approaches to Policy Convergence in Europe." *Social Policy & Administration* 6 (2003): 539–54.

Wilensky, Harold. "Comparative Social Policy: Theories, Methods, Findings." In *Comparative Policy Research: Learning From Experience,* edited by M. Dierkes and A. Antal. Aldershot, England: Gower, 1987.

XIV. PUBLIC SECTOR ECONOMICS

Boadway, R. *Public Sector Economics.* London: Basil Blackwell, 1984.

Culyer, A. J. *The Political Economy of Social Policy.* Oxford: Martin Robertson, 1980.

Glennerster, Howard. *Paying for Welfare: The 1990s.* New York: Harvester Wheatsheaf, 1992.

Musgrave, Richard. *The Theory of Public Finance.* New York: McGraw-Hill, 1959.

Musgrave, Richard A., and Peggy B. Musgrave. *Public Finance in Theory and Practice.* London: McGraw-Hill, 1989.

Samuelson, Paul A. "Pure Theory of Public Expenditure." *Review of Economics and Statistics* 36 (1954): 387–89.

Stiglitz, Joseph E. *Economics of the Public Sector.* New York: W. W. Norton, 1986.

Tiebout, C. "A Pure Theory of Local Expenditures." *Journal of Political Economy* 64 (1956): 416–24.

Wagner, A. "Finanzwissenschaft (1883)." Reproduced partly in *Classics in the Theory of Public Finance,* edited by Richard A. Musgrave and Alan Peacock. London: Macmillan, 1962.

Walker, Alan, ed. *Public Expenditure and Social Policy.* London: Heinemann, 1982.

Wilensky, Harold. *The Welfare State and Equality: Structural and Ideological Roots of Public Expenditures.* Berkeley: University of California Press, 1975.

XV. PUBLIC CHOICE

Borcherding, Thomas E. *Budgets and Bureaucratics: The Sources of Government Growth.* Durham, N.C.: Duke University Press, 1977.

Buchanan, James M., and Robert Tollison, eds. *The Theory of Public Choice II.* Ann Arbor: University of Michigan Press, 1984.

Friedman, Milton, and Rose Friedman. *Free to Choose.* Harmondsworth, England: Penguin Books, 1981.

Harris, R., and A. Seldon. *Welfare Without the State: A Quarter Century of Suppressed Public Choice.* London: Institute of Economic Affairs, 1987.

Mueller, Dennis C. *Public Choice.* Cambridge: Cambridge University Press, 1979.

———. *Public Choice III*. Cambridge: Cambridge University Press, 2003.

Niskanen, W. A., Jr. *Bureaucracy and Representative Government*. Chicago: Aldine-Atherton, 1971.

XVI. CRISIS OF THE WELFARE STATE

Alber, J. F. *"Is There a Crisis,"* *European Sociological Review, 4,3: 181–207, 1988.*

Block, F., Cloward, R., et.al. *The Mean Season: The Attack on the Welfare State*. New York: Pantheon Books, 1987.

Culpitt, I. *Welfare and Citizenship: Beyond the Crisis of the Welfare State?* London: Sage, 1992.

Esping-Andersen, Gøsta, Martin Rein, and Lee Rainwater, eds. *Stagnation and Renewal in Social Policy: The Rise and Fall of Policy Regimes*. Armonk, N.Y.: M. E. Sharpe, 1987.

Habermas, Jürgen. *Legitimation Crisis*. London: Heinemann, 1976.

Mishra, Ramesh. *The Welfare State in Crisis: Social Thought and Social Change*. Brighton, England: Harvester Wheatsheaf Books, 1984.

Munday, Brian, ed. *The Crisis in Welfare: An International Perspective on Social Service and Social Work*. Hemel Hempstead, UK: Harvester Wheatsheaf, 1989.

O'Connor, James. *The Fiscal Crisis of the State*. New York: St. Martin's Press, 1973.

Offe, Claus. *Contradictions of the Welfare State*. London: Hutchinson, 1984.

Organization for Economic Cooperation and Development (OECD). *The Welfare State in Crisis*. Edited by A. H. Halsey. Paris: OECD, 1981.

Pierson, P. *Dismantling the Welfare State? Reagan, Thatcher and the Politics of Retrenchment*. Cambridge: Cambridge University Press, 1994.

Therborn, G., and J. Roebroek. "The Irreversible Welfare State." *International Journal of Health Services* 16 (1986): 319–338.

Whynes, David, ed. *In Defence of Welfare*. London: Tavistock, 1985.

Wicks, M. *A Future for All: Do We Need the Welfare State?* Harmondsworth, England: Penguin Books, 1987.

Wilding, P., ed. *In Defence of the Welfare State*. Manchester, England: Manchester University Press, 1986.

XVII. VOLUNTARY ACTIVITIES

Baine, S., J. Benington, and J. Russell. *Changing Europe: Challenges Facing the Voluntary and Community Sectors in the 1990s*. London: NCVO Publications and Community Development Foundation, 1992.

Beveridge, William *Voluntary Action*. London: Allen & Unwin, 1948.

Kramer, R. *Voluntary Agencies in the Welfare State*. Berkeley: University of California Press, 1981.

Morris, Mary. *Voluntary Work in the Welfare State*. London: Routledge & Kegan Paul, 1969.

XVIII. POLITICAL SCIENCE AND THE WELFARE STATE

Buchanan, James M. *The Political Economy of the Welfare State*. Stockholm: Almqvist & Wiksell, 1988.

Deakin, Nicolas. *The Politics of Welfare: Continuities and Change*. Hemel Hempstead, UK: Harvester Wheatsheaf, 1994.

Esping-Andersen, Gøsta. *Politics Against Markets*. Princeton, N.J.: Princeton University Press, 1985.

———."Power and Distributional Regimes." *Politics and Society* 14 no. 2 (1985): 223–56.

Gutmann, A., ed. *Democracy and the Welfare State*. Princeton, N.J.: Princeton University Press, 1988.

Hadley, R., and S. Hatch. *Social Welfare and the Failure of the State*. London: Allen & Unwin, 1981.

Hancock, M.D. *Politics in the Post-Welfare State: Responses to the New Individualism*. New York: Columbia University Press, 1972.

Harris, D. *Justifying State Welfare*. Oxford: Blackwell, 1987.

Hills, J., ed. *The State Welfare*. Oxford: Clarendon Press, 1990.

Hirschman, A. *Shifting Involvement: Private Interest and Public Action*. Oxford: Martin Robertson, 1972.

Korpi, Walter. *Class, Power and State Autonomy in Welfare State Development*. Stockholm: Swedish Institute for Social Research Reprint Series, 1987.

———. *The Democratic Class Struggle*. London: Routledge & Kegan Paul, 1983.

———. *The Working Class in Welfare Capitalism*. London: Routledge & Kegan Paul, 1979.

Loney, Martin. *The Politics of Greed: The New Right and the Welfare State*. London: Pluto, 1986.

Luhmann, Niclas. *Political Theory in the Welfare State*. Berlin: De Gruyter, 1990.

McCarthy, M., ed. *The New Politics of Welfare*. Basingstoke, England: Macmillan, 1989.

Oakley, A., and A. Susan Williams, eds. *The Politics of the Welfare State*. London: UCL Press, 1994.

Pampel, F. C., and J. B. Williamson. *Age, Class, Politics and the Welfare State*. Cambridge: Cambridge University Press, 1989.

Taylor-Gooby, Peter. *Public Opinion, Ideology and State Welfare.* London: Routledge & Kegan Paul, 1985.

Weale, A. *Political Theory and Social Policy.* London: Macmillan, 1983.

XIX. SPECIFIC BENEFITS

Espina, A. "Reform of Pension Schemes in the OECD-Countries." *International Labour Review* 135, no. 2 (1996): 181–206.

Evandrou, M., J. Falkingham, J. Hills, and J. Le Grand. *The Distribution of Welfare Benefits in Kind.* London: London School of Economics Welfare State Programme, 1991.

Gough, I., et al. "Social Assistance in OECD Countries *Journal of European Social Policy* 7, no. 1 (1997): 17–43.

Myles, John. *Old Age in the Welfare State: The Political Economy of Public Pensions.* London: University Press of Kansas, 1989.

Palme, Joakim. *Pension Rights in Welfare Capitalism. The Development of Old Age Pensions in 18 OECD Countries 1930 to 1985.* Edsbruk: Swedish Institute for Social Research 14, 1990.

Wilson, T., ed. *Pensions, Inflation and Growth: A Comparative Study of the Elderly in the Welfare State.* London: Heinemann Educational Books, 1974.

XX. LABOR MARKET

Atkinson, Anthony B., and Gunnar Viby Mogensen, eds. *Welfare and Work Incentives: A North European Perspective.* Oxford: Clarendon Press, 1993.

Brittan, S. *Beyond the Welfare State: An Examination of Basic Incomes in a Market Economy.* Aberdeen, Scotland: Aberdeen University Press, 1990.

Gershuny, John. *Social Innovation and the Division of Labour.* Oxford: Oxford University Press, 1983.

Mogensen, Gunnar Viby, ed. *Work Incentives in the Danish Welfare State: New Empirical Evidence*, Århus, Netherlands: Århus University Press, 1995.

Scharpf, Fritz, and Vivian Schmidt. *From Vulnerability to Competitiveness: Welfare and Work in the Open Economy*, Oxford: Oxford University Press, 2000.

Sinfield, Adrian. "The Necessity for Full Employment." In *The Future of the Welfare State,* edited by H. Glennerster. London: Heinemann, 1983.

———. *What Unemployment Means.* Oxford: Martin Robertson, 1981.

Sinfield, Adrian, and Neil Fraser. *The Real Cost of Unemployment.* Newcastle, England: BBC North-East, 1985.

Teague, Paul. *The European Community—The Social Dimension: Labour Market Policies for 1992*. London: Kogan Page, 1992.

XXI. SOCIAL DIVISON OF WELFARE

Greve, Bent. "The Hidden Welfare State, Tax Expenditure and Social Policy." *Scandinavian Journal of Social Welfare* 3 (1994): 203–211.
Sinfield, Adrian. "Analysis in the Social Division of Welfare." *Journal of Social Policy* 7, no. 2 (1978): 129–56.
Titmuss, Richard. *Commitment to Welfare*. London: Allen & Unwin, 1968.
———. *Essays on the Welfare State*. London: Allen & Unwin, 1958.

XXII. SOCIAL SECURITY AND SOCIAL POLICY

Aaron, H. J. *Economic Effects of Social Security*. Washington, D.C.: Brookings Institution, 1982.
Ashford, D. E., and E. W. Kelly, eds. *Nationalizing Social Security in Europe and America*. London: JAI Press, 1986.
Atkinson, Anthony B. *Poverty and Social Security*. Hemel Hempstead: Harvester Wheatsheaf, 1989.
Clasen, Jochen, ed. *Comparative Social Policy. Concepts, Theories and Methods*. Oxford: Blackwell, 1999.
———. *Social Insurance in Europe*. Bristol, England: Policy Press, 1997.
———. *What Future for Social Security? Debates and Reforms in National and Cross-National Perspective*. Bristol, England: Policy Press, 2001.
Dean, H. *Social Security and Social Control*. London: Routledge & Kegan Paul, 1990.
Glazer, N. *The Limits of Social Policy*. Cambridge, Mass.: Harvard University Press, 1988.
Glennerster, Howard, and John Hills, eds. *The State of Welfare: The Economics of Social Spending*. Oxford: Oxford University Press, 1998.
Goodin, Robert. *Protecting the Vulnerable*. Chicago: University of Chicago Press, 1985.
Greve, Bent. "Economics and Social Security in Europe." In *Social Security in Europe*, edited by Danny Pieters. Bruylant, Belgium: Maklu, 1991.
Hill, Michael. *Social Policy: A Comparative Analysis*. London: Harvester Wheatsheaf, 1996.
Hill, Michael, and G. Bramley. *Analysing Social Policy*. Oxford: Blackwell, 1986.
Jones, Catherine. *Patterns of Social Policy: An Introduction to Comparative Analysis*. London: Tavistock, 1985.

Kemshall, Hazel. *Risk, Social Policy and Welfare*. Buckingham, England: Open University Press, 2002.

Le Grand, Julian, and Will Bartlett. *Quasi-markets and Social Policy*. Basingstoke, England: Macmillan, 1993.

Madison, B. Q. *The Meaning of Social Policy*. London: Croom Helm, 1980.

Marshall, T. H. *Social Policy*. London: Hutchinson, 1961.

Martin, G. T. *Social Policy in the Welfare State*. Englewood Cliffs, N.J.: Prentice Hall, 1990.

Mishra, Ramesh. *Society and Social Policy: Theories and Practice of Welfare*. London: Macmillan, 1977.

Morris, R., ed. *Testing the Limits of Social Welfare*. London: Brandeis University Press, 1981.

Organization for Economic Cooperation and Development (OECD). *The Future of Social Protection*. OECD Social Policy Studies, no. 6. Paris: Organization for Economic Cooperation and Development, 1988.

Pinker, R. *Social Theory and Social Policy*. London: Heinemann Educational Books, 1971.

Plant, R., H. Lesser, and P. Taylor-Gooby, eds. *Political Philosophy and Social Welfare*. London: Routledge & Kegan Paul, 1980.

Rein, Martin *Social Policy: Issues of Choice and Change*. New York: Random House, 1970.

Silburn, R. *The Future of Social Security*. London: Fabian Society, 1985.

Smith, G. *Social Needs: Policy Practice and Research*. London: Routledge, 1988.

Sullivan, M. *The Politics of Social Policy*. Hemel Hempstead, UK: Harvester Wheatsheaf, 1992.

———. *Sociology and Social Welfare*. London: Allen & Unwin, 1987.

Titmuss, Richard. *Problems of Social Policy*. London: His Majesty's Stationery Office and Longmans, Green, 1950.

Townsend, Peter. *Sociology and Social Policy*. London: Allan Lane, 1975.

Walker, C. *Changing Social Policy*. London: Bedford Square Press, 1983.

Williams, F. *Social Policy: A Critical Introduction: Issues of Race, Gender and Class*. Cambridge: Polity Press, 1989.

Wilson, Thomas, and Dorothy Wilson, eds. *The State and Social Welfare*. Harlow England: Longman, 1991.

XXIII. ADMINISTRATION AND THE WELFARE STATE

Adler, Michael, and S. Asquith. *Discretion and Welfare*. London: Heinemann, 1981.

Appleby, P. H. *Public Administration for a Welfare State*. London: Asia Publishing House, 1962.

Clarke, J., A. Cochrane, and C. Smat. *Ideologies of Welfare*. London: Routledge & Kegan Paul, 1987.

Crozier, M. *The Bureaucratic Phenomenon*. Chicago: University of Chicago Press, 1964.

Davies, B. P. *Universality, Selectivity and Effectiveness in Social Policy*. London: Heinemann, 1978.

Davis, K. C. *Discretionary Justice*. Baton Rouge: Louisiana State University Press, 1969.

Donnison, D. V., et al. *Social Policy and Administration*. London: Allen & Unwin, 1965.

Greve, Bent. *Advantages and Disadvantages by Local Provision of Social Policy*. Roskilde, Denmark: Roskilde University, Department of Social Sciences, 1994.

Johnson, Norman, ed. *Private Markets in Health & Welfare. An International Perspective*. Berg, USA: Oxford/Providence, 1995.

Lerman, Paul. *Deinstitutionalization and the Welfare State*. New Brunswick, N.J.: Rutgers University Press, 1982.

Lipsky, Martin. *Street-level Bureaucracy, Dilemmas of the Individual in Public Services*. New York: Russell Sage, 1980.

Papadakis, Elim. *The Private Provision of Public Welfare: State, Market and Community*. Brighton, England: Harvester Wheatsheaf, 1987.

Scott, D., and P. Wilding. *Beyond Welfare Pluralism*. Manchester, England: Manchester Council for Voluntary Service and Manchester Social Administration Department, 1984.

Smith, S. R., and M. Lipsky. *Nonprofits for Hire—The Welfare-State in the Age of Contracting*. Cambridge: Harvard University Press, 1993.

Taylor-Gooby, Peter. "Privatization, Power and the Welfare State." *Sociology* 20, no. 2 (1986): 228–46.

Weber, Max. *The Theory of Social and Economic Organizations*. Edited by A. M. Henderson and T. Parsons. Glencoe, Ill.: Free Press, 1947.

Wilensky, Harold. *"The New Corporatism": Centralization and the Welfare State*. London: Sage, 1976.

XXIV. CITIZENSHIP

Coote, A., ed. *The Welfare of Citizens*. London: Rivers Oram Press, 1992.

Friedman, K. V. *Legitimation of Social Rights and the Western Welfare State: A Weberian Perspective*. Chapel Hill: University of North Carolina Press, 1981.

Janoski, Thomas. *Citizenship and Civil Society: A Framework of Rights and Obligations in Liberal, Traditional and Social Democratic Regimes*. Cambridge: Cambridge University Press, 1998.

Marshall, T. H. *Citizenship and Social Class.* Cambridge: Cambridge University Press, 1950.
Meehan, E. *Citizenship and the European Community.* London: Sage Publications, 1993.

XXV. FAMILY AND GENDER

Abrahamsson, Peter, Thomas Boje, and Bent Greve. *Families and Family Policy in Europe.* Aldershot, England: Ashgate, 2005.
Dale, J., and P. Foster. *Feminists and State Welfare.* London: Routledge & Kegan Paul, 1986.
Daly, Mary, ed. *Care Work: The Quest for Security.* Geneva, International Labour Organization, 2001.
Dominelli, L. *Women Across Continents: Feminist Comparative Social Policy.* Hemel Hempstead, UK: Harvester Wheatsheaf, 1991.
Donzelot, Jaques *The Policing of Families.* London: Hutchinson, 1980.
Drew, E. et al., eds. *Women, Work and the Family in Europe.* London: Routledge, 1998.
Fagan, C., and B. Burchell. *Gender, Jobs and Working Conditions in the European Community.* Dublin: European Foundation of Living and Working Conditions, 2002.
Fraser, Nancy. "Women, Welfare and the Politics of Need Interpretation." In *Politics and Social Theory,* edited by P. Lassman. London: Routledge & Kegan Paul, 1989.
Glendinning, Carol, and Jane Millar. *Women and Poverty—Exploring the Research and Policy Agenda.* Brighton, England: Harvester Wheatsheaf, 1987.
Hantrais, Linda. *Gendered Policies in Europe: Reconciling Employment and Family Life.* London: Macmillan, 2000..
Langan, M., and Ilona Ostner. *Gender and Welfare.* Bremen, Germany: Bremen University, 1991.
Larsen, Trine P. "Work and Care Strategies of European Families." *Social Policy & Administration* 38, no. 6 (2004): 654–77.
Leira, Ann. *Working Parents and the Welfare State: Family Change and Policy Reform in Scandinavia.* Cambridge: Cambridge University Press, 2002.
Lewis, Jane. "Gender and the Development of Welfare Regimes." *Journal of Social Policy* 2, no. 3 (1992): 333–66.
———. *Women's Welfare, Women's Rights.* London: Croom Helm, 1983.
———, ed. *Gender, Social Care and Welfare Restructuring in Europe.* Aldershot, England: Ashgate, 1998.
Millar, Jane. "Gender, Poverty and Social Exclusion." *Social Policy and Society* 2, no. 3 (2003): 181–88.

Pascall, G. *Social Policy—A Feminist Analysis*. London: Tavistock, 1986.

Sasson, A. S., ed. *Women and the State: The Shifting Boundaries of Public and Private*. London: Hutchinson, 1987.

Sipilä, Jorma, and Teppo Kröger. "European Families Stretched between the Demands of Work and Care (Editorial Introduction)." *Social Policy & Administration* 38, no. 6 (2004): 557–64.

Skocpol, Theda. *Social Policy in the United States: Future Possibilities in Historical Perspective*. Princeton, N.J.: Princeton University Press, 1995.

Trattner, W. I. *From Poor Law to Welfare State: A History of Social Welfare in America*. London: Macmillan, 1974.

Ungerson, Clare. *Women and Social Policy: A Reader*. London: Macmillan, 1985.

Wilson, E. *Women and the Welfare State*. London: Tavistock, 1977.

XXVI. SOCIAL MOVEMENTS

Docherty, James C. *Historical Dictionary of Organized Labor*. Lanham, Md.: Scarecrow Press, 2003.

Habermas, Jürgen. "New Social Movements." *Telos* 49 (1981): 33–37.

XXVII. SOCIAL CAPITAL

Evers, Adalbert. "Social Capital and Civic Commitment: On Putnam's Way of Understanding." *Social Policy & Society* 2, no. 1 , 2003:, 13–21.

Franklin, Jane: "Social Capital: Policy and Politics." *Social Policy and Society* 4, no. 4 (2003): 349–52.

Putnam, R. D. *Bowling Alone: The Collapse and Revival of American Community*. New York and London: Oxford University Press, 1995.

Roberts, John Michael, and Fiona Devine. "The Hollowing Out of the Welfare State and Social Capital." *Social Policy & Society* 2, no. 4 (2003): 309–18.

XXVIII. GLOBALIZATION AND WELFARE STATES

Esping-Andersen, Gøsta. *Welfare States in Transition: National Adaptations in Global Economies*. New York, Sage, 1996.

Greve, Bent, and Jesper Jespersen, eds. *Globalisation and Welfare*. Roskilde Denmark: Roskilde University Press, 2003.

Jessop, Bob. *The Future of the Capitalist State*. Cambridge, Polity Press, 2002.

Leibfried, Stefan, and E. Rieger. *Limits to Globalisation: Welfare States and the World Economy*. Cambridge: Polity Press, 2003.

Sykes, Rob, Bruno Palier, and M. Prior, eds. *Globalisation and European Welfare States: Challenges and Changes.* Houndmills, New York: Palgrave, 2001.

Tsukada, Hiroto. *Economic Globalisation and the Citizen's Welfare State: Sweden, UK, Japan, US.* Aldershot, England: Ashgate, 2003.

Weiss, L., ed. *States in the Global Economy: Bringing Domestic Institutions Back In.* Cambridge: Cambridge University Press.

About the Author

Bent Greve received a M.A. in economics at Copenhagen University in 1977, a Ph.D. in public administration from Roskilde University in 1992, and a Dr. Scient. Adm in public administration in 2002. He is a professor in welfare state analysis and head of the Department of Social Sciences, Roskilde University, Denmark, and director of the Jean Monnet European Center of Excellences at Roskilde University.

He is an expert on the analysis of the welfare state and its development, mainly in a comparative European perspective. His research on the welfare state covers areas such as social security, the labor market, financing, and tax expenditures. He has been the Danish expert to several European Union Commission studies on financing and its implications, labor market policies, tele-working, and free movement of workers. He has done evaluation of welfare state policies and initiatives in core areas of the welfare state. He is also actively involved in and coordinates several programs on European Social Policy Analysis. Among other things, he is a deputy member of the board of the European Institute of Social Security and member and vice chair of the Danish Central Board of Taxation.

His recent publications include, *Velfærdssamfundet: Myter og Facts* (*Welfare Society: Myth and Facts*), *Velfærdsstat and velfærdssamfund* (*Welfare State and Welfare Society*), *Vouchers—nye styrings- og leveringsmåder I velfærdsstaten* (*Vouchers: New Ways of Steering and Delivery in the Welfare State*), *Fordelingsteori og fordelingsbeskrivelse, Væksten i de offentlige udgifter, Skatteudgifter i teoretisk og empirisk belystning, Social Policy in Europe* (ed.), *Comparative Welfare Systems: The Scandinavian Model in a Period of Change* (ed.), as well as several articles in professional journals such as Social Policy & Administration, Journal of European Public Policy, and European Legacy.